MANAGING ADJUNCT & PART-TIME FACULTY

FOR THE NEW MILLENNIUM

Donald E. Greive, Editor
Catherine A. Worden, Editor

Published by Info-Tec
1005 Abbe Road North
Info-Tec **Elyria, OH 44035**
(440) 366-4632

Library of Congress Data
Catalog Card Number: 99-95581

ISBN 0-94-00-17-24-5 (Hard cover)
ISBN 0-940017-25-3 (Paperback)

Jacket & Book Design: Brian Sooy & Co.
Cover Image: Corbis

Acknowledgements

It is difficult with a complex publication such as this to adequately recognize all individuals who were instrumental in its conception and development. There are, however, several whose contributions are of such significance that they merit recognition.

First and foremost, of course, are our chapter authors: Tinnie A. Banks, Helen Burnstad, Roy A. Church, Jo Lynn Autry Digranes and Swen Digranes, William Murphy, Michael Parsons, Mark Smith and David Wright, Al Smith-Bonita Butner-Brent Cejda-John Murray, Sharon Stoops, and Elizabeth Reynolds Welfel. We thank all for their patience and perseverance in sticking with us through this project and for the quality of their contributions.

Significant contributions from others include: Steve Sefchik for his work on cover design and layout, Peggy Nesbit and Iona Abraham for their efforts in manuscript preparation, and Brian Sooy & Co.for design communications expertise.

Of special mention is the encouragement received from Dr. Roy A. Church, President of Lorain County Community College whose support helped make this dream a reality, and to Dr. David Leslie for same.

Our appreciation is noted to our regional advocacy committee whose input was invaluable: Doris Salis of the University of Findlay, Richard McCarbery of Lorain County Community College, Darby Williams of Bowling Green State University-Firelands Campus, Ralph Bishop of the University Partnership at Lorain County Community College, David Richardson of Cleveland State University, Robert Dudash of Lorain County Community College, Richard France of Cuyahoga Community College, and Sue Richenberg of the University of Akron.

Without the cooperation and efforts of these people, this publication would not have been possible.

Donald E. Greive, Editor
Catherine A. Worden, Editor

Contents

Preface

With the continuing growth in the number of adjunct and part-time faculty, managers in the new decade will experience not only increased challenges due to their numbers, but also the impact of technology and the internet. In addition, the increase in activity of non-traditional educational delivery systems and entities will play a greater role in higher education.

These factors will not only impact the training and utilization of adjunct faculty and their managers, they will also lead to related issues such as intellectual property rights, legal issues, and ethical concerns. The purpose of this publication is to address these and elated issues and provide information necessary for effective management of adjuncts in the coming years.

In the introductory chapter, Dr. Roy Church raises futuristic questions concerning the multitude of issues confronting institutions as we move from the information age to the digital economy. He discusses not only the impact of technology on the teaching-learning process, but a number of related issues such as intellectual property rights, the "one college concept," and institutional assessment. In Chapter 2, Don Greive examines new entities and organizations and their potential impact on traditional colleges and universities. In addition, he discusses the "learner centered college" and organizational arrangements to address the changing academic environment.

Chapter 3 provides insight into contemporary management of the orientation process(es) necessary to acclimate new adjunct faculty to their teaching and institutional role. Mark Smith and David Wright also present exemplary programs and models for orientation. Keeping with the concept of contemporary management needs, Helen Burnstad in Chapter 4 presents a model for a comprehensive faculty development program. In it she discusses the faculty development role in the entire process: hiring, new faculty orientation, mentoring, and teaching preparation, workshops, and seminars.

Elizabeth Reynolds Welfel in Chapter 5 discusses the importance of ethical concerns as they relate to adjunct faculty in the new millennium. She discusses the foundation of ethical practice in higher education, teaching, and competency, the responsible use of power, as well as respectful professional relationships. Another contemporary topic and possibly more important, that of legal issues, is discussed in Chapter 6 by Bill Murphy. In this chapter he gives significant attention to: sources of law, employment responsibilities, general liability, duty of teachers, and other legal issues as they relate to adjunct faculty.

"Five Steps to Parity" described by Michael Parsons in Chapter 7, identifies five areas in which adjunct faculty can reach parity with full-time faculty. They are: recruitment/integration, orientation/assimilation, instructional support, evaluation, and the parallel progression. Tinnie Banks in Chapter 8 provides a valuable and informative look into the future of adjunct faculty training. In this chapter she guides us through the basic understanding of the utilization of distance education and media. Also discussed is supporting distance education technology, synchronous and asynchronous distance education as well as required skills and training.

With more and more institutions opting for off-campus sites, Jo Lynn and Swen DiGranes in Chapter 9 guide us through the "care and maintainances" of an effective off-campus operation. They identify potential problems as well as necessary components of effective management such as administrative structure, recruitment and selection, professional development of off-campus faculty, and support services. Chapter 10, by Sharon Stoops, identifies the many facets of good faculty evaluation programs including the student evaluation factor, conditions for good evaluation, evaluation instruments, and the evaluation instrument development process.

Last, but certainly not least, the importance of maintaining institutional quality with the increased impact of adjunct faculty roles is effectively described in Chapter 11 by Al Smith and his colleagues: Bonita Buttener, Brent Cejda, and John Murray. They provide considerable insight into hiring and developing quality part-time faculty, instructional quality and the use of part-time faculty, and program evaluation for enhancing quality.

Donald Greive
Catherine Worden

1 A Vision of the Future-From the CEO

By Roy A. Church

AS WE ENTER THE NEW MILLENNIUM, INSTITUTIONS OF HIGHER EDUCA-
TION FACE MANY CHANGES IN THEIR ROLE AS KNOWLEDGE GENERATORS,
ARBITERS, AND BROKERS. AND PERHAPS THE GREATEST CHANGES WILL BE
IN THE DELIVERY OF INSTRUCTION. ONE FACTOR REMAINS CERTAIN, HOW-
EVER, COLLEGES AND UNIVERSITIES WILL CONTINUE TO USE SIGNIFICANT
NUMBERS OF PART-TIME FACULTY AND THE USE OF WHAT DONALD
KENNEDY CALLS "PARA-FACULTY" WILL EXPAND IN DIFFERENT AND OFTEN
UNEXPECTED WAYS (KENNEDY, 1997).

The impact of new technology on the delivery systems of education will affect all of the operating units of academic institutions. Full-time faculty will have the opportunity to become involved in creative endeavors such as the delivery of education in new formats while continuing to meet the demand of high quality classroom instruction, regardless of place or time.

Adjunct faculty will be called upon to develop new skills to deliver new kinds of knowledge and competencies to the students of the future. Many part-time faculty may be employed on a project basis rather than course-by-course basis and will be able to offer the institution their considerable professional competencies and technological expertise. The evolution of the traditional college to a learning, community, or education center will impact not only full- and part-time faculty, but also the management, support, and financial structure of the institution.

The arrival of the new millennium will see the culmination of the transition of our society from the industrial revolution to the information age and from that to the digital economy. It has been reported that presently more Americans make computers than all forms of transport; more work in accounting firms that in the whole energy industry; more work in biotech technology than machine tools; and more work in the movie industry than the automotive industry (Maitland, 1998).

It is generally accepted that there has been more information produced in the last 30 years than the previous one thousand. There has appeared on the scene new types of institutions, utilizing new technology that provides educational services to students of all kinds at their own place and time. These institutions are market-oriented, independent, client-centered, competency-based, and degree-granting. They also award certificates that are recognized by both employers and the academic community. In order for traditional institutions to meet the challenges in support of this technological revolution in education, new types of delivery systems will need to be developed. This will no doubt include greater utilization of adjunct and part-time faculty as well as adjunct and part-time specialists and project directors.

Not only will technology affect the goals of future educational institutions, but the movement toward community-centered and student-centered colleges and universities will have considerable impact. With the movement off the main campus to delivery sites near the students' home, educational programs presented by full- and part-time faculty will encounter addition-al challenges. Without the direct support of the home campus services, sig-nificant effort and off-campus resources will need to be allocated to support the faculty (many part-time) in accommodating the diverse needs of the stu-dents. Technology will be able to assist certain aspects of this transition; however, the overwhelming challenge to institutions is to retain the human touch for both staff and students.

It is possible that a whole new concept of accreditation will need to be developed for awarding of credit by modules rather than by course and for the accommodation of processes to award certificates and professional cre-dentials. Add to this the emergence of workforce/career change education and one realizes the potential for enormous changes within educational institutions. To some degree, institutions will need to depend upon part-time adjunct faculty and information specialists for instructional delivery in this new era of education.

Administrators and managers working in this new institution will encounter significant challenges that were not evident in the traditional institution. Some of these border on legal and ethical issues. For example, what is the institution's position on part-time faculty and specialists' intel-lectual property rights, including: copyrights, patents, proprietary classroom materials, courseware, and fair use issues?

In addition to the academic and intellectual property questions, we will need to examine the role of adjunct faculty and specialists in terms of facul-ty rank, compensation, seniority, tenure, and retirement. The institution of tomorrow will be a much more exciting place for professionals than in the past. New creative ideas and processes will be stimulated, some will be valu-able and contribute, while others may be valued less, possibly adding stress and frustration to the management process.

With these concerns and the others elaborated upon in this book, one very important consideration is the need to maintain an environment in which all participants feel that they are an integral part of a human endeavor and not just a cog in the system. The challenges confronting institutions of the new millennium should call for dialogue to reexamine institutional priorities relating to adjunct faculty. For institutions that have worked through the TQM process, it might be time to revisit this process with a stated objective of addressing the new delivery systems, new educational institutions, and adjunct faculty/specialists roles. Such a dialogue would need to address several questions:

1. Are we a learner-centered institution or an institution-centered organization? Who is our community and how do we respond to that community in terms of what we deliver educationally and how we deliver it?

2. Is there a clear definition of the roles of all institutional professionals involved in the evolving academic institution, including the role of full-time faculty and its institutional support of the curriculum, as well as support of part-time faculty? What is the role of the part-time faculty in terms of delivery of traditional instruction as well as specialist assignments and other projects? A clear definition of the role of support services across the institution and a delineation of responsibilities therein is critical. In the traditional institution, campus agencies have been developed with the mission and goal of supporting the ongoing internal degree-granting educational process. In the future we may not find this sufficient.

3. How do we assure the continuation of general education in the liberal arts mission while dealing with the pressures being placed upon the institution by our culture for greater attention to career development and career change opportunities for our students?

4. What is the process of faculty and administration for assuring the delivery of quality instruction through the utilization of technology in the new millennium?

On the operational level it appears that an institutional self-examination would intend to resolve some current issues. There is a general feeling nationally that a goal of a 60/40 faculty assignment with 40% part-timers is the optimum. This may or may not be true in all cases. Each institution will need to examine its activities to determine the appropriate percentage of part-time participation for that institution. The literature is also rampant with reports of "abuse" of part-time faculty and their misuse by institutions of higher education. There is, however, evidence that most adjunct are happy with their institutional roles and would like to become more involved in the institutional mission. If, in fact, it is found that there are inequities, then the inequities will need to be identified and addressed.

Finally, institutional quality, which has always been a concern to institutions of higher education through any evolutionary period, needs to be monitored closely. In the recent past, the influx of non-traditional students has tested institutions on their ability to sustain quality. The impact of new delivery systems and new off-campus clientele will present an additional test. Each institution in its own way will need to establish processes to monitor the quality of educational offerings in order to assure that the highest quality educational product is being delivered.

The institution of the new millennium may also force us to examine our definition of the "faculty." Traditionally we have viewed faculty as full-time tenure tract, earning seniority and benefits. With increasing numbers of support personnel traditionally given titles such as adjunct and part-time, future institutions may be required to consider "one faculty" made up of many contributors to the instructional process, including: full- and part-time instructors, specialists, consultants, project developers, curriculum developers, etc. This arrangement will obviously require an analysis of how the different components of the educational process are compensated, how titles are given, and what and how awards/rewards are distributed. If, as Donald Kennedy suggests, tenure as a means of guaranteeing faculty ideological freedom has served its purpose, then perhaps it is time to consider multi-year contracts for both full- and part-time faculty (Kennedy, 1997).

Assessment is ultimately linked to an institution's mission and learning goals. The overriding purpose of assessment is to understand how educational programs are working and to determine whether they are contributing to student growth and development. Thus, the definition of assessment used on any particular campus may not work well on other campuses. In order to gain the most benefit from assessment, faculty and administrators at each institution must develop their own understanding of assessment. If we look at assessment as being "student progress or outcomes" assessment, the emphasis is placed on student learning and development as opposed to faculty evaluation or comprehensive program review. It is clear that knowing where students wind up in the educational process is important but really only part of the story.

What students encounter along the way is just as important. Given the ratio of full-time to part-time faculty, have institutions developed the means for including part-time faculty in the ongoing assessment process? As alumni, employers, and community members, part-time faculty can make valuable contributions. Widespread engagement will help to guarantee that assessment will focus on the most important learning issues and maximize the likelihood that assessment information will be used. Although degrees of involvement will vary among institutions, extensive awareness about what assessment is and what it is trying to accomplish must exist.

*** *** ***

This book covers a number of issues important to the future of the management of adjunct and part-time faculty. The topics of these chapters were especially selected to address those issues and concerns that the adjunct and part-time faculty manager will most need information on in the future. The intention is that any manager or faculty member may find valuable insights here from some of their most accomplished fellows in academia.

Below are brief descriptions of each chapter.

In the following chapter, entitled Leadership Issues of the New Millennium, co-editor Dr. Donald Greive draws on his long association with adjunct training and his contemplation of the possibilities of the future of academics to discuss some of the new developments and trends that will influence the management of adjunct faculty. These trends include: new kinds of institutions such as the virtual university, mega or open university, commercial marketing initiatives, and learner-centered institutions; the different administrative structures for support of adjunct faculty, incorporating andragogical techniques in adjunct faculty management; the stance of accrediting bodies on adjuncts; as well as recommendations on the future of faculty rank and titles for adjunct faculty and the concept of "One Faculty".

Dr. Mark Smith and Dr. David Wright of Indiana Wesleyan University, Marion, Indiana look at the principles of orientation of adjunct and part-time faculty through various exemplary models. This chapter focuses on four primary areas: the necessity for orientation programs, the issues that need to be addressed in an orientation program, the important features that need to be incorporated into a program, and the differences involved in orienting distance education adjunct faculty.

Well-known in the area of adjunct and part-time faculty programs, Dr. Helen Burnstad of Johnson County Community College, Overland Park, Kansas outlines the best processes and procedures for a comprehensive faculty development program in Chapter 4. Dr. Burnstad discusses what constitutes an excellent comprehensive adjunct faculty development program, including these topics: determining the needs of newly hired adjunct faculty, using the initial interview and orientation as developmental tools, creating and encouraging opportunities for faculty training through workshops and seminars, as well as examining the models of other institutions for their development strategies.

In Chapter 5, entitled Ethical Issues for Adjunct Faculty and Their Managers, Dr. Elizabeth Reynolds Welfel, an ethicist and professor of counselor education at Cleveland State University, Ohio, handles the often confusing concerns over ethical issues related to higher education. These issues include competency to teach, the responsible use of power, respectful relationships with coworkers and students, as well as offering ethical guidelines for adjunct faculty and their managers.

William Murphy, Esq. of Cuyahoga Community College, Cleveland, Ohio serves as General Counsel and Assistant Attorney General for a large three-campus metropolitan community college. As such, he is more than qualified to address the legal issues concerning adjunct faculty and their managers. In chapter 6 adjunct faculty and their managers are given general information concerning the following legal issues: legal rights of adjuncts based on institutional types and common law; adjuncts' employment relationships; constitutional rights of adjuncts, including due process; forms of adjunct faculty liability including general and tort liability, as well as negligence; protections against discrimination including sexual harassment; and issues of academic freedom as outlined by AAUP Guidelines.

The particular concerns of the academic manager of adjunct and part-time faculty and the need for parity between full- and part-time faculty programs are discussed in Chapter 7 by Dr. Michael H. Parsons of Hagerstown Community College, Hagerstown, Maryland. Five areas in which adjunct faculty can reach parity with full-time faculty include: sources and strategies for recruitment/integration; individual and group opportunities for orientation/assimilation; contractual, personal, and technical instructional support; substance and structure of evaluation; and the Parallax Progression of identification, professional development, and civic value.

Perhaps one of the most daunting innovations in higher education, the technology associated with distance education are reviewed by Tinnie Banks, M.S., Instructional Design Media Coordinator at Lorain County Community College, Elyria, Ohio. This chapter discusses the following topics: the types of distance education technologies and the necessary support for each type, the selection and training of adjunct distance education faculty, the types of and equipment needed for synchronous and asynchronous delivery systems, the development of programming for both delivery systems, and a discussion of copyright and fair use issues related to distance education programs.

The next chapter by Dr. Jo Lynn Autry Digranes of Connors State College and Dr. Swen H. Digranes of Northeastern State University, both in Oklahoma, address the special concerns associated with managing adjuncts at a distance. In Management of Adjunct Faculty on Branch and Off-Campus Sites, the co-authors discuss issues that include the administrative types of branch and off-campus sites; the recruitment, orientation, professional development, and evaluation of adjuncts; and the special needs of adjunct faculty involved in distance instruction.

Sharon L. Stoops of Ivy Tech State College in Muncie, Indiana provides thoughtful comments on issues related to the evaluation of adjunct faculty.

The issues in this chapter include: evaluation practices, the historical background of faculty evaluation, student evaluation practices and procedures as well as student biases, other tools for use in faculty evaluation, and the process for developing faculty development instruments.

And finally, chapter 11 entitled Maintaining Quality in Higher Education by Drs. Albert B. Smith, Bonita Butner, Brent Cejda, and John Murray of Texas Tech University, Lubbock, Texas, consists of four major sections related to maintaining and improving quality in institutions of higher learning: quality management and part-time faculty, hiring and developing quality part-time faculty, instructional quality and part-time faculty, and program evaluation for enhancing quality. Each section offers some specific recommendations for academic managers who are looking for new ways to enhance the quality of their programs and their work with part-time instructors.

References

Kennedy, D. (1997). *Academic Duty*. Cambridge, MA: Harvard University Press.

Maitland, C. (1998). "Technology: Will It Replace Us?" Washington D.C.: National Education Association. Available at http://www.nea.org/he/webpt/cgu2/index.htm (permission).

Dr. Roy A. Church is president of Lorain County Community College, Ohio.

Leadership Issues of the New Millennium

By Donald E. Greive

Overview

This chapter will examine some of the new developments and trends that will influence the management of adjunct faculty. They include:

- New kinds of institutions that include the virtual university, mega or open university, commercial marketing initiatives, and learner-centered institutions;
- Different administrative structures for support of adjunct faculty;
- Incorporating andragogical techniques in adjunct faculty management;
- The stance of accrediting bodies on adjuncts;
- Recommendations on the future of faculty rank and titles for adjunct faculty; and
- The concept of "One Faculty".

Introduction

If traditional degrees offered to traditional students on traditional campuses at unlimited cost [are] valued, then perhaps traditional faculty careers are sustainable. On the other hand, if society wants and needs just-in-time preparation for new careers at different stages in life without regard to physical location and reasonable price, then perhaps a more nimble and adaptable kind of institution is needed—one in which the faculty may or may not hold traditional doctorates, may or may not be full-time employees of one institution, and may or may not be even physically present in a particular place at a particular time. Current employment arrangements for part-time faculty may or may not provide the claimed flexibility, creativity, adaptability and efficiency that such an imagined institution would need. Would it be better to reconsider the conditions under which all faculty work and to build opportunities to combine ways to make intellectual contributions—clearly the most intrinsic motivator for most faculty—with protections and rewards that allow good people to do so with enough security to make lasting commitments? (Leslie, 1998).

This statement best identifies the challenges of the new millennium to be discussed in this chapter. It presents evidence of the dramatic role that part-time faculty may be asked to play in the delivery of education in the future.

Affected by the utilization of technology in delivery systems, the changing demands and differing attitudes of students, and competition in the education marketplace, new strategies will need to be considered. Today's literature is rampant with the discussion of the delivery of education in modules without time and place restraints. Much of this will take place through competency-based career-oriented instruction. More specifically, "short- and long-term curricula will be linked and it will become the responsibility of the college to maintain lifelong learning portfolios for its students. Resources will be allocated to learning and assessment centers based upon need and performance" (Baker, 1999).

Given the established role of full-time faculty on campuses, many institutions will look to adjunct and part-time faculty (and even commercial agencies) for the delivery of instruction. During the next century we will reach the culmination of another evolution in the change from the industrial revolution to the information age, and then from the information age to the information economy. Thus, it appears that the delivery of information at the convenience of the learner (who may be changing careers or upgrading professional competencies) will need to be closely examined. Many authorities feel that education of the future will be more market-oriented with high quality standards to be met and will focus on the needs of students rather than the dictates of the institution.

Although there has been considerable study and discussion concerning the amount of participation of part-time faculty in higher education institutions, there is no evidence that the trend toward using less part-time faculty will develop. Present figures indicate that approximately 40% of college instruction is delivered by part-time faculty. It is highly likely that this practice will continue and, with the introduction of different types of instructional systems, may even increase. For example, it is estimated that over 20,000 courses are presently being delivered through distance education techniques to over a half million students (Maitland, 1998). It is also probable that this trend will continue to increase and require additional attention by adjunct faculty managers.

New Institutions

In addition to the responsibilities placed upon colleges and universities due to technology implementation, client demands, and changing delivery systems, new institutions have appeared that compete with traditional colleges and universities. Many institutions are delivering Internet courses, and in some cases an entire college curriculum, thousands of miles from their home campus, without the benefit of campus walls and buildings. Two of these new institutions have been labeled the *virtual university* and the *open* or *mega university.*

The Virtual University

The virtual university, which has risen to prominence during the last decade, is destined to be a major player in the future of higher education. The virtual university is Internet-oriented and relies almost exclusively upon the transmission of Internet courses and the admission of students from sites that may be miles from the main campus. Courses are transmitted from a central web site and may involve one or more institutions for the delivery of instruction. The virtual university may assist students in obtaining college degrees based partially on what they already know (experiential credit) and what they are willing to teach themselves by any method they choose. It is difficult to determine the number of institutions who are involved in the delivery of virtual education. Kentucky has recently opened a virtual university that provides students with a directory of on-line courses offered by both public and private colleges (*www.kcvu.org,* 1999).

Two of the major players in the virtual university scene are The Western Governors University and the University of Phoenix. They are unique and worth discussion simply because they are pioneers and take slightly different approaches to delivery of their instruction. The University of Phoenix, which has been in business for over a decade, operates independently and primarily as a home campus for the site; whereas the Western Governors Conference (University) may call upon web sites from several participating institutions.

The University of Phoenix currently enrolls over 60,000 students and is a private accredited university intended basically for working adults. It provides degree and certificate programs over the Internet as well as at regional on-site centers. Accredited in 1978, it was among the first to recognize the need for degree and continuing education programs for adult learners. The University of Phoenix recognizes the distinction between the younger student and the undecided adult student who has established personal professional goals. It makes accommodations for the daily demands of the working adult schedule. The University of Phoenix has approximately 75 outlet campuses. Twelve percent of the offerings by the University of Phoenix are produced by Internet-managed and delivered coursework (Noone, 1999).

The Western Governors University itself develops no courses. Instead it "brokers" courses provided by others. During the pilot phase, for instance, its smart catalog will list 150-200 courses offered via distance learning by about 200 institutions. Western Governors University consultant Dennis Jones of the National Center for Higher Education Management Systems, Boulder, CO, says "more than anything else, it will change the conversation about higher education." Some suggest it already has. In just three years WGU's architects have created a model that challenges just about every convention in higher education (Marklein, 1998).

It is not unusual to find major accrediting organizations willing to accredit "cyber" universities. Recently the North Central Association of Colleges and Schools accredited Jones International University which exists completely on-line and does not have a traditional bricks-and-mortar campus. Other providers accredited by North Central include Northwestern University, University of Chicago, Michigan State University, University of Notre Dame, Arizona State University, Ohio State University and the University of Michigan. One Jones official states "this announcement is a milestone in the history of education as it signifies the great strides taken by the providers of on-line education" (*Community College Times*, 1999).

Most institutions of this type draw upon a faculty composed of leading experts in their fields at various institutions across the United States. These faculty members serve as content experts in the design of courses and set evaluation standards for student performance.

The virtual university will require that a faculty compensation formula be developed for different types of instruction. This will include, besides the formal credit arrangement, compensation for modular instruction and development, time for delivery of instruction, and possibly some recognition based on the number of students being served since in a virtual setting that number could vary from a very few into the hundreds and even the thousands. These institutions will also need to determine how adjunct faculty will be compensated for product and program development as well as their time spent on support and development activities. Since competency-based and experiential credit is awarded by many virtual institutions, the question of the validation of standardized tests for awarding credit will need to be assessed. The problem is magnified when managers realize they may be calling upon adjunct faculty members to evaluate experiential credit without established standards required of both full- and part-time faculty.

However, a key question in the virtual university remains: "who is the faculty?" There obviously will be full-time university-trained faculty members teaching in such an institution. In addition, however, there will be technology specialists, curriculum specialists, part-time modular instructors, part-time course instructors, and various other entities, not yet identified (*Community College Times*, 1999).

There are several related challenges presented to adjunct faculty managers with the rise of the virtual institution. They are as follows:

- virtual colleges' sometimes extensive dependence upon the use of part-time faculty,
- the new level(s) of legal issues involved in intellectual property rights,
- their dependence on competency-based and modular instruction,
- their reliance on commercial agencies for the delivery of their instruction,
- the introduction of a whole new scheme of compensation for faculty and agents who provide delivery of instruction (Is it really necessary to have a master's degree in computer science to teach a software course in word processing?) and may even change the definition of "faculty".

Additional problems for the virtual university and their use of part-time faculty include their recruitment and qualifications and the steps taken to maintain institutional quality. It also places emphasis on faculty training and development which includes not only the fundamentals in the delivery of classroom instruction but also the appropriate delivery to students at a distance. Upon the institution is also placed the responsibility to maintain the institutional mission and the problem of understanding students and their needs, especially students that are not physically on a campus.

The issue of intellectual property rights is currently being discussed in many institutions and organizations. Questions are being raised. If the institution compensates the faculty member for the development and the delivery of the course, does this give the institution the intellectual property rights to the course materials? In fact, can an institution, without an author, retain copyrights? These and related issues that may require compensation will need to be resolved. Many universities presently are in a phase of transition and are experimenting with their copyright dilemma.

The Mega University/Open University

The Open University, although gravitating more recently to the characteristics of the virtual university, has been around for a much longer time. Some authorities say the open university actually commenced with colleges offering correspondence courses over 100 years ago. Although the open university is more closely related to distance education, there is a significant difference. The open university will accommodate many modes of instructional delivery, including the World Wide Web, cable, television, videotape, CD-ROM, satellite, and even chat rooms. One need merely visit the World Wide Web to realize the number of institutions involved in open university activities.

In our country, The University of Wisconsin has been involved in open university activities for over 30 years and Penn State has also developed an extensive program. However, probably the most renowned institution is the Open University of the United Kingdom which is credited with setting the standards for the modern mega or open university.

Speaking primarily of the United Kingdom Open University (founded 1969), Sir John S. Daniel describes the mega university as "a large university without walls operating through the use of technology [in] a much more efficient manner than the present colleges and universities" (Daniel, 1997). The mega university, according to Daniel, provides the maximum amount of flexibility and allows lifelong learners to study whenever they choose and wherever they are. The enrollment of a mega university can be from 100 to 500,000 students, and usually operates on a national or international basis. A significant factor, however, is the fact that the academic staff of the mega university is made up of predominately adjunct faculty.

A key characteristic of the mega university is that the programs and curriculum are student driven rather than institution and faculty driven. Daniel points to four keys for success, all of which have implications for the development and training of adjunct faculty:

- **Very high quality multimedia learning materials** produced by multi-skilled academic teams. Study materials must be excellent and varied to make the campus in the home a congenial university experience.
- **Dedicated personal academic support.** Each open university student has her or his own tutor for each course. They comment on and mark the students' assignments, hold group meetings, and give support by phone and e-mail.
- **Slick logistics.** Each individual student must receive the right materials and information at the right time. With over 100,000 students that requires careful attention to detail.
- **A strong research base.** When thousands of students use the materials for each course and millions of people view each TV program, the content must be academically up-to-date.

Closer to home, the open university is more easily understood. The difference lies in the fact that in conventional education the teacher teaches as curriculum demands, whereas in distance learning, the university teaches as a unit. Thus, instruction is a result of the development of materials and curriculum by a group of experts. This has significant implication for the organization of a distance learning program and for managers of adjunct faculty.

Commercial Marketing

The virtual college has introduced a new factor that will need to be considered by educators in the coming years. Commercial firms are prepared technologically to deliver distance education in an efficient and effective manner. Many institutions will consider this option in the future. Commercial agencies are being utilized by colleges for two basic reasons: (a) they have the equipment, the materials and the technology at hand which eliminates the need for institutions to make expensive purchases, and (b) they have staff, or can obtain staff, on a project basis to develop modules that address the specific needs of the market. Because this type of commercialization carries the potential danger of control over content, systems will need to be put in place to provide assurance that the institutional mission is being addressed. The logic for using commercial agencies is very simple. Why should institutions divert resources within their own organization to duplicate what has already been developed and researched in the commercial market? Thus, a new concept of hiring private commercial agencies to deliver the educational product will face academic managers.

The issues of cost and control over content are very important, and with the large number of institutions offering distance courses on the Internet, time is a major consideration in the delivery of the product. In some larger institutions, the time to develop and perfect the delivery systems may be prohibitive, and in smaller institutions the cost involved cannot be accommodated.

Most such commercial companies offer a similar core of products, a software platform from which professors can present an array of textual and multimedia course material, conduct on-line discussions with students in real time, and manage testing. Some even offer the services of converting courses to the Internet and of training staff.

This new concept confronts educational leaders with many questions. Not only the justification of the cost of establishing such a system, but how are the tuition costs to be passed to students versus the tuition costs that an on-campus student might pay. These are but a few of the challenges facing the virtual educational society in the years to come (Blumensty, 1999).

Learner-Centered Institutions

Recent literature describes an additional movement that will impact higher education, that of the learner-centered institution. Although in place in many institutions for years, the concept of the learning college, or the community-centered institution, is gaining ground as emphasis shifts to technology use and community demands. O'Banion describes the learning college as one that has options for the learner. They may include:

- prescribed, preshrunk portable modules in such areas as general education;
- core courses of specific skills training;
- stand-alone technological expert systems that respond to the idiosyncrasies of a specific learner, guiding and challenging the learner to a rich maze of information experiences;

- opportunities for collaboration with other learners and small groups through technological links;
- tutor-led groups, individual reading programs, school-to-work service learning lectures and laboratories;
- all established learning options, since many of these still work well for many learners (O'Banion, 1997).

The learning college will contract with many specialists to provide services to learners. Specialists will be employed on a contractual basis to produce specific products or to deliver services. Some will work full-time but many will work part-time, often from their homes, linked to the learner through technology.

A model of the learning college is based upon the assumption that educational experiences should be designed for the convenience of the learners. It is based upon six key principles:

1. The learning college creates substantive change in individual learners.
2. The learning college engages learners as full partners in the learning process, with learners assuming primary responsibility for their own choices.
3. The learning college creates and offers as many options for learning as possible.
4. The learning college assists learners to form and participate in collaborative learning activities.
5. The learning college defines the roles of learning facilitators by the needs of the learners.
6. The learning college and its learning facilitators succeed only when improved and expanded learning can be documented for its learners.

O'Banion states "we will start where we are then use our emerging technology to deliver instruction and to allow students to interact with faculty in the anytime, anyplace environment" (O'Banion, 1997).

The implications of the learner-centered institution in the new century should be evident to academic faculty managers. The problems concerning the role of full- and part-time faculty need to be identified and specific strategies put in place. Decisions will need to be made concerning the assets that can be brought to the learning process. Some questions to be answered include:

- Is the most efficient method to address the learning-centered institution the training or retraining of full-time faculty or the employment, training, and managing of part-time faculty?
- Will much of the faculty role be assumed by professionals and business entities who are already knowledgeable of training in the industrial and commercial world?
- How will faculty be reimbursed for the scheduled time and place assignments?
- Will there remain a distinction between the reimbursement of full-time and part-time faculty assigned to this delivery system?
- Will an entirely new faculty be developed that will concentrate on new and innovative types of activities and will it be a tenure-track continuous type of appointment or will institutions opt to retain greater flexibility with the use of all part-timers?

The tremendous challenge of training these instructors in this new mode of educational endeavor will force the marriage of technologically trained individuals to faculty development programs.

An example of the community-centered learning institution is presented at Hagerstown Community College in Maryland. Dr. Michael Parsons states that Hagerstown Community College has adopted a core value system as part of their recent reorganization. Of this core value, the first has identified the college as a learning community that fits in with the core value approach, stating that "it is essential that we involve adjuncts in the intellectual community at the college and assist them in enhancing the quality of their courses" (Parsons, 1999).

Administrative Organizations for Adjunct Faculty Management

The institutional organization for the management and support of adjunct faculty varies considerably depending upon the type, size and location of the institution. The two major positions in developing organizational process seems to be the discipline- or department-centered approach and the college-wide approach. However, they may not be mutually exclusive.

The typical traditional/contemporary college is organized with the responsibility for the support of adjuncts provided by the academic department. This includes curriculum development, syllabi, and support materials, as well as recruitment and evaluation of faculty. The advantages of this arrangement are numerous. In traditional colleges, curriculum and teaching is the jurisdiction of the faculty and this arrangement assures that provision. The disadvantages of this approach is that some activities and services may be duplicated across campus. For example, there is frequently the need for a college-wide orientation and faculty development activities that address college-wide issues not necessarily restricted to the academic discipline. This arrangement may require modification in the future to accommodate extended in-service and technological support.

The second organizational structure is one that provides for a central office that provides support services and activities necessary for involving adjunct faculty as part of the total institution. The central office sometimes is the provost's office or a special director or dean of part-time services. This office assumes the responsibility of providing a full range of services for adjunct faculty during the hours when they are on campus. The advantage of this system is that it is more efficient in terms of orientation, employment, maintenance of records, and support personnel. This arrangement normally allows the academic department to concentrate on the selection, hiring, and evaluation of adjunct faculty. The central office concept also provides the opportunity to work closely with staff development and teaching excellence centers by providing a comprehensive in-service program for adjunct and part-time faculty as well as full-time faculty.

Academic departments, colleges, and the office of provost need to be concerned about finding a systematic approach to structuring a part-time faculty organization that lessens the burdens on individuals and ensures adequate support for the learning environment. One university, Towson State University, has taken steps to ensure a better environment for adjunct faculty. Their statement includes:

1. **Establishing a series of lecture appointments for a few part-time faculty.** Institutions should experiment with continuing appointments for some part-time faculty that teach for the institution year after year. These individuals would be [given] a semi-permanent status and would be provided office space, telephones, computer access, communication facilities, etc.

2. **Delegating overall responsibility for part-time faculty policies and communications through a person or office,** in our case, the office of the provost. We have a newsletter and part-time faculty receptions that include the president, provost, deans and chairs, invitations to adjuncts to major university events and specific orientation programs for part-time faculty.

3. **Recognizing that part-time faculty are an important element in the faculty mix and that changes must be made to the existing structures of faculty life.** Changes in department membership, advising, and representation in the university senate are included. University-wide advising systems must be rethought so that not all advising is dropped on full-time faculty.

4. **Enhancing university guidelines for departments to ensure that part-time faculty can be successful in the classroom.** Can a determination be made of the percentage of part-time faculty by department? Can departments be orchestrated so that students receive the benefits of the regular faculty, including advising, as well as the expertise of the part-time faculty? (Haeger, 1998).

Following are sample organization charts reflecting the arrangements described in the previous paragraphs.

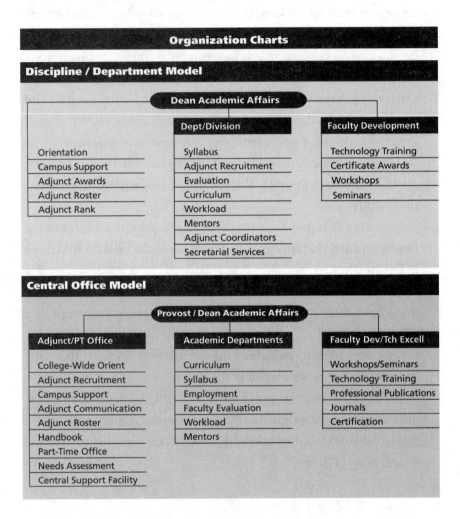

Figure 2.1 — Organizational Chart Models

Management Strategies

Using the Techniques of Andragogy for Management of Adjunct and Part-time Faculty

Although this chapter is intended primarily to examine future challenges, it seems fitting to address one of the adjunct manager's major concerns. With the continuous growth in the utilization of adjunct faculty and the progress made for the support of faculty development initiatives, one area appears to have been neglected. That is the management techniques to best accommodate the adjunct faculty's contributions. It is recognized that many adjunct faculty come from a non-academic background and are not in sync with the academic structural organization and hierarchy, therefore strategies to accommodate their varying needs should be considered. For suggestions in this discussion we turn to the works of Malcolm Knowles (who is best known for his influence in the teaching of adults) and the concept of andragogy. Knowles gives suggestions for the management of people that are of value in the management of adjunct and part-time faculty. They are as follows:

1. **Creative leaders make a different set of assumptions (essentially positive) about human nature from the assumptions (essentially negative) made by controlling leaders.** This consideration calls for managers to provide challenging opportunities and to delegate responsibilities to people. Although there are considerable restrictions in the assignment of adjuncts in most institutions, there is still ample opportunity to provide positive support to adjuncts through a consideration of assignments, involvement in campus affairs, personal notes, individual conferences, feedback, awards and rewards.

2. **Creative leaders accept as a law of [human] nature that [a person's] commitment to a decision is in proportion to the extent they feel they have participated in making it.** Certainly it is possible in most institutions to more actively involve adjunct faculty members in the determination and support of their role. Many institutions have addressed this issue by appointing adjunct advisors or coordinators selected from the adjunct faculty staff. Inclusion in department meet-

ings, planning orientation programs and planning in-service programs in which adjuncts themselves do the presentation are also important.

3. **Creative leaders believe in and use the power of self-fulfilling prophecies.** This implies that telling good teachers that they are good and communicating to them in meaningful ways is important to building the morale as well as the quality of life for adjunct faculty. This can also be addressed by merit recognition, promotions, innovation and good teaching awards as well as publication of adjunct faculty works.

4. **Creative leaders highly value individuality.** Most creative people perform at a higher level if they operate from their strengths. Adjuncts should be allowed to develop creative approaches to their disciplines and to share them with others. They should also be given assignments in the areas of their strengths and encouraged to develop improvement strategies for courses and curriculum. Publicizing adjunct faculty successes also is important.

5. **Creative leaders stimulate and reward creativity.** Providing the opportunity for change and creativity and making it legitimate for people to experiment can energize instructors. In the new millennium many opportunities for development of technologically oriented learning materials and delivery systems will be available. In many cases the adjunct faculty member may be the best person to consider for such an assignment.

6. **Creative leaders are committed to a process of continuous change and are skillful in managing change.** Many adjunct faculty members have spent five or more years at their institutions. In most cases these faculty have had a repetitious assignment of teaching the same course time after time. Is it possible to make available challenging sessions of assignments, research and other roles?

7. **Creative leaders emphasize internal motivators over external motivators.** Studies show that most part-time faculty teach because they enjoy it. To make it easy for them to achieve satisfaction in their teaching, provide technical professional support of their teaching activities, provide human support by the assignment of mentors, and avoid unnecessary bureaucratic procedures, forms, and reports (Knowles, 1990).

Accreditation

One of the myths concerning the use of part-time faculty is that accrediting agencies may challenge the accreditation of institutions that are using too many adjunct faculty. The realities of the situation are that some institutions that use adjunct faculty for as much as 90% of their instruction are fully accredited. The question seems to be twofold: (a) Does the institution maintain academic quality? and, (b) Does it have selection and development processes in place to assure that only qualified part-time faculty members are employed? Formal statements from accrediting agencies below outline the position concerning part-time faculty.

Middle States Association of Colleges and Schools

There is no precise formula for determining the balance between full-time and part-time faculty. Part-time faculty usually accept teaching appointments as a commitment secondary to other responsibilities. They do not have the time to devote to committees, counseling, and other normal faculty duties. The full-time faculty bears an increased burden in these areas as the proportion of part-time faculty rises with direct implications for the morale and effectiveness of the full-time faculty.

New England Association of Schools and Colleges

The faculty includes adequate numbers of individuals whose time commitment to the institution is sufficient to assure the accomplishment of classroom and out-of-classroom responsibilities. It avoids undue dependence on part-time faculty, adjuncts, and graduate assistants to conduct classroom instruction.

North Central Association of Colleges and Schools

Faculty responsibilities at an institution are best fulfilled when a core of full-time teaching faculty has as its primary commitment the educational programs provided by the institution. There is no precise mathematical formula to determine the appropriate number of full-time faculty each institution should have. However, it is reasonable to expect that an institution would seldom have fewer than one full-time faculty member for each major that it offers.

Northwest Association of Schools and Colleges

Part-time and adjunct faculty are qualified by academic background, degree(s), and/or professional experience to carry out their teaching assignment and/or other prescribed duties and responsibilities in accord with the mission and goals of the institution. (Accreditation Handbook, 1999).

Southern Association of Colleges and Schools

The employment of part-time faculty members can provide expertise to enhance the educational effectiveness of an institution but the number of part-time faculty members must be limited. Part-time faculty members teaching courses for credit must meet the same requirements for professional, experiential and scholarly preparation as their full-time counterparts teaching in the same disciplines.

Western Association of Schools and Colleges, Senior College Commission

There must be a core of full-time faculty whose primary employment obligation is teaching and research at the institution... With regard to the obligations and responsibilities of part-time faculty, the institution has a policy designed to integrate them appropriately into the life of the institution.

Western Association of Schools and Colleges, Community College Commission

The institution has sufficient qualified full-time and part-time faculty to support its educational programs wherever offered and by whatever means delivered. (Copyright 1997, *The Chronicle of Higher Education. Reprinted with permission*).

The Faculty

Although there are various reasons that adjunct/part-time faculty teach, they will differ from one individual to another. These reasons, identified by Gappa and Leslie, include: the pursuit of professional growth, the economic motive, personal development, social interaction, community and professional service. It appears that much of the motives for adjunct faculty teaching are intrinsic (Gappa & Leslie, 1993).

Many institutions and organizations are beginning to take a more serious look at the future in relation to adjunct faculty. A recent study by the American Association of State Colleges and Universities entitled "Facing Change-Building the Faculty of the Future" is an extensive study of faculty policies—several of which address part-time faculty issues. These include:

1. **Faculty development opportunities** (including advancement and rewards) should be made available to part-time faculty. Given the increasing importance of part-time faculty mix, investing in part-time faculty is just as important as it is to invest in full-time faculty. Institutions should support faculty development opportunities in instructional technology as well as recognize and reward all aspects of curriculum innovation. Used as a teaching, learning, research and communications tool, technology has the potential to transform and expand the higher education experience.

2. As the institutional mix of full-time, part-time and adjunct and other employment arrangements is developed, it is critical that an **effective annual performance evaluation** be integrated into the faculty role in rewards systems in the institution.

3. A **"continuing expectation of employment" or multi-year contracts** are high on the list of desirable working conditions of part-time faculty. As with full-time non-tenure track faculty, institutions can reap the benefit of long-term planning and greater faculty commitment when they offer multi-year contracts (AASC, 1997).

Faculty Rank/Titles

It is impossible to identify the contract status of adjunct/part-time faculty for all types of institutions. Therefore this will consist primarily of a discussion of potential and possible academic rank assignments and some practices concerning the same.

Many institutions, probably a majority, identify their adjunct and part-time faculty by just those names. That is, all individuals working part-time delivering instruction will be called either adjunct or part-time faculty. Some institutions are required to call them part-time faculty. Other institutions identify all part-timers as adjunct faculty. Generally speaking, the trend in higher education is to assign the adjunct title to someone who returns year after year or has a continuous appointment (with or without seniority) and leave the part-time classification for individuals who teach occasionally.

There are, however, many deviations from this practice.

Some colleges call their adjunct faculty "associate faculty". Even the term "guest faculty" is used. Johnson County Community College in Kansas uses the titles of adjunct assistant professor, adjunct associate professor, etc., based on longevity. Some institutions use the full-time faculty titles with the same qualifications for promotion and simply put the adjunct title in front of the faculty rank, i.e., "adjunct associate professor". At Roosevelt University in Chicago, the college of education has a permanent part-timer classification, awarding two-year contracts to some part-time faculty who teach two courses per semester and are assigned advising duties. These individuals are paid at a higher level (Head, 1999). At Phoenix University, all of their faculty are called "practitioners" (Noone, 1999). The University of Louisville in Kentucky has adopted a "senior lecturer" program. This program recognizes the service experience of teachers by providing senior status to qualified lecturers who have taught for three years. The selection process involves submitting documentation in three areas: teaching excellence, significant program contributions and professional development activities (Hall, Atnip, 1992). At a recent workshop for adjunct managers, many titles were mentioned by participants including: specialists, practitioners, agents, trainers, professors, instructors and lecturers, depending upon the assignment given the individual.

It is likely that in the future, there will be many "specialist" kinds of titles assigned to adjunct and part-time faculty depending upon their roles and differing assignments outside of the classroom. Such "specialists" may also challenge the traditional position concerning academic credentials, e.g., is it really necessary for a computer expert to have a computer science master's degree to teach the latest software program?

The NEA has recently devoted considerable effort to the study of adjunct faculty utilization. They use such terms as: contingent, temporary, visiting, or adjunct faculty. In a recent study, it was observed that temporary appointment faculty (TAF's) given appointments of a year or more have slightly more job stability than others. Thus they suggest that scholars have begun to study the demography, working conditions, and outlook of this previously ignored contingent workforce. The study also notes that only 9% of adjuncts belong to unions (Rhoads, G., Hendrickson, R., 1997).

Although there is little in the literature to support the following two concepts, it deserves mention. There has been considerable concern expressed about the need to fill many of the full-time faculty positions that will become vacant during the next decade due to the retirement of experienced faculty members. Little has been mentioned, however, concerning the concurrent problem of the pending retirement of many experienced, competent adjunct faculty members. It is estimated that nearly 40% of the adjuncts plan to leave their current positions in the next three years. This raises two questions: (a) Are colleges and universities prepared for the training and development of their replacements? and (b) Is there a need for the possible recognition of emeritus part-time faculty members? A second and nearly revolutionary proposition would be that, much in the same manner that full-time faculty are recognized, institutions would strive to establish "chairs" for adjunct faculty members which would promote and support an adjunct faculty member in a teaching or research role for an entire year. Some managers feel that local business and industry would sponsor such an individual to enhance their community support initiatives and provide a meaningful relationship with the college or university.

Adjunct Faculty Support Systems

With the advent of permanent part-time faculty, the growing utilization of project experts, and the demands of distance education and technology, institutions will need to provide enhanced support systems. Many colleges presently provide central conference and work areas where adjunct and part-time faculty obtain not only secretarial support, mail services, telephone services, office space, etc. but also support in the form of computers with e-mail capability, PowerPoint™ materials, and other technological supports.

In order for part-time faculty to remain abreast of diverse student populations, changing student styles, and the student culture, it is important for them to have sufficient reading and resource materials that chronicle the changes in the institution of the future.

These demands in the new millennium will require an extensive in-service program beyond the "how to teach" and "orientation to teaching" sessions. Such a comprehensive in-service program may provide opportunity for the adjunct/part-time faculty member to receive promotion in rank, pay or possibly certification. The days of the curriculum or subject expert coming to class from an outside job to "tell" the students what they need to know about a specific topic are past.

One Faculty

As we near the new millennium we may be faced with the question: "Is it not time that we abandon the traditional institutional acceptance of the bifurcated faculty?" Rather than a divided faculty, should we not have "one faculty?" With the curriculum of the future enhanced with new and student-centered offerings, it will be necessary to call upon members of the community to deliver instruction. Many of these individuals will be "specialists" and not a duplications of the traditional full-time on-campus instructor. The "one faculty" arrangement would incorporate the strengths and assets of both full- and part-time faculty, recognizing all of their contributions to the institution.

Already we are seeing the recognition and acceptance of part-time faculty by professional agencies, associations, and unions. Some institutions have incorporated the "one faculty" concept through the integration of adjunct faculty members into departmental roles. Many institutions have made significant progress in the assimilation of part-time faculty. Maricopa Community College in Phoenix and Jackson Community College in Michigan, while working through the continuous quality improvement process, found it necessary that adjunct faculty become a part of this activity (O'Banion, 1997). At the University of Phoenix, their faculty, called "practitioners", are all considered a part of "the faculty" (Noone, 1999). At

Baldwin-Wallace College in Ohio, the computer/mathematics department welcomes adjunct faculty by posting their pictures along with those of the full-time faculty, provides conference/work/and library space, and the opportunity for them to participate in the "Excellence in Teaching" awards. Adjuncts who have won the award have a certificate of recognition placed in the department for public display (Riggle, 1999).

In developing the "one faculty" concept it is important that the process incorporate all segments of the academic community: full-time faculty support, technology, administration, part-time faculty, department chairs, adjunct coordinators and adjunct faculty. The process may not be easy, but the risk of continuing with a bifurcated faculty may be more costly. It would benefit full-time faculty who are entering emeritus status to assist adjuncts as part of their role to maintain institutional quality. With this in mind, the following questions are presented for examination to help formulate an institutional assessment of reaching the goal of "one faculty":

- Are part-time faculty members invited to department meetings?
- Do they participate in academic activities such as commencement?
- Do they qualify for professional travel stipends?
- Are they assigned faculty rank?
- Do they qualify for promotion?
- Are they held to the same evaluation standards as full-time faculty?
- Do they have the opportunity to serve on standing committees?
- Are they knowledgeable of and dedicated to the mission of the institution and to community standards?
- Are they willing to undergo the appropriate training and faculty development programs to assist them in the age of technology and the digital economy?

Conclusion

The suggestions and challenges put forth in this chapter and this book verify the complex issues in the management of adjunct faculty in the new millennium. It was found in researching this chapter that at each turn it seems that, rather than finding answers and solutions, more questions were raised.

There is no one organizational system for all colleges and universities. The management style necessary for the management of the adjuncts depends upon the institution's relationship with the adjuncts and their ranking in the institutional hierarchy. Individuals, who were employed part-time to fill a short-term teaching need, have now become educational specialists upon whom we rely for delivery of a variety of educational services.

Some truths are self-evident, however. Technology has and will continue to affect the delivery of instruction, its content and its place of reception. New types of institutions and educational organizations will emerge. Education will become more student and client centered. Education will become community centered and at the same time more and more individuals will be learning from a distance.

This important challenge exists: adjunct managers, at a time when many institutions do not have a comprehensive system for adjunct development in an institutional setting, will now be confronted with the problem of employing adjunct faculty in a technology-centered, competitive, and possibly even a commercial environment away from the institution.

Yet with a close examination of the topics in this book, it appears that academic managers are left with many of the same tasks in the new millennium as in the current college environment. Adjunct faculty need to be supported by their institution, whether on campus or in cyberspace, need to have training, need to be selected carefully and nurtured, need to be assimilated, need to be evaluated, and need to provide instruction to meet the mission of the college and university. Through this, the college or university which employs them will be assured of the maintenance of institutional quality in the eyes of the community and their students.

References

Accredited virtual university. (1999, March 23). *Community College Times*, p. 4-5.

American Association of Colleges and Universities. (1999). *Facing change-building the faculty of the future*. Washington, DC: Author.

Baker, G., III. (1999). Building the comprehensive community college. *Community College Journal*, 69(4), 35.

Blumensty, K.G. (1999, April 9). The marketing intensifies. *Chronicle of Higher Education*, pp. A27-28.

Commission on Colleges. (1999). *Accreditation Handbook*. Bellevue, WA: Author.

Daniel, J.S. (1997, July-Aug). Why universities need technology strategies. *Change-The Magazine of Higher Learning*, 8-9.

Gappa, J.M., & Leslie, D.W. (1993). *The invisible faculty: Improving the status of part-timers in higher education*. San Francisco, CA: Jossey-Bass.

Haeger, J.D. (1998). Part-time faculty, quality programs, and economic realities. *New Directions for Higher Education-The Growing Use of Part-time Faculty: Understanding Causes and Effects*. (ed. Leslie, D.W.) San Francisco, CA: Jossey-Bass.

Hall, C., & Atnip, C. (1992). *Rewarding part-time/adjunct faculty: A senior lecturer program*. University of Louisville, KY. ERIC Clearinghouse on Higher Education (ERIC Document Reproduction Service No. ED 343 544).

Head, T. (1999). E-mail correspondence.

Kentucky Virtual University. (1999). <www.kcvu.org>.

Knowles, M. (1990). *The adult learner-A neglected species*. Houston, TX: Gulf Publishing.

Leslie, D.W. (Ed.). (1998, May). *Part-time, adjunct, and temporary faculty: A new majority*. A report of the Sloan Conference on Part-time and Adjunct Faculty. Williamsburg, VA: College of William and Mary.

Maitland, C. (1998). "Technology-will it replace us?" Washington DC:

National Education Association.
<http://www.nea.org/he/webpt/cgu2/index.htm>. (permission).

Marklein M.B. (1998, June 9). Virtually a university-Western Governors put higher education on-line. *USA Today*, D1.

Noone, L.P. (1999). Provost, University of Phoenix. Telephone interview.

O'Banion, T. (1997). *A learning college for the twenty first century*. American Association of Community Colleges, American Council on Education Series in Higher Education. Phoenix, AZ: Oryx Press.

Parsons, M. (1999). E-mail correspondence.

Rhoades, G., Hendrickson, R. (1997). Reconfiguring the professional work-force. *Almanac of Higher Education*. Washington, DC: NEA.

Riggle, T. (1999). Professor and Chair, Baldwin-Wallace College. Personal Interview.

Dr. Donald Greive is presently an author and consultant for adjunct and part-time faculty programs. He is author of A Handbook for Adjunct/Part-Time Faculty and Teachers of Adults *and the editor of* Adjunct Info-A Journal for Managers of Adjunct Faculty. *He has published numerous articles and studies concerning adjunct faculty.*

3

Orientation of Adjunct and Part-time Faculty – Exemplary Models

By Mark Smith and David Wright

Overview

This chapter will focus on four primary areas:

- The necessity for orientation programs,
- The issues that need to be addressed in an orientation program,
- The important features that need to be incorporated into a program,
- The differences involved in orienting distance education adjunct faculty.

Introduction

A comprehensive orientation program for adjunct and part-time faculty has a two-fold purpose: (a) to provide a connection between these individuals and the institution and (b) to prepare them to succeed in the classroom. As colleges and universities change to meet current challenges, part-time and adjunct faculty are bearing more of the teaching load. Successful orientation of these key faculty members is becoming an important variable affecting institutional effectiveness.

The diverse and often conflicting challenges facing institutions of higher education are the focus of intense discussion within the higher education community. These challenges include rapid expansion at some institutions, heightened competition for most, budgetary constraints for others, and the introduction of new models of learning that affects all institutions. Corporate models are forcing a paradigmatic shift that will have far-reaching impact. As students become more consumer-oriented, their expectations of colleges will change. One of these areas of institutional life on which most of these challenges eventually focus is the make-up and role of the faculty. Faculty members are being asked to envision their role differently. Perhaps more significantly, institutions are rethinking accepted notions of who makes up the faculty and what place they occupy in the institution. Institutions are hiring new kinds of faculty members, offering them different relationships, and "deploying" them in new ways.

Thompson (1995) summarizes the trend in the following way. "Like many businesses across the country, institutions of higher education have been increasing the use of part-time and/or temporary staff. Nationally, adjuncts teach between 30%-50% of all credit courses and between 95%-100% of noncredit courses." Leatherman (1997) believes that adjuncts account for 64% of the faculty members in two-year colleges.

As is to be expected, such a process of change brings confusion, anxiety, and conflict. It is not the purpose here to offer judgment about these changes but to simply make two points. First, the reality is that adjunct and part-time faculty are doing more and more of the front-line instructional work of higher education. And, second, in order to prepare them well enough to begin this work, institutions must offer these faculty members a comprehensive program of orientation tailored to their unique needs.

Though the focus here is on the orientation of adjunct faculty, it should be noted that these social and educational changes present new full-time tenure-track faculty with enormous communication, pedagogical, and professional challenges as well. The days are gone when a newly minted Ph.D. could move directly from graduate school into the college classroom and expect to command the respect and attention of students. The speed of technological innovation gives every student instant access to knowledge-bases that, in the past, required years of intense research and study. The influx of adjuncts and part-time faculty into academic institutions further confuses traditional faculty roles. All of this has bearing on the orientation of adjuncts.

In the midst of this change, some constants remain – faculty members need to connect with their institution, to understand its mission and values, and to be prepared to meet the needs of its students. In this context, colleges can no longer avoid the responsibility to provide a comprehensive orientation program for their part-time and adjunct faculty members. Institutions must understand that the quality of this orientation and initial faculty development is a key determinant of their institutional effectiveness. John Scott (1997) argues that, "By supporting and fully integrating adjuncts, an institution's quality of instruction, collegiality, and communication increases."

The Need for Orientation Programs

Adjunct and part-time faculty can be a most valuable resource in helping an institution meet its instructional mission. They can bring to the institution a diversity of perspectives, a passion for teaching, a wealth of personal and professional experience, and the freedom from entanglement in institutional politics. But for this to occur, they must be treated as a valuable resource and not simply as a temporary set of hired hands. The way in which an institution selects, orients, and cultivates a different but significant long-term relationship with its adjunct faculty is a key determinant of the quality that will be brought to the institution.

The presence of a comprehensive orientation program can serve as a foundation for creating quality adjunct and part-time faculty. The need for one may seem self-evident. Understanding exactly why it is needed will help clarify what such a program should do, and when, where, and how it should be conducted.

Faculty are the front-line guardians of institutional quality. They are at the heart of a learning institution. In large measure they determine the kind of experience students have with the institution. Paradoxically, though faculty quality is perhaps the single most crucial element in a student's education, it is usually neither the most visible nor the most scrutinized element of institutional life. Students tend to take what happens in the classroom for granted. While they may grumble to their peers, they will typically not petition the President about a perceived lack of quality among their professors. If anything, they will vote with their feet by avoiding the courses of those professors whom their peers give bad marks. Nevertheless, the quality of the classroom experience is far more critical to their education than the amount of convenient parking, the quality of ancillary services, or the stance that the administration takes on the latest political issue.

One of the simplest and most important steps an institution can take to lay the groundwork for quality learning experiences in its classrooms is to ensure that every member of the teaching faculty participates in comprehensive and ongoing orientation and professional development programs. The need for a comprehensive faculty orientation program increases proportionally with an institution's reliance on adjuncts and part-time faculty. When colleges use adjuncts sparingly to fill holes in the academic term's teaching schedule, the overall quality of instruction in the institution will likely not be greatly affected by those adjuncts who are not well oriented to the institution. When institutions, whether by choice or by default, rely on adjuncts and part-timers (including teaching assistants, one might add) to carry a substantial portion of the teaching load, the need for such an orientation increases exponentially.

Adjunct faculty members do not need to be oriented because they are adjuncts. They need to be oriented because all teaching faculty need to understand the institutional context in which they work, the curriculum they will be expected to cover, and the students with whom they will be working.

The relationship of an institution with its adjunct and part-time faculty is obviously different from the relationship with its full-time faculty. When a full-time faculty member joins an institution, he or she joins a peer group of other faculty members who collectively serve the educational needs of their students and govern the academic activity of the institution. Adjuncts and part-timers are often relegated to the fringes of the institution, only doing the work for which they are paid, but not becoming part of the tenure-track academic community at the heart of the institution. The extent to which part-timers are relegated to the fringes of the institution's academic community is the extent to which the college has failed to prepare some of those people most responsible for the success of its core teaching mission. Therefore, the goal of the faculty orientation program should be to bring adjuncts in from the cold.

The quality of learning taking place in an institution's classrooms will always be a function of several combined factors. Among them are these:

- the clarity of the college's institutional mission and the extent to which that mission is embraced by faculty and reflected in their classroom work,
- the instructional skill displayed by faculty,
- the faculty mastery of the knowledge-bases within their disciplines, and
- the accuracy and effectiveness of measures that provide formative and summative assessment of student academic achievement.

In reality, institutions are employing adjunct and part-time faculty members not simply to fill gaps in the teaching schedule, but as an essential segment of the faculty of the institution. This fact highlights the increased need for a comprehensive plan of orientation for this integral part of more and more institutions of higher education.

Simply put, if a prospective student wishes to know the quality of instruction he or she will receive at an institution, the primary question should not be, "How many adjunct and part-time faculty will I have?" Instead, the student should ask such questions as these:

- How current are the professors in their disciplines?
- How passionate are they about their disciplines?
- Do they know how to facilitate learning for people like me?
- Will they care about my needs and give me their time outside of class?
- Will they know about their institution's support systems and help me use them?

This, then, is the point of departure for a comprehensive orientation program for part-timers and adjuncts.

Foundations of an Orientation Program

At the heart of any comprehensive orientation plan must be a process whereby adjunct and part-time faculty members come to "own" the institution where they work. There are several key elements that connect faculty to and help them understand the institution. Before moving on to more practical issues, an orientation program must address the following three areas – purpose, mission, and core values.

1. **Faculty members must understand the *purpose* of the institution in which they work.**

   At its most simple level, the purpose is the reason for the institution's existence. Edward Shils (1983) suggests that "universities have a distinctive task. It is the methodical discovery and the teaching of truths about serious and important things." It is particularly important that adjunct faculty, most with primary references to other organizations with different purposes, wrestle with this fundamental question. The issue is particularly important in this period when for-profit universities are challenging the status quo in higher education. It is of vital importance for those involved in the enterprise to understand whether their college has the purpose of making money (for shareholders or for the larger non-profit institution) or whether it exists for some other reason. This is important both from a conceptual and a practical standpoint because the fundamental purpose of an institution is the final arbiter when practical decisions must be made. The orientation program must give adjuncts the chance to obtain ownership of the purpose of their academic institution.

2. **Adjunct faculty must understand the *mission* of the institution in which they work.**

    Academic institutions accomplish their basic purpose in many different ways and the mission is what the institution does to live out its purpose. For example, within the overarching purpose of discovering knowledge and facilitating learning, individual institutions may diverge. Some exist primarily to serve as centers for the creation of new knowledge through research. In actual practice, teaching becomes an ancillary activity at those institutions. Other schools exist to serve as centers for student learning. Faculty must understand the unique mission of their institution because it has direct bearing on the expectations brought to bear upon them by colleagues, students, and administrators.

3. **Adjunct faculty should be able to share the *core values* that shape the ethos of an institution.**

    Values may be thought of as the ideals that guide an institution's choices and actions. Examples of core values in higher education are freedom of inquiry, academic integrity, quality of instruction, and commitment to service. No matter what an institution's public rhetoric may say, its core values are what govern daily life at the institution. An adjunct faculty member who does not know and understand the core values of his or her institution is at a disadvantage. On the other hand, adjunct faculty members who understand the purpose, mission, and values of the institution where they work are more likely to succeed in making the contribution expected of them. An effective orientation program builds on the foundation of an institution's purpose, mission, and core values.

Content of an Orientation Program

The practical goal of a comprehensive orientation program is to insure that adjunct and part-time faculty members are prepared to offer students the very best possible learning experience in an institution's classrooms. An effective orientation program gets the relationship between adjunct faculty and their

institution off to a good start. It lays the groundwork for a mutually rewarding relationship in which the adjunct faculty member helps the institution
accomplish its mission and finds personal satisfaction in doing so.

Both parties bring their own set of needs to this relationship. In general, institutions need help meeting their obligations to students. Adjuncts
need help understanding the expectations of those students and of the institution that asks for their assistance. These mutual needs set the context for
and help to delineate the outlines of an effective plan of orientation.
Orientation must include a short-term process that prepares the faculty
member for initial entry into the institution. It should also include a longer-
term process that keeps the faculty member abreast of changes within the
institution. If possible, the long-term professional development process
should involve adjunct faculty members in the evaluation and development
of institutional policy and practice. If an institution is to allow adjunct faculty to be more than a temporary set of "hired hands" who fill gaps in the
teaching schedule, it must prepare them to contribute to the conceptualiza-
tion, assessment, and oversight of the academic programs in which they participate. A strong program of orientation lays the groundwork for this kind
of collaboration.

To this end, building on the foundations of purpose, mission, and core
values, an effective plan of orientation should address these three phases of
orientation for adjuncts.

- The hiring process
- Connecting with the institution
- Preparing for the classroom

The Interview Orientation

The hiring process for adjunct and part-time faculty members has been
notoriously haphazard. All too often it has followed a scenario something
like this: A quick perusal of the *vita* (sometimes optional), coupled with a
perfunctory interrogation, followed by directions to the classroom — "The
class meets Monday, Wednesday, and Friday at 7:30 a.m. in room 231. Please
be there on Monday morning."

This is an invitation to disaster. Even in the most pressured situations, where a department head must fill a teaching assignment at the very last minute, time can be taken to do better than this. The initial orientation previous to the first assignment must properly set the stage for the relationship that will follow. Here are some guidelines to follow for the interview orientation:

1. **The interview orientation should articulate the process that will be used for the selection of adjuncts.**

   This process should be used consistently and should not be compromised except for the most extreme emergencies. It should provide for the review of the candidate's *vita*, an overview of the institution's documentation, a review of the criteria by which candidates will be selected and assigned, and a set of interviews with key representatives (i.e., department chairs, associate deans, and full-time faculty).

2. **The interview orientation should articulate the institution's faculty selection criteria as applied to adjuncts.**

   This helps the adjunct to understand how the institution views adjuncts and how the criteria for selecting them are to be applied. This orientation process can be especially beneficial if it is explicit about the strengths that adjunct faculty can bring to the institution – strengths such as a wealth of professional experience or involvement in unique or unusual positions and projects.

3. **The interview orientation should give the candidate a quick overview of the institutional context.**

   This is not the place to cover the foundational or the practical elements in-depth, but the interview orientation should give the candidate the chance to opt in or out of the process before commitments are made on either side.

4. **The interview orientation should include an unambiguous discussion of the institution's expectations of the adjunct.**

   The middle of the academic term is not the time for adjuncts and department heads to come into conflict because expectations were not made explicit from the outset.

5. **The interview orientation should provide the candidate with an opportunity to ask questions and state his or her expectations.**
   Giving candidates the chance to clarify what will be required of them and to make their own expectations known lays the groundwork for a healthier relationship later on.

   The goal of the interview orientation, then, is to allow the institution to consistently identify individuals who match the institutional mission and who can contribute value to its students. A good interview orientation process will give candidates the chance to opt in or out of the institution based on their other commitments as well as their own strengths and weaknesses.

The Initial Orientation — Connecting with the Institution

Once a candidate has been asked to serve as an adjunct faculty member, the focus of orientation shifts from selection to connection. Adjunct and part-time faculty members usually do not have the benefit of the formal and informal systems that help full-time faculty connect with the institution. There are typically no formal interview with the personnel department, no departmental dinner with introductions, no informal invitations to lunch or to the fitness center, no passing conversations in the hallways, no frank talks about the structure of the institution and the relationships between its departments, and no departmental meetings. In short, there will be few opportunities for established members to pass along the ethos of the community. There will be no opportunity for adjuncts to gather those all-important tips and cues about "the way things get done around here."

Two things must certainly be true in this situation. First, adjunct and part-time faculty will serve the institution better if they understand its ethos. Second, part-time faculty will not become connected to the institution without a purposeful system of orientation. Some institutions have responded to this need by creating intensive orientation experiences that bring part-time faculty to campus and, in effect, treat them as full-time faculty members during their initial exposure to the institution.

The initial orientation plan that connects the adjunct to the institution, then, should incorporate the following features:

1. **The initial orientation must provide ample opportunity for the adjunct to become familiar with the mission, purposes, and core values of the institution.**

   While these will have been communicated in overview fashion in the interview orientation, the initial orientation provides an opportunity for in-depth coverage of these foundational elements. The faculty member must be given the opportunity to find his or her own points of connection and tension with these elements. In doing so, the aim will be to understand the contribution he or she will make to the fulfillment of the mission.

2. **The initial orientation must acquaint the faculty member with the "nuts and bolts" of the policies and procedures he or she will be expected to follow.**

   Here is an all-too-frequent scenario from the classroom of an adjunct professor. A student, quite innocently and appropriately, asks a question about a procedure or policy of the institution. Because adjuncts don't wear nametags to differentiate them from the institution's "real" professors, students expect them to be able to give guidance. But since the adjunct was not oriented well, does not know the answer, and more importantly, does not see himself as a part of the university, he or she dodges the question by saying, "I don't know. You'll have to ask the institution." When this happens, everyone in the situation loses. Both the faculty member and the institution lose credibility. The student loses faith. It becomes harder for the adjunct to accomplish the job for which he or she was hired. This is why adjunct faculty need to understand the policies and procedures of the institution — not to spare the registrar's or the department chair's office headaches but to serve students better and to preserve credibility. Ultimately, the goal of this part of the initial orientation is not to master policies, but for the adjunct faculty member to be able to act as part of the university community.

3. **The initial orientation should assist adjunct and part-time faculty members in forming departmental relationships.**

    Colleges and universities are made up of people who accomplish their work by means of a diverse set of relationships. The value of the education offered within the context of a healthy academic department is not determined simply by the quality of the discrete classroom experiences of each student. Instead, much of the value comes from the comprehensive experience of being exposed to an academic team working together. The whole makes a greater impact on the student than the sum of its parts. In a healthy academic department, faculty colleagues refer to one another's work, publicly agree and disagree with one another, bolster one another's arguments, and contribute to one another's work by critical interaction. By doing this, the faculty of the department challenge students to find their own points of view. An adjunct that has not been invited into this community, nor given the chance to form the relationships it requires, is at a distinct disadvantage. But even more importantly, the students who sit in this faculty member's courses are disadvantaged. Therefore, the orientation that connects the adjunct to the university must provide him or her with the opportunity to form these departmental relationships.

4. **The initial orientation should provide opportunities for adjunct faculty to identify and link up with a mentor.**

    New full-time faculty often select such mentors informally. For example, an established professor may serve as a young faculty member's informal guide and champion through the tenure process. This role is even more important for adjuncts since most of them will have their primary professional relationships elsewhere. They need someone to whom they can turn for answers when problems arise, when they need new ideas, or for growth within the discipline.

5. **The initial orientation must establish a reliable and clearly understood means of communication between the adjunct and his or her departmental leadership.**

    Adjuncts can become "lone rangers" who become adept at solving their own problems, answering their own questions, and guiding students according to their own lights. The orientation program, however, should give them clear communication links with those to whom they can turn when answers are needed.

Classroom Preparation

Traditionally the preparation of most academics focuses almost solely on the content of their disciplines. When a new faculty member walks into his or her first classroom, almost nothing has been done to prepare him or her to facilitate learning. For full-time faculty, this hole is filled by trial and error within the classroom and by informal collegial sharing within the department. Neither of these two resources is available to the same degree for adjunct and part-time faculty members. They teach less than full-time faculty and take longer to build up the volume of instructional experience of full-time faculty members. As has been pointed out earlier, they are not able to draw from the same informal collegial relationships as a full-time faculty member. For the most part, they are on their own. For these reasons, a portion of their orientation program must give them at least the basic instructional tools that they will need in the classroom. Some of the key areas of this orientation should include:

1. **New adjuncts should be able to prepare and use a course syllabus effectively.**

    Some departments provide adjuncts and part-time faculty with prepared syllabi. This can be an important tool for ensuring the quality of course content. Even so, adjunct faculty members will be more effective if they understand the function of a syllabus, know what their institution requires the syllabus to contain, and anticipate the questions and pressures that students will bring to bear on the syllabus.

2. **New adjuncts should be conversant with the basic concepts of student evaluation and should have a thorough grasp of their institution's grading criteria and grading scales.**

    No other area of classroom work will place more pressure on the adjunct than this one. The more tenuous the adjunct's grasp of the institution's policies, practices, and commitments, the more susceptible he or she will be to the pressure students bring to bear on the grading process.

3. **New adjuncts should be able to develop basic lesson plans for their classroom sessions.**

Unfortunately, this is a skill most college professors learn by default rather than by design. The days are gone when faculty members can succeed by relying on a single-skill instructional strategy. Students have come to expect something more than a steady pattern of lectures. But neither will they succeed with a disjointed and chaotic jumble of "learning activities." Adjunct faculty should know how to prepare a coherent plan that focuses the content and guides the events of each class session.

4. **New adjuncts should be forearmed with basic techniques to overcome initial anxiety and to avoid "rookie" mistakes.**

Anxiety can be a hurdle for all new faculty and an especially formidable one for adjuncts. More than one adjunct who could have become an excellent facilitator of learning gave up after one or two assignments because they were unable to face a class full of students with confidence. New adjuncts will be better prepared if they use such basic techniques as:

- establishing rapport with students before a class begins,
- being clear with the class about one's abilities and one's role as a facilitator of learning,
- indicating the strengths one brings as a resource for students (without shading into braggadocio),
- being willing to admit ignorance when it exists, and
- being clear and firm about course expectations without being inflexible.

5. **New adjuncts will benefit from an orientation in the theoretical foundations of their work.**

Some discussion of the differences between pedagogy and andragogy can generate new insights about learning. Finally, the orientation must include a discussion of the institution's expectations of adjuncts as they relate to scholarship and professional development.

Some Features of Exemplary Orientation Programs

Several universities have developed comprehensive orientation programs that embody a core set of "best practices." These programs were studied to identify those common experiences that can serve as models for others to emulate.

University of Findlay, Ohio

Dr. Doris Salis (1998) at the University of Findlay suggests several elements involved in the proper orientation of faculty. A primary focus of the orientation program should be to produce a handbook to guide both full- and part-time faculty. Each year the University of Findlay publishes a handbook that "contains information for part-timers teaching in the university's evening, weekend and off-campus programs" (Salis 1998). This handbook serves as a critical knowledge-base for all faculty.

Salis (1998) identifies another important component by suggesting that faculty should be provided with such vital information as "phone numbers or important procedures." Many institutions fail to give their adjuncts the basic tools that will allow them to get the job done. What does an adjunct do if there is a problem in the classroom? Whom should the person call? These simple but often overlooked pieces of information are essential in equipping the faculty member to adequately represent the university.

The University of Findlay incorporates another important factor in its orientation program – adequate time spent with the new faculty member. For example, each new adjunct is "invited to an orientation session held in mid-August on the main campus. New faculty who are not able to attend are sent a packet of materials on pertinent topics covered at the orientation" (Salis, 1998). Salis adds some very practical advice.

> Remember that it is not necessary to devise elaborate systems for supporting part-timers. They must have the necessities that support their teaching, receive information in a timely manner, and know who to contact for help and clarification. Often, adjunct faculty need the answers to simple questions such as "how do I get to the site?" At other times they may need guidance on more complicated student or teaching problems.

The University of Findlay's orientation program is designed to equip adjuncts with these key fundamentals.

Thus, while institutions may not need elaborate systems to support adjuncts, they must understand the importance of covering the essential details in the orientation they offer their new adjuncts.

William Rainey Harper College, Palatine, Illinois

William Rainey Harper College offers an exemplary model in their intensive four-day orientation session for new faculty members. This program has been studied internally for many years and about 50% of the faculty at the institution believe the program has been important to their professional growth. One important concern with this type of program of orientation such is the need for part-time or adjunct faculty to dedicate large blocks of time for training. Since most of these candidates have primary commitments elsewhere, this can be a difficult practical hurdle. William Rainey Harper College reports that 42% of the faculty have not been able to attend their extended sessions. Nevertheless, while it is important for administrators to understand that adjunct faculty have other primary commitments, William Rainey Harper College exemplifies the belief that a commitment to their classrooms is important enough to demand special time from their adjunct candidates. This communicates expectations at the outset and sets the stage for the relationship that develops over time. Their determination not to allow any new faculty members to enter the classroom unprepared is an exemplary "best practice."

Indiana Wesleyan University, Marion, Indiana

Indiana Wesleyan University (IWU) has dealt with the challenge of preparing over 650 part-time faculty members by developing an extensive selection and orientation program. This program is built on the conviction that the corporate leaders it recruits have the appropriate academic credentials to teach but that they will not succeed as facilitators in its adult degree programs without careful preparation. To prepare them, IWU has focused their orientation process on four key areas:

- Understanding the mission and purposes of the institution,
- Understanding IWU policies and practices,
- Understanding the characteristics and needs of non-traditional students, and
- Understanding both pedagogical and andragogical approaches to the facilitation of learning.

In order to become familiar with the IWU mission, all new adjunct faculty members are required to attend a one-night orientation program that emphasizes the important distinctions of this university. In this development session, the institutional mission statement is reviewed and the core values of the university are discussed. In addition, the session includes an explanation of the learning outcomes that the university hopes each student will achieve. New faculty members are challenged to embrace the fundamental goal of providing high quality instruction for every student in every class by creating a challenging academic framework for the knowledge-base and by applying this knowledge-base to the real world in which students live. Once this foundation has been laid, faculty members are able to progress to the more practical issues of institutional policies and practices.

Faculty members are introduced to the policies and practices of the university through a carefully designed set of exercises that present a particular policy, acquaint the new adjunct with the potential problems that might arise around that policy, and present possible solutions to those problems. For example, a role-playing exercise centering on a tardy student focuses attention on the attendance policy, highlights the problems that experience shows occur among these classes when students habitually arrive late, and gives the opportunity to practice ways to defuse the situation. An interesting sidebar discussion can reverse the situation and focus on the impact on the class when a facilitator arrives late. Another activity focuses on the correct completion of a grade sheet for the Records Office (a simple but surprisingly problematic activity). The evening proceeds with practice/drill types of situations that aim to make institutional policies come to life through situations that experience has shown will occur in their teaching experience. At

IWU, this segment of the orientation is geared to get the attention of the faculty but also to reinforce the importance of following policies that have grown out of hard experience. Faculty members are presented with the Faculty Handbook, designed explicitly for IWU's part-time and adjunct faculty members.

The third component of the orientation program at IWU includes a second required four-hour evening session for the purpose of exploring the characteristics and needs of adult learners and matching these needs with appropriate teaching methodologies. This session begins with an in-depth exploration of the comparison between teaching today's adult learners and the practices of the past. IWU believes that new faculty members must be introduced to this approach since most of them will not have seen newer methodologies modeled in their own education.

The last area of focus for IWU's orientation program is on the development of effective pedagogical and andragogical practices. This is particularly important since most of the adjunct candidates are practitioners rather than educators. These individuals are highly skilled leaders with a wealth of valuable experience to bring to the classroom. All of them possess the requisite academic credentials, many from benchmark institutions. But almost none of them have been trained in effective facilitation practices. One's grasp of the knowledge-base may be outstanding, but in order to effectively facilitate learning, one must understand the different approaches to teaching. The specific topics of this session include: "Best Teaching Practices," "Grading — An Extension of the Teaching Process," "Teaching the Visual Learner," "How to Build a Syllabus," and "Preparing a Lesson Plan."

Larry Renihan, coordinator of the IWU faculty orientation program, indicates that the single most effective change in the institution's process was the commitment to require all faculty to attend two full evenings of orientation. Internal assessment processes have shown a decline in negative student feedback about the quality of their classes since the second night of orientation was required. Institutions that spend time on faculty preparation reap rewards.

IWU has followed up on the orientation program with the implementation of a mentor system and professional development requirements for each faculty member. These continue to enhance the process of student learning at the university. IWU is addressing the concerns about part-time and adjunct faculty by establishing faculty teaching goals, implementing a faculty observation system with over 200 peer and administrative class visits each year, requiring a faculty growth and development plan for all full- and part-time faculty, as well as following the orientation process.

Cuyahoga Community College, Greater Cleveland Area, Ohio

Dr. Richard France, Dean at Cuyahoga Community College, has approximately 900 faculty members to prepare for the classroom. Under his leadership, Cuyahoga has established some exemplary "best practices" worthy of emulation. These practices may begin to sound familiar. This is to be expected since research and experience suggests that effective orientation programs follow common patterns. France (1996) suggests that "part-time faculty need to know about the institutions for which they work, including an introduction to the college's history and organization. They need to know procedures regarding employment and academic affairs, and they need to have knowledge of the support services available to them in supporting their teaching." France concludes that one of the key areas of concern with part-time faculty is their need to develop effective teaching skills. An effective orientation program should not only focus on the short-term preparation of the faculty but should be followed up with regular development workshops that continually improve the faculty member. In other words, there may be a requirement for development processes at the beginning of each academic term.

Cuyahoga Community College adds another important element to the orientation process by suggesting that video technology be utilized as a method of orientation. These videos are developed each academic term to assist faculty with new processes or to introduce new administrative team members. Videos are also used to share new teaching practices with the faculty members.

One of the most important aspects of successful orientation programs is the academic institution's commitment to support faculty with clear incentives for attending the orientation sessions. Both IWU and Cuyahoga acknowledge the importance of faculty support. France (1996) emphasizes that "we provide clear incentives for participation in the orientation process, along with college-wide availability at convenient times, resulting in a high level of attendance by part-time faculty."

McLennan Community College, Waco, Texas

McLennan Community College offers yet another approach to the orientation of faculty. This college also relies on the use of off-campus experts. Schorman (1994) indicates that faculty members at McLennan are oriented through the following methods:

- Courses offered for credit on topics directly affecting classroom instruction,
- In-house faculty mentoring by off-campus experts,
- Four-hour noncredit workshops,
- Faculty development meals, and
- Participation in "Great Teacher Workshops."

Again, one can see similar threads with distinct institutional differences in the approach to the orientation of the faculty.

- Effective Orientation Program's "Best Practices"
- Faculty handbook for full- and part-time faculty
- Faculty procedures and services (phone numbers, contact points, etc.)
- On-campus orientation sessions from one or two 4-hour sessions to an intensive 4-day session
- Emphasis on the mission, purpose, core values, history and distinctions of the institution
- Focus on effective teaching practices
- Video and technology training
- Incentives for attendance at orientation sessions
- Professional development courses offered for credit
- Required attendance at orientation sessions before teaching

These best practices show that an institutional commitment of people and dollars is required to effectively orient the part-time faculty member. The faculty, for their part, must also commit time to learn the appropriate procedures and best practices for becoming an effective member of an institution's faculty.

Addressing the Orientation of Distance Education Faculty

In addition to teaching in traditional classrooms, adjunct faculty are increasingly being asked to teach distance education classes. Their orientation will include many of the same elements already discussed but with key differences.

Distance education has been defined as education in which the instructor and students are not physically in the same location at the same time. The mediating link between the participants in the distance education course is some form of communication technology. One IWU faculty member recently observed that good teaching is not about technology. And while this observation is certainly true as far as it goes and can be a refreshing reminder in an age when technology can feel both intimidating and intrusive, in the distance education arena good teaching is all about using technology appropriately. Without it, there would be no teaching at all. The orientation program that prepares faculty for distance education must wrestle with the centrality of its enabling technology.

It has been a very long time indeed since anyone tried to teach without the aid of enabling technologies. Perhaps truly Socratic teaching requires no mediating technology. But few faculty members would attempt to conduct courses without textbooks, and though this is easily overlooked, a book is merely a form of communication technology grown so familiar as to have become reified. This technology has shaped education. Some would say it has shaped thinking. Most faculty members could improve their use of textbooks in the classroom, let alone their use of electronic presentation and communication tools.

Like many institutions testing the waters with various forms of distance learning, Indiana Wesleyan University's orientation program for distance education faculty has grown in sophistication as its distance education systems have evolved. In 1995 IWU chose the Internet as its platform for the delivery of distance education courses. During 1996 a task force composed of faculty, academic administrators, programmers and technical experts developed a standardized Online Course Interface. This interface was designed to provide all online IWU students with a common, integrated course structure, regardless of the discipline or the course content. In the simplest terms, the online interface provides the student with a structure in which course content is presented, a suite of supplemental tools, and a rich medium for communication that links students with each other and with their facilitator. To properly prepare faculty to succeed with a mediating technology as encompassing as this one, several key elements must be covered.

1. **The orientation program must make the medium commonplace.**
   Learning has always taken place on two levels. On one level students must master the medium. But on another level, they must be able to use the medium to interact with content. The medium always constrains the learning in one way or another. The task of well-prepared faculty members is not only to know content, but to know how the medium constrains interaction with that content. This is as true of books as it is of the Internet. Just as an illiterate faculty member is unthinkable, so should a faculty member unable to use a distance education technology be unthinkable. The goal of the orientation program, then, should be both to put the faculty member at ease with the medium, and to help him or her think through the way in which this particular medium will constrain the education of his or her students.

2. **Faculty who teach at a distance need to be prepared for the psychological loss they will feel in the distance setting.**
   In the online setting, experience is showing that being separated in space and time brings both advantages and disadvantages to the distance learning "classroom." Before they can engage the strengths of the medium, however, faculty members must cope with a sense of not being "truly connected" with the students. Without the familiar visual and auditory cues to rely on, faculty members wonder whether students are learning, and how to monitor and evaluate this learning. In time, as

they come to understand the medium better, this feeling dissipates. The orientation program must help faculty members know in advance that they will feel this sense of loss, and prepare them to counter it. To do this, the orientation process should provide faculty with direct experience of the medium so that they can experience the different psychological dynamic at work before they face "live" students for the first time. It should give them the chance to discuss and practice the tools they will need to help students thrive in this new learning environment.

3. **The orientation program must help faculty develop the instructional practices demanded by the medium.**

    Maintaining the interest level of students participating in a class by means of a two-way video/audio link requires specific instructional skills. Generating and guiding meaningful and enlightening discussion in online chat rooms requires specific instructional skills. The orientation program must alert faculty to these skills and give them an opportunity to practice them.

In addition to the normal orientation discussed elsewhere in this chapter, the following methods can be useful in the orientation of distance education faculty members:

- An orientation course that is taken using the medium itself, so that the faculty member becomes immersed in the medium as a student before he or she must use it as a facilitator;
- A written guide that thoroughly explains the medium and its use;
- An internship with an experienced distance education faculty member, including "shadowing" a facilitator in a live class;
- Availability of a mentor; and
- Follow-up meetings (online and in person) to foster ongoing skill development and to resolve problems and concerns.

In conjunction with distance education issues is one of the fastest growing trends in higher education — the return of the adult population to institutions of higher learning. This population brings unique challenges that must be addressed in order to adequately serve their learning needs. Many of these students are professionals who are unimpressed by the traditional format and pedagogical approach of higher education. For example, for many years higher education has focused on the faculty member as the "knowledge giver." Faculty members have been trained in research universities with a focus on the theoretical underpinnings of the discipline. In their own education, they have not only learned the content of their field, but they have learned that the role of the faculty member is to select which knowledge is to be shared. With the large-scale return of adults to higher education, faculty are now faced with students who challenge this role and who complain of the lack of real world applications in their education. While adults appreciate the intrinsic value of learning when thinking about their college courses, they do tend to focus on variations of this question: "How does this class affect my ability to perform better at my job or cope better with my life?" Faculty members must be hired, oriented, and developed who understand this mindset and can address the issues this adult population brings to the classroom. In response, many adult degree programs use a model that explicitly recruits corporate practitioners who can serve as facilitators of adult learning by synthesizing theory and practice.

Conclusion

Future trends in higher education point to the need for an increase in faculty orientation. As more adjunct faculty members are added, distance education initiatives are multiplied, and institutions are faced with the cultural need for diversification, effective orientation programs, utilizing the "best practices" suggested here, must be implemented. Comprehensive programs of orientation must address the hiring process, the need to connect adjuncts and part-timers with the institution, and the need to prepare them for the classroom. In the years ahead, the quality of these orientation programs will become an even more critical factor in helping institutions achieve their instructional missions within a continuously changing environment.

References

France, R. (1996). Comprehensive orientation leads to quality academic program. *Adjunct Info: A Journal for Managers of Adjunct and Part-Time Faculty, 4,* 1-2.

Leatherman, C. (1997). Do accreditors look the other way when colleges rely on part-timers? *USA Today,* A12.

Lucas, J. A. (1975). Evaluation of faculty orientation. Palatine, IL: Clearinghouse for Community Colleges. (ERIC Document Reproduction Service No. ED 118 190).

Salis, D. (1998). Supporting Adjuncts at a Distance. *Adjunct Info: A Journal for Managers of Adjunct and Part-Time Faculty, 7,* 1.

Shils, E. (1983). *The Academic Ethic.* Chicago: University of Chicago Press.

Schorman, R. S. (1994). An ongoing, multi-level orientation and renewal plan: An original and an update. Princeton, NJ: Clearinghouse for Higher Education. (ERIC Document Reproduction Service No. ED 382 278).

Scott, J. (1997). Many adjuncts support strategies emerging in the literature. *Adjunct Info: A Journal for Managers of Adjunct and Part-Time Faculty, 5,* 1-2.

Thompson, D. M. (1995). Alternative approaches to adjunct faculty development. Princeton, NJ: Clearinghouse for Community Colleges. (ERIC Document Reproduction Service No. ED 384 392).

Dr. Mark Smith is currently the Associate Academic Dean of Adult and Professional Studies at Indiana Weselyan University. Dr. David Wright is currently the Vice President for Adult and Professional Studies at Indiana Weselyan University.

The Comprehensive Faculty Development Program

By Helen Burnstad

Overview

This chapter will discuss what constitutes a comprehensive adjunct faculty development program, including:

- Determining the needs of newly hired adjunct faculty,
- Using the initial interview and orientation as developmental tools,
- Creating and encouraging opportunities for faculty training through workshops and seminars,
- As well as examining the models of other institutions for their development strategies.

Introduction

Faculty development for adjunct faculty—a necessity or an oxymoron?

When considering an adjunct faculty development program, the first step should be to examine the program currently in place for full-time faculty. Each institution will have a different arrangement for the delivery of faculty development and extent to which the program applies to adjunct faculty. The institution might have either a discipline/department model or a central office model. Another organizational pattern is possible, however, that modifies a central office model by using a staff development/human resources model. In this model the support for adjunct faculty is neither separate from nor different from that for full-time faculty. By using a centralized approach, this model presents faculty development as supportive of the organizational development effort to improve student learning or student success. Johnson County Community College has developed just such a model. (See Figure 4.1 — JCCC Staff and Organizational Development Model.)

In such a centralized model, the institution's activities for full-time faculty would also serve part-time faculty. This faculty development program for adjunct faculty can be presented as a comprehensive program serving all faculty in an institution. The elements of a comprehensive human resources model begin with the hiring process and conclude with the awards and recognition process.

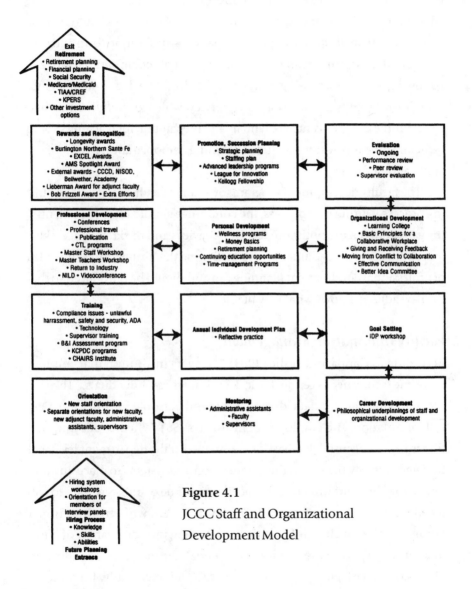

Figure 4.1

JCCC Staff and Organizational Development Model

A Comprehensive Faculty Development Program
Hiring

As much care should be taken in hiring adjunct instructors as when hiring full-time instructors. The posting of positions should be specific about the educational and/or work experience required. This process should include completing an institutional application packet—application form and submission of a current resume, portfolio, letters of recommendation, etc. Following a careful screening by a committee from the department including full-time faculty and the chair, an interview which is carefully structured to determine the applicant's credentials and preparation for teaching should be held. Some institutions include a teaching demonstration as part of the application process.

The faculty development program for adjunct faculty starts with the hiring process. During that process, the committee should be able to identify the gaps between the optimum faculty behaviors and the knowledge, skills and abilities the new adjunct possesses. During the hiring process, the idea of professional development planning can and should be introduced so that the new adjunct knows what is available.

Faculty Information Management

According to Gappa and Leslie (1993) " ... every institution that employs part-time faculty needs certain basic data about these individuals." They list the following types of data: demographic and personal information, payroll information, and employment history (p.238). Whether this information is kept in a central database or maintained at the department level will be determined by the size of the organization and systems in place. In addition to the above information, the facilitator at time of hire may want to collect data that will help frame future development work by the adjunct faculty member. Such an information sheet might include a variety of information gleaned from the application material, the interview, or follow-up discussions. (See Figure 4.2 — Sample of JCCC Adjunct Faculty Data Sheet.)

Figure 4.2 — Sample of JCCC Adjunct Faculty Data Sheet

JCCC ADJUNCT FACULTY DATA SHEET

Name:_____

Address:_____

Telephone number:_____

How to contact during the day:_____

Major:_____Minor:_____

Areas of interest to teach:_____

Past teaching experiences (if any):_____

Courses approved to teach:_____

_____

_____

Start date:_____

Schedule for first semester:_____

_____

Rate of pay for first semester:_____

Did this faculty member attend the orientation?:_____

Is this faculty member interested in the certification program?:_____

Notes from student feedback:_____

_____

_____

_____

Professional Development interests:_____

Individual Development Plan (IDP) completed?:_____

Date:_____

Adjunct Faculty Needs Assessment

Asking adjunct faculty about their needs can easily be accomplished with a traditional pencil and paper questionnaire. Information can be gathered either through a targeted questionnaire to adjunct faculty members or through a general questionnaire to all faculty, asking each to indicate if they are full or part time. At JCCC, the Kansas City Professional Development Council (KCPDC) conducts a needs assessment for each of three employee groups every three years. The part-time faculty are included in the faculty needs assessment. Sample questions include such things as classroom management/leadership, developing instructional media, multimedia/electronic instruction formats, increasing student motivation, student learning styles, writing across the curriculum, critical thinking, active learning techniques, service learning, managing classroom behavior, ethics, creating a "learner"-centered class and more.

The instruction/research question section is followed by a general section that includes questions about time management for retirement, family relationships, conflict management/human relations skills. The needs assessment asks respondents to indicate on a Likert scale from 1 — not likely to 5 — very likely whether they would participate in professional development programs. The survey also asks about program format preferences including online chat rooms, demonstrations, hands-on workshops, lectures, group dialogue, or one-on-one consulting. Finally the survey collects preferences for day and time of delivery. The data are analyzed for each of the member schools as well as the total group. Careful attention is given to providing professional development consistent with the information received. Based on the information gathered, an individual college will schedule the activities or a specific activity will be scheduled for all member schools.

In addition, every two years the associate deans at JCCC convene a committee to review the program for adjunct faculty. During that time they work with the Dean and the Dean's Advisory Council to survey adjuncts regarding their needs for training and development as well as benefit enhancements. This data usually frame some programs especially designed for adjunct faculty to learn to work more effectively with our students.

A very traditional way of determining where adjuncts might need help is gleaned from the use of the IDEA evaluation form. Each semester the adjunct's classes complete the standard form with departmental questions. That information is reported back to the adjuncts, including written comments, and compared against similar classes. Academic Directors use the information to provide feedback for instructors. This information is used as part of the evaluation process and to help design an improvement plan if one is indicated.

The total evaluation system provides ways of designing a faculty development plan for adjuncts. Each adjunct works with an Adjunct Facilitator who is responsible for assisting him or her in the classroom. The facilitator provides one leg of the evaluation system when they visit the adjunct member's classroom and provides feedback. In tandem with the Academic Director, the facilitator compiles the data from the adjunct faculty member's self-evaluation, the student feedback and the classroom visitation. Together the three hold a conversation regarding the status of the adjunct faculty member's teaching and make recommendations for growth.

Adjunct faculty needs are not dramatically different from needs of full-time faculty. Therefore, all faculty can be considered together when designing a faculty development program.

New Faculty Orientation

The paper portion of orientation can be done by providing the new adjunct faculty member with documents that describe the college, the department, academic policies, beliefs about students, and services to support adjunct faculty. A packet of information, in addition to the current Faculty Handbook, should be prepared. However, a more personalized way of welcoming new adjunct faculty would be with a centralized orientation program. Orientation is an ideal time for all new faculty to learn some basic information about the learning environment of the college.

Figure 4.3 — Contents of the JCCC Faculty Orientation Packet
Faculty Orientation Packet

Orientation Agenda

Community Colleges & JCCC

JCCC Viewbook

Current JCCC Catalog of Courses (separate)

Ombuds

JCCC Foundation-Employee Campaign Pledge

Teaching

    Center for Teaching & Learning

    Handbook for Adjunct & Part-time Faculty

    101 Teaching Tips from JCCC Master Teachers

    Fifty Favorite Faculty Teaching Tips

    100 Ideas for Your First 3 Weeks of Class

    Adjunct Info

Training & Development

    http://www.johnco.cc.ks.us/acad/sd

    Staff Development Directory

    Individual Development Plan

    In-service Schedule (see home page)

    Staff Development Programs (see home page)

    Technology Talk-Newsletter of Training (see home page)

    Voice Mail Training Guide

Additional Important Information

    Who's Who in Support Services

    JCCC Library

    Reminder from Human Resources

    JCCC Recycles

    Word Production Services

At JCCC we invite all new faculty to a dinner and short meeting before classes begin. We prepare a packet of print material for all new faculty. Our system includes our faculty handbook, provided to new faculty at time of hire. The handbook is also available on the Web.

The program includes a welcome and short speech by the Dean of Instruction who sets expectations for student learning, followed by a short presentation by the Dean of Student Services who addresses the issues of behavior in the classroom as well as support for students needing special accommodation. The Director of Staff Development overviews the material in the packet and invites participation in other in-service activities, programs, and activities during the academic term.

Following the general dinner, each academic area has its own content-focused orientation. For some academic areas this is an opportunity for new adjunct faculty to meet returning adjuncts as well as full-time faculty members. If the program has an adjunct facilitator, they have an opportunity to meet their new staff members at this time. The program then holds its own orientation about the systems and procedures in that teaching area. The design is different for each program but the standard is to cover any special requirements and the adjunct's relationship with the facilitator and director.

Mentoring

The system, role, and outcomes of mentoring programs for adjunct faculty were studied by Cynthia Hoss in 1998. She reported:

> Professional developers with formal [mentoring] programs identified structured induction elements of matching, training for both participants, monitoring and assistance, and assessment/evaluation. In contrast, informal mentoring programs tended to depend on the fortuitousness of a protégé. The success of formal mentoring programs depended on how they were arranged, managed, and sanctioned ... [m]entoring programs depend heavily on the skill of a mentor. (Unpublished dissertation)

The advantage of a strong mentoring program is the encouragement that adjunct faculty receive to participate in professional development activities.

Therefore, in an ideal program each new adjunct faculty member should be assigned a mentor. The mentor will usually be a member of the same academic program and be charged with assisting the new adjunct in preparing for the content to be taught as well as assisting him or her with

79

logistical problems around the college. Ideally both the mentor and protégé should receive training.

In some organizations the adjunct facilitator is also designated mentor for at least eight adjuncts in a program. The mentor position is a voluntary one; this assignment serves as a very good professional development opportunity for the full-time faculty member. The mentor can provide the link between the chair and the classroom for the adjunct faculty member. A mentor will typically work with the adjunct faculty member for the first year of employment.

Individual Development Plan (IDP)

Institutions which use a "career planning" model for faculty development can adapt their system for the use of adjunct faculty. A model IDP, modified for use by adjunct faculty, is detailed in Appendix 4.1.

Teaching Preparation
Teaching Materials and Supplies

The current literature (Hoss, p.88) focuses on the integration of part-time faculty. To that end, many institutions have developed systems to provide for their "creature comforts." Such supports as office space, storage cabinets, files, access to telephone service including voice mail, e-mail address, mailbox, teaching supplies, secretarial support, and copying service are typically standard. In addition, departments provide copies of the textbook(s) for the course(s) assigned, sample syllabi, and resource materials that include sample assessment tools.

Syllabus

New adjunct faculty members should be provided with a standard, sample syllabus that conforms to the campus academic requirements. The adjunct faculty member then has the opportunity to prepare his or her own course timeline and specific syllabus requirements such as attendance policy, grading system, and caveats. A workshop can be held early in the term to assist adjunct faculty in preparing their syllabus, if needed. Depending on the calendar, this workshop may be on the first Saturday of the semester so those adjuncts may receive help with the preparation. Many avenues of assistance are available, including the mentor, chair, Writing Center, Center for Teaching and Learning, and Staff Development.

When developing a comprehensive faculty development program for adjunct faculty, considerable attention should be given to classroom performance. Some excellent materials are available to support such areas, see Greive, McKechie, and others. In addition, the individual institution may have prepared sample teaching strategies material examples like the handbook from Butler County Community College, KS or the Teaching Tips brochures from University of Nebraska at Lincoln and Johnson County Community College, KS.

Educational/Training Opportunities
Workshops and Seminars
Another way of reaching adjunct faculty is through workshops scheduled at times when they can participate, i.e. in the evenings or on weekends. Some institutions do conferences targeted for adjunct faculty. In looking at some recent programs, such workshops as "Creating Classroom Climate", "Writing Assignments Across the Curriculum", "Using Technology in the Classroom", "Writing an Effective Syllabus", "Understanding Learning Styles", "Cooperative Learning", "Critical Thinking", and "Using Movies Across the Curriculum" appear. These workshops may be held as part of an institution's in-service or professional development day program or a consortium's series.

Financial Support for Faculty Development
Adjunct faculty may receive financial support for development from their program budget or division budget. At JCCC, an alternative is to apply to the Special Grants Committee for support. Through the Special Grants Committee, there are five types of grants available: Center for Teaching and Learning (CTL) Grants, Project Grants, Specialized Training Grants, Conference Presentation Grants and Conference Attendance Grants. The three most often accessed by adjunct faculty are CTL, conference attendance, and conference presentation grants. These grants require an IDP and the sig-

nature of the Academic Director. Adjunct faculty members may receive from $400 to $2,000 depending on the type of activity they are involved in. Appendix 4.2 shows the JCCC Special Grants Application Form.

Master Teachers Workshop

Involving adjunct faculty in local "Master Teachers Workshops" has result-ed in outstanding improvement in communication between full- and part-time faculty. The Master Teachers Workshop is an adaptation of the Great Teachers Seminar held nationally in various locations. A single college or a consortium of colleges can use this format to immerse faculty members in an exploration of successful teaching strategies, a contemplation of issues of concern for teaching faculty, a search for solutions to issues at the insti-tution, and a bonding opportunity for faculty members. At JCCC, the Master Teachers Workshop is held during three days of in-service time at the open-ing of the Spring Semester. As many as 46 faculty, both full- and part-time, are taken to a retreat setting where they workshop under the leadership of faculty members. In 1999 the workshop staff was made up of 10 faculty members, equally divided between full- and part-timers. The theme, "Making Connections", examines the strategies and techniques used to enhance student learning from discipline to discipline.

"Teaching in the Community College" Course

A number of colleges, including Miami-Dade Community College, FL and JCCC, offer a graduate credit course to prepare faculty members for teaching. With many adjunct faculty, teaching skills have not been learned elsewhere. These courses are usually offered in conjunction with a neighboring university.

Adjunct Certification Training (ACT)

In-house certification programs have been developed by some schools, including: Tompkins-Cortland Community College, NY; Butler County Community College, KS; Fredrick Community College, MD; and JCCC. A sample of the activities of one such program can be seen in Appendix 4.3. Adjunct Certification Training (ACT) benefits the students, adjunct faculty and JCCC. The goal is to provide tools and resources to help assimilate and integrate adjunct faculty into the academic community by helping them become even more effective educators in the classroom. Not specific to any discipline, ACT consists of an Instructional phase and a Professional Development phase. Certification requires that an adjunct faculty member enroll in the seven required modules plus an elective module. The eight modules can be completed within a two-semester sequence with the option to extend for one additional year.

Upon completion of ACT, the adjunct faculty member should:

- be cognizant of the College's mission,
- be aware of policies and procedures of the Academic Branch,
- be comfortably assimilated into the College's learning community, and
- be able to enhance student learning in the classroom.

ACT is limited to 30 participants each year. Adjunct faculty with limited or no teaching experience and adjunct faculty whose long-range goal is full-time teaching are encouraged to apply for ACT. Applicants must provide a letter of recommendation from their Academic Director. Upon completion of ACT, an adjunct faculty member moves up one step in the adjunct pay schedule.

Micro-teaching

The activity of micro-teaching is an outstanding way to encourage adjunct faculty to examine their teaching style and skills. In this process, the Faculty Director of the Center for Teaching and Learning convenes five to seven new adjunct faculty members, each of which presents a 7-10 minute videotaped mini-lesson. The entire group then discusses the experience, giving feedback on what worked and what did not work. Later in the term the faculty member is then videotaped a second time in the classroom so the two experiences can be compared. The activity of examining one's own behavior is very enlightening and has received excellent feedback from all involved. The CTL Director must be skilled in giving feedback in a way that is encouraging and supportive. Significant growth and change in classroom behavior has been observed from this activity.

Portfolio Development

Portfolios are being used more consistently in higher education for a variety of purposes, including: teaching, faculty role, and recognition. Adjunct faculty should be encouraged to prepare a portfolio that reflects their understanding of the teaching function. This teaching portfolio should include: their statement of teaching philosophy; artifacts to demonstrate how that teaching philosophy is carried out, i.e. syllabus, student work, exams; activities designed for the students; and reflections on the year.

Faculty role portfolios would include materials that reveal the faculty member's teaching activity as well as materials reflecting their professional activities, such as published articles, creative works, professional presentations and/or other community activities.

Awards and recognition portfolios would include all of the above materials but be slanted in such a way as to demonstrate the excellence of the adjunct faculty member. At JCCC, for example, the Lieberman Teaching Excellence Award for Adjunct Faculty invites the nominated adjunct faculty member to submit a portfolio that includes their answers to questions about their contributions to the college. In addition, the portfolio includes a current resume, letters of nomination, letters of support, and student-produced materials. An external expert on adjunct faculty issues judges the portfolios.

Adjunct faculty should be encouraged to produce a portfolio to have available when they may wish to apply for a full-time position.

Awards and Recognition
Years of Service (Longevity)

At JCCC, adjunct faculty are recognized for their years of service to the college just as all other employees are. Academic Directors determine the adjunct faculty member's academic period of service and present that information to the Staff and Organization Development office which then notifies the faculty member that they will be recognized at the January In-Service All Staff Meeting. Jeweled lapel pins with the college logo are given for five years (10 semesters for adjuncts) and subsequent five-year intervals.

Teaching Excellence

At JCCC, adjunct faculty are recognized for teaching excellence by the Lieberman Award. This award was established to parallel the Burlington Northern Santa Fe Award for full-time faculty. The announcement and system of portfolio preparation are indicated in Appendix 4.4.

Exemplary Programs

While much of this chapter has included ideas and examples from the comprehensive faculty development program for adjunct faculty at Johnson County Community College, KS, there are many other examples of good practices to support adjuncts. First, reference the material covered in the Roueche, Roueche and Milliron and Gappa and Leslie books.

Many other practices abound. Here are a selected few.

Central Michigan University, Michigan

CMU has a compressed weekend program offered throughout the country. They use approximately 800 adjunct faculty in any semester. Some features of their staff development program for adjunct faculty include an orientation organized regionally and held all day on a Saturday. The content focuses on the unique needs of the adult students being served in the program. The demands by students include focus on the core content, use of technology to support learning, and the need for hand-on learning strategies and application examples rather than "fluff". CMU provides a standardized template for the development of the course syllabus that is provides on disk to adjunct faculty. They prepare their syllabus and send it back to the main campus where it is generated for use. New adjunct faculty members are assigned a mentor who supports them during their first semester of teaching. The mentor's activities are designed with the adjunct faculty member to meet their needs and may include classroom observation/feedback, syllabus critique and assistance, and help with course adjustments if needed.

Wright State University, Ohio

WSU holds an orientation for new adjunct faculty on Saturday morning.

They serve breakfast and provide a program including a panel of faculty discussing methods used in the classroom. The program then includes 45-minute sessions on various topics identified from a survey of adjunct faculty. One standard session is presented by a representative from the Dean's Office who speaks on college directions and the state of university initiatives.

Carroll Community College, MD

In addition to a very nice adjunct faculty handbook, Carroll Community College uses a checklist system. One checklist is for supervisors of adjuncts to be sure they have completed all the administrative paperwork for adjuncts. They have also developed an Adjunct Faculty Check-Off Sheet, printed on card stock, which reminds adjuncts of responsibilities they have to the division and the college.

Penn Valley Community College, one of the Metropolitan Community Colleges, Kansas City, MO

Penn Valley has a position identified to work with adjunct faculty. The position title is Mentor/Ombudsman for Instructional Improvement. This is a part-time position for which they have a very thorough job description. This position offers support to new adjunct instructors primarily but is also available to support continuing adjunct instructors or full-time instructors as requested.

Included in the duties of the position is the publication of a newsletter for adjuncts containing teaching tips and articles highlighting programs with many adjuncts or unique or outstanding contributions of adjunct instructors. In addition this positions is responsible for maintaining a resource library and publishing a bibliography which is available to adjuncts.

Butler County Community College, KS

Butler has 26–32 sites where courses are offered throughout their service area. They hold an orientation for a full day on a Saturday. Their agenda includes a welcome by the Vice President for Academic Affairs; a structured activity designed for them to meet their colleagues; sessions on: "Non-

Traditional Student", "Classroom Teaching Strategies", "BCCC Policies and Procedures"; Lunch; "Syllabus Writing", and "Professional Development Opportunities." This packed orientation day receives rave reviews. Adjuncts especially appreciated the syllabus writing workshop.

Another element of the Butler program is their Adjunct Faculty Professional Development Plan in which participants accomplish 15 hours of attendance/participation or presentation in development activities over the course of two semesters. Upon completion they receive a $200 stipend. They also have an opportunity to participate in the "Summit Plus" drawing which is held among those who have accomplished the 15 hours and the winner receives another $100. The 15 hours may be earned through attending meetings (five points), Instructional Development (minimum of five points from this area), and General Development (pre-approval required for these activities).

Support for this comprehensive program includes an adjunct faculty facilitator position, a Faculty/Staff Development office, a Center for Teaching Excellence, and a host of full-time faculty and/or chairs that serve as Peer Consultants. Butler also has prepared a Teaching Handbook which they self publish.

Virginia Community College System

The Virginia Community College System developed a plan for supporting adjunct faculty on all their campuses. The Virginia system includes 23 community colleges coordinated through the Chancellor's Office that has committed to a major staff development program. The program began in 1994 under the direction of Bernadette Black. One of their working committees focused on adjunct faculty. The result of their work was a publication entitled "Enhancing Support for Adjunct Faculty" published in January 1997. The publication includes "Suggested Practices" and "Further Suggestions" in each of four areas: Recruitment, Selection and Appointment; Professional Development and Orientation; Support Services; and Supervision, Evaluation and Recognition.

Conclusion

The task of establishing a comprehensive program for the professional development of adjunct faculty is a challenging one. When undertaking this task, the manager should tailor the program to the culture of his or her institution, the resources available, and the current level of professional development for full-time faculty. A few recommendations follow:

- Create a program to meet the needs of the adjunct faculty you will be serving. Ask them what they want and need.

- If you have a comprehensive staff development program for full-time faculty, do all you can to parallel that program for adjunct faculty.

- Be creative in scheduling and delivery modes. Adjunct faculty cannot attend programs at the same time as full-time faculty especially during the workday. Involve your full-time faculty in the design and delivery of your program.

- Explore programs and activities available at surrounding institutions or at the state level. Some states such as Iowa and Ohio have statewide conferences for adjunct faculty. Support your adjunct faculty in attending those conferences.

- DO NOT do more for adjunct faculty than you do for full-time faculty in your institution.

References

Biles, G.E., & Tuckman, H.P. (1986). *Part-time faculty personnel management policies*. New York: American Council on Education/Macmillan Series on Higher Education.

Gappa, J., & Leslie, D.W. (1993). *The invisible faculty: Improving the status of part-timers in higher education*. San Francisco: Jossey-Bass.

Hoss, C.J. (1998). *The mentoring and professional development of part-time faculty*. Unpublished Doctoral Dissertation, University of Nebraska Lincoln, Nebraska.

Millis, B.J. (1994). Forging the ties that bind: Peer mentoring part-time faculty, mentoring revisited: Making an impact on individuals and institutions. In Marie A. Wunsch, (ed.). *New Directions for Teaching and Learning, #57*. San Francisco: Jossey-Bass.

Roueche, J.E., Roueche, S.D., & Milliron, M.D. (1995). *Strangers in their own land: Part-time faculty in America's community colleges*. Washington, DC: Community College Press.

Dr. Helen Burnstad is currently the Director of Staff and Organizational Development at Johnson County Community College, Kansas.

Chapter 4 Appendices

Appendix 4.1 — Individual Development Plan

INDIVIDUAL DEVELOPMENT PLAN

Johnson County Community College is committed to the personal, professional, and career development of all staff. Within the framework of Staff Development, many opportunities are available for improving the quality of your personal life, professional activity and career potential. This INDIVIDUAL DEVELOPMENT PLAN (IDP) offers you a means to analyze your own development needs, set specific short- and long-term goals, and decide which opportunities best meet those needs and goals. Since the promotion of lifelong learning is one of the goals of JCCC, it supports your continued growth efforts. Your IDP will also assist your immediate supervisor in supporting your development. Information shared may result in budget decisions at the program, division or staff development levels.

The IDP process should stimulate useful introspection and focus your planning. Your IDP should be reviewed and updated annually. Keep one copy, provide one copy to your immediate supervisor and file the original in the Staff Development Center, Box 43.

Completion of the IDP is voluntary. However, its completion may be an eligibility requirement for funding through the Staff Development Center.

Professional development opportunities are available to all employee groups as noted in the Staff Development directory.

DEFINITIONS OF TERMS

1. Short-term — will be accomplished in 1-2 years.
2. Long-range — reachable within a 3-5 year period.
3. Personal goals — those skills or activities you want to undertake because they will improve your personal life, e.g., time management skills in order to improve the work and personal environment.
4. Professional goals — those activities which will contribute to effectiveness of what you are currently doing, e.g., a staff member who wants to become computer-literate in order to use computers in the college.
5. Career goals — activities undertaken to advance your career beyond what you are currently doing, e.g., running for a national office in order to assist with a career change.

GOAL SETTING

1. Be sure your goals are your own — not what you feel others think you should do. They should be. . .
2. S — specific
3. M — measurable
4. A — achievable
5. R — realistic
6. T — time-bound

Name_____ Job Title_____

Division_____ Box No._____

© 2000 JCCC

You are now ready to begin the exciting process of career planning and development. It might be helpful for you to consider the following question as you complete your IDP.

1. What do you want to be doing in five (5) years? If you know, complete the rest of this form.

(If you are not sure what you want to be doing in five (5) years, assistance is available in the Career Planning and Placement Center. They will provide help for you to complete this section.)

Please consider the following as your personal **strategic plan** (I and II) and your **action plan** (III and IV).

I. PERSONAL/PROFESSIONAL PROFILE — ASSESSMENT OF SELF
   a. Strengths, interests, and areas of proficiency or
   b. Areas of potential growth

II. GOAL SETTING
   a. Short-term individual goals:

   b. Long-range individual goals:

III. DEVELOPMENT ACTIVITIES
   Select activities currently available at JCCC or elsewhere listed on pages 3 and 4 of this form. Provide specifics in the limited space available. Immediately below, list the letters corresponding to the programs, workshops, and activities you selected on pages 3 and 4.

IV. ADDITIONAL RESOURCES
   a. List new programs and/or services that would help you accomplish your goals:

   b. What budget or funding requirements must be available to you to accomplish your goals?

Using the Staff Development directory, indicate the specific programs you wish to take advantage of to support the goals you have set.

a. Computer skills training_____

b. Workshops and seminars_____

c. Division-sponsored activities (travel, retreats, curriculum development, etc.)_____

d. Wellness for Life activities (nutrition, exercise, etc.)_____

e   Sabbatical leave_____

f. Special grants_____

g. OPL/AKCCOP/Office and Technical Staff Development/Master Staff Workshop_____

h. Education (tuition reimbursement, Teaching in the Community College course, technical updating)_____

i. Exchanges (CCEP, international, "return to industry," etc.)_____

j. Professional conferences (AACC, KACC, discipline-specific)_____

k. Travel for credit_____

l. Consortium activities (NISOD, CCC:UMMSU/MSU)_____

m. League for Innovation projects_____

n. Special opportunities (leadership program, management training, writing or computing across the curriculum, etc.)_____

_____

o. Develop in-house program (colloquy, college forum lecture series, seminar series, etc.)

_____

_____

p. Award program (Burlington Northern, NISOD, etc.)_____

_____

q. Individual research, writing or special project_____

_____

r. Service (college committee, task force/community organization, professional association, etc.)_____

_____

s. Other:_____

_____

Once your INDIVIDUAL DEVELOPMENT PLAN (IDP) has been completed, please discuss your plan with your supervisor.

_____
Staff Member's Signature   Date

COMMENTS:_____

_____

_____

_____
Supervisor's Signature   Date

COMMENTS:_____

_____

_____

_____
Division Director's Signature   Date

Send completed form to Director of Staff Development.

Appendix 4.2 — JCCC Special Grants Application Form

Applicants are encouraged to meet with the representative from their division.

STAFF DEVELOPMENT

SPECIAL GRANTS APPLICATION
Applicant's Name

_____

Name of Project/Training or Conference

_____

The purpose of Special Grants is to provide an alternate source of funds for the professional or personal development of Johnson County Community College staff in the areas of:
1.　College-wide or discipline research and development projects.
2.　Specialized training.
3.　Conference participation.

All awards are predicated on the fact that funds are not presently provided for in normal division and college-wide budgets. Special Grants is NOT to be considered a source of monies for standard ongoing curriculum or departmental development or for expected and ongoing technical updating.

Have you requested funds from your division and been denied? ___ yes ___ no

OR have you been granted partial funding? Please indicate amount. _____.

GENERAL GUIDELINES:
1.　Staff member must have an "Individual Development Plan" (IDP) on file in the Staff Development Center. (The committee will not have access to any staff member's file.)
2.　Staff member must relate request to goals as indicated on the IDP. (Staff may update or add goals at any time during the year.)
3.　Staff member must have the completed grant application reviewed and signed by immediate supervisor or division director or dean or v. p. Contact any member of the Special Grants Committee for assistance.
4.　Staff member must accept the responsibility to have the application approved by Special Grants at least **two (2)** months prior to activity participation.
5.　Staff member will be required to submit to Special Grants a summary paper detailing the professional or personal worth of the completed activity to the person's goal as set forth in number 2 above. (Failure to do so will preclude consideration for future special grants.) Provide a copy to the program director.
6.　Staff member may receive only one grant per year.
7.　Grants will be awarded on activity merit and availability of funds. Reimbursement will be the total of the approved request only.
8.　Your registration form must indicate your JCCC affiliation and a copy of it must accompany this application.

GRANT OPTIONS:
1.　Project Grant — up to $1500
　　a.　may be college-wide or discipline applicable.
　　b.　must be original in nature, resulting in product or service.
　　c.　must go beyond regular contract responsibilities.
　　d.　may be eligible for reapplication for more than one year.
2.　Specialized Training Grant — up to $1,000
　　a.　may be professional or personal in nature.
　　b.　must be an "active participation" type of training.
　　c.　will be awarded for one's individual training.
　　d.　are one-year awards only.
3.　Conference Presentation Grant — up to $600
　　a.　must have prior written permission from conference.
　　b.　Special Grants will contribute up to $600 but no more than one half (1/2) the total cost.
4.　Conference Attendance Grant — up to $400
　　Funds available only for adjunct faculty and staff with no out-of-district travel funds.
　　a.　must be job-related.
　　b.　will be awarded on individual's rationale for attendance and funding.
　　c.　are one-year awards only

Describe how this activity will help your professional and personal development. How will your participation in this activity benefit your program, division, or the College?

_____

_____

_____

_____

_____

_____

ATTACH TO THIS FORM:

1. Copy of agenda, program, or other supporting material.
2. Completed Travel Authorization Form if required.

TOTAL BUDGET FOR ACTIVITY

ITEM	AMOUNT
Air Fare (call designated JCCC travel agent for cost)	_____
Transportation (personal auto rate $0.29 per mile)	_____
Meals (reasonable and customary)	_____
Lodging	_____
Registration (Please attach completed registration form)	_____
Other* (i.e., tips, materials, supplies — please specify)	_____
Total	_____

*Other (specify) _____

1. Place the information above on a Travel Authorization Form if one is required.
2. If additional funds will be coming from division account, add division account number to Travel Authorization Form and have form signed by division director.
3. Send completed form to Staff Development Center for account number and director's signature.
4. After trip, contact Staff Development for reimbursement instructions. Reimbursement will be no more than the total of the approved request.

_____ IDP on file (in Staff Development Center)

SPECIAL GRANT APPLICATION

NAME_____ EXT._____

DIVISION_____ JOB TITLE_____

FULL TIME_____ ADJUNCT_____

DATES OF ACTIVITY_____ LOCATION_____

NAME OF PROJECT/TRAINING OR CONFERENCE_____

For which of the following grant options are you applying? Choose only one:

_____   Project Grant — up to $1500
_____   Specialized Training Grant — up to $1000
_____   Conference Presentation Grant — up to $600
_____   Conference Participation Grant — up to $400

Describe the project/training or conference below (objectives, outcomes, completion date).

_____

_____

_____

_____

_____

Attach a detailed description of your project.

Which goal(s) of your Individual Development Plan will be satisfied by this activity? (Please list the goals.)

_____

_____

_____

_____

_____

_____

AGREEMENT: I have read the guidelines and rules for Special Grants and agree to adhere to them in completion of this activity. I consider this grant to provide primarily _____ professional _____ personal development (check one or both if appropriate). I would be willing to share the results of my activity as requested.

_____   _____

Signature   *Date*

The committee reserves the right to interview applicants if deemed necessary.

ROUTING CHART FOR APPROVAL:

_____

Program Director's, Division Administrator's or Dean's Signature

_____ Approved (Check one: ___ with or ___ without division funds)
_____ Not Approved

Rationale for decision (required) _____
_____
_____
_____
_____

SPECIAL GRANTS COMMITTEE ACTION:

_____ Approved   Amount Approved _____
_____ Not Approved

Comments:_____

Report received_____

Sharing requested and provided _____

Appendix 4.3 — Adjunct Certification Training Activities

ADJUNCT CERTIFICATION TRAINING PROGRAM

PART I
INSTRUCTIONAL PHASE
Module 1: *Employment Policies and Procedures--1 hour (required)*
The module includes teaching expectations, classroom policies, disciplinary procedures, instructional support and media services/resources, employment policies, faculty mentor, faculty handbook, and job description. The module will be available by viewing a videotape in the Staff Development Office or as an activity during the departmental adjunct orientation.
Module 2: *Instruction--3 hours (required)*
The module will includes syllabus design, instructional strategies, student assessment, curriculum development and student learning styles.
Module 3: *Challenges of Our Students--3 hours (required)*
This module covers topics pertaining to diversity; "Gen X"; adult learning; pedagogy; brain research, styles of learning & teaching; and instructor as facilitator, coach, leader, mentor and learner.
Module 4: *Legal Issues/Diversity--3 hours (required)*
This module covers the topics of sexual harassment and ADA Compliance issues.

PART II
PROFESSIONAL DEVELOPMENT PHASE
Module 5: *Video Taping of Classroom Activity (required)*
Videotaping will involve two sessions during the semester. The first video, to be taped during the beginning of the semester, is a micro-teaching session (7-10 minutes) which will illustrate the instructor's teaching techniques. Feedback will be provided by one's peers and the Facilitator. A second video, taped later in the semester, will be used to determine progress made in teaching style/format as identified by the adjunct instructor and the Facilitator. The adjunct faculty member will retain the video.
NOTE: Academic Director WILL NOT view the tape, nor will it be used in the adjunct faculty member's performance appraisal unless the adjunct wishes to share it with his/her Academic Director.
Module 6: *Technology--3 hours (required)*
This module provides the adjunct faculty member with the opportunity to learn technology skills as needed.

- Web-for-Faculty: Learn how to use a web browser to access your class roster and student information directly from our BANNER Database using the Web-for-Faculty product.
- Grade Machine: Learn how to download rosters and import student names directly into this electronic grade-book. This program provides individual and group reports for your class.
- E-Mail/Voice Mail: Every employee at JCCC is entitled an e-mail account and voice-mailbox. Learn how to use these technologies both here on campus and remotely (e-mail requires ISP).
- Smart Classroom: JCCC has invested a large amount of time and money into bringing technology into the classroom. Learn how to utilize this technology in your classroom.

Module 7: *Reflective Narrative (required)*
This module -- a journal describing how the adjunct instructor processes information learned during the certification training -- will include experiences and consequences of actions taken by the adjunct instructor as he/she implements the tools and strategies learned through ACT into the classroom setting.

ELECTIVES (select one)
Elective 1: *Effective Communication and Listening Skills--2 hours*
This module provides participants an opportunity to interact with other teachers as they learn the dynamics of effective listening and communication.
Elective 2: *Professional Development--(2 activities must be completed)*
The activities of this module are:

- Development of an Individual Development Plan (IDP).
- Attendance/Presence at professional meeting. Credit will be given for attendance at professional meetings in one's discipline as well as attendance at other professional and staff development conferences.
- Observation of an instructor in the classroom teaching the same/similar discipline. Adjunct faculty selecting the observation section will be given a list of instructors who are known to be highly

effective in classroom instruction and must visit at least two different classes taught by JCCC instructors.

- Awards and Recognition.
- Serving on Committees.

Upon completion of this module, the adjunct faculty member will provide a written summary of the conferences and/or classroom observations.

Elective 3: *Master Teacher Workshop–3 days and 2 nights*
Elective 4: *Teaching in the Community College–3.5 hours an evening for a 10-week period*
Elective 5: *CTL/CPDC–Saturday Mornings*
The following modules will lx, offered: Enhancing Teaching & Learning Conference and Critical Thinking Conference.

Elective 6: *Journal and Portfolio*
This module includes a journal of the first year plus a portfolio that will include the following items: syllabus, tests and artifacts, student evaluations, video, and awards.

Elective 7: *Basic Principles for a Collaborative Workplace–2 hours*
This module is an overview session providing a foundation for interaction in the JCCC learning community. The five basic principles serve as guidelines for behavior that put the organization's shared values into practice while developing a strong network of productive relationships at every level of the organization.

Appendix 4.4 — Lieberman Award

Johnson County Community College
Lieberman Teaching Excellence Award for Adjunct Faculty
1998-

NOTIFICATION

Through a gift honoring George and Floriene Lieberman and support from JCCC, six monetary awards will made to recognize outstanding performance by an adjunct faculty member at Johnson County Community College. The program was initiated in 1997 with the first awards given in 1998.

ELIGIBILITY

Adjunct faculty members who have been employed at JCCC for a minimum of six semesters cumulatively may be considered. Employment longevity will be determined by review of program division records. Previous award recipients may not receive the award again for four semesters.

NOMINATIONS

A nomination may be submitted to the adjunct faculty member's program office by any of the following:

- an eligible employee him/herself
- a divisional colleague
- a program or division administrator
- another college staff member
- a student

The division will review the nominations and select their nominees. Each division will establish its own applicant review process. The division nominations will be submitted to Staff and Organizational Development.

The number of nominees will be based on the number of adjunct faculty employed by the program – one nominee for every 15 adjunct faculty members in the program. If a program has fewer than 15, that program may nominate one adjunct faculty member each year. Divisions may combine remaining numbers to allow for an addition nominee, if desired.

PORTFOLIO

Nominees who wish to be considered for the award are invited to submit a portfolio to include the following material, at minimum:

- a current resume
- copies of their IDEA evaluations (student evaluations)
- minimum of two letters of support
- copies of performance reviews (adjunct facilitator/academic director review)
- complete four-statement questionnaire (provided as part of the preparation packet) in a maximum of three pages.
- supporting documents (no more than 10 separate documents of no more than 30 pages)
- Completed portfolio materials will be submitted to an external adjudicator for selection.

AWARDS

Nominees: All nominees will receive a plaque.
Award Recipients: The external judge will select six recipients--one of $750 and five of $250.

These awards are given at the Lieberman Dinner during the Spring semester. The external judge serves as the speaker for the dinner. Nominees and their families are invited to the dinner. In addition, the Dean of Instruction, Academic Directors, Adjunct Facilitators and other interested support persons are invited. Each nominee for the award received an engraved walnut plaque while the selected recipients receive the financial awards through supplemental contracts.

5

Ethical Issues for Adjunct Faculty and Their Managers

By Elizabeth Reynolds Welfel

Overview

This chapter will cover the concerns over ethical issues including:

- Competence to teach,
- Responsible use of power,
- Respectful relationships with coworkers and students,
- As well as offering ethical guidelines for adjunct faculty and their managers.

Introduction

Adjunct faculty typically serve under short-term contracts for low wages and with no job security. Full-time faculty and administrators view them as temporary workers outside the mainstream of higher education even though they spend an average of 6.5 years in this position (American Association of University Professors [AAUP], 1993) and are responsible for approximately 40% of the courses offered at any given time (Clery, 1998). Consequently, adjunct and part-time faculty have relatively little power in the institution and are vulnerable to exploitation and mistreatment from unscrupulous college administrators. They receive less careful scrutiny in hiring, less adequate orientation to their jobs, less supervision while under contract, and less support in carrying out their duties (Clery, 1998). Their limited power, desire for full-time appointments, or commitment to another full-time profession result in their reluctance to seek redress for administrative mistreatment, even when it is egregious.

In spite of these problems, the great majority of adjunct and part-time faculty carry out their duties competently and interact with students respectfully. Most are surprisingly loyal to the institutions that employ them and some are quite ingenious in finding ways to wrestle resources for students from the institution. Their "real world" experience offers a perspective and knowledge-base students cannot always obtain from full-time faculty. Nevertheless, the laxity with which this group of professionals are often supported and supervised leaves their students vulnerable to incompetent, unfair, or exploitive treatment on occasion. Needless to say, most administrators who are responsible for hiring and supervising adjuncts intend to act responsibly and make these decisions with the best interests of students in mind. The multiple demands on the time and budgets of administrators often make it difficult for them to give this task the priority it deserves. This chapter will describe the primary ethical issues facing administrators and adjunct faculty and offer a set of practical strategies for preventing and correcting unethical practice.

At the start, though, it is important to emphasize again how crucial part-time faculty are to the operation of institutions of higher education. Their numbers have increased by 91% since 1976 (compared to 27% for full-time faculty) and they now constitute a majority of faculty in many two-year colleges (Gappa & Leslie, 1993). As of 1993, 64% of community college faculty hold part-time employment (AAUP, 1997a, 1997b). Of all undergraduate sections taught, 20-50% are taught by temporary faculty members (Gappa & Leslie, 1993). Courses in English, humanities and languages have the highest percentages of adjunct faculty, but adjunct teaching is a part of nearly every department in a college or university. These numbers mean that virtually all department heads are hiring, supervising, and evaluating the work of adjuncts. Indeed, it is possible that some managers oversee more adjuncts than regular faculty, especially in the humanities and languages.

Foundation of Ethical Practice in Higher Education

The process of identifying the major ethical issues for adjunct faculty is complicated by the lack of a single enforceable "code of ethics" for them or any faculty or administrators in higher education. Institution-specific codes of conduct do exist and professional organizations have written ethical guidelines for faculty, but the former are not enforceable beyond the particular college and the latter are purely advisory. The American Association of University Professors (AAUP), for example, has issued a series of statements on ethical issues for faculty, beginning with its broad "Statement of Professional Ethics" of 1987. This brief document includes a preamble and five brief sections, each identifying a major responsibility of faculty. These include (in paraphrase form):

- to seek and state the truth as they see it,
- to encourage the free pursuit of learning in their students,
- to respect and defend the free inquiry of associates as members of a common community of scholars,
- to seek to be effective teachers, and
- to separate statements they make as private citizens from those made in their roles as professors.

As an advisory statement, this document broadly defines the components of ethical behavior by faculty, but it does not speak directly to the concerns of adjunct faculty nor does it flesh out the particulars of ethical action in each section. Moreover, it offers only minimal guidance in addressing complex and/or confusing ethical questions. Consequently, we must seek out other sources of guidance on the subject.

One relevant resource is a report published by AAUP entitled, "Guidelines for Good Practice: Part-time and Non-Tenure-Track Faculty" (AAUP, 1997a) that suggests a set of standards for institutional policies and procedures for such faculty. These guidelines are directed primarily at the ethics of hiring, overseeing, and terminating adjunct faculty. Specifically, these guidelines recommend the following:

- All faculty appointments should include a description of the required duties.
- Performance of faculty should be regularly reviewed based on those duties.
- Compensation and promotion decisions should be based on job performance.
- Compensation of part-time faculty should be similar to full-time faculty for corresponding responsibilities.
- Non-reappointment notices should be timely.
- Institutions are responsible for providing the supports and conditions necessary for part-time faculty to carry out their duties.
- Adjunct faculty should be included in governance structures and should be given fair consideration for full-time positions when they arise.

Although they are useful, these guidelines function more as personnel policies than as ethical duties. To gain a clearer picture of the truly ethical dimensions of this work, we must look to the scholarly literature in the field. That literature has identified three major ethical issues: competence to teach, responsible use of power with students, and respectful relationships between adjunct faculty, students, managers and other faculty.

Competence to Teach

The primary mission of education is to assist students to become adults who can live "self-examined" lives, act as responsible citizens in a democracy, and embark on an occupation that allows them to be self-sufficient and contributing members of society. When colleges and universities accept student tuition and other monies, they are contracting with students to teach them the skills to reach those goals. The ability of students to evaluate the competence of faculty before paying tuition is limited; they have neither the competency themselves to fully assess the expertise of the faculty nor the access to the data they need to make that determination. In essence, they are paying "in good faith", hoping that the college will be honoring the implicit promise to provide competent teaching. Because the institution so heavily promotes its value and worth to potential students, its most fundamental responsibility is to deliver competent teaching (Robinson & Moulton, 1985).

Competence in teaching includes both (a) knowledge of the subject to be taught, and (b) skill in communicating that knowledge in a way that makes it accessible to students. Expertise in the subject matter not only includes a graduate degree in the field, but also a specific background in the particular topic of the class. A doctorate in psychology, for example, does not qualify an adjunct faculty member to teach any course in that field. Similarly, the knowledge of a topic must be relatively current. A person who has not kept up-to-date with the literature in macroeconomics is not competent to teach a course in that area unless he or she engages in a systematic effort of re-education, no matter how prestigious the degree in the field once was.

Compliance with this ethical responsibility seems easier in theory than in practice. Administrators rarely have the luxury of an extensive search for adjunct faculty to teach a particular course nor do they usually have a large pool of applicants for such positions. They often must make decisions on short notice and rarely can offer a salary that would attract the best practitioners in the given academic field. Those who are interested in adjunct positions are also attempting to present themselves in the best possible light and may be reluctant to be completely frank about the limits of their competency. In addition, practitioners who are new to adjunct teaching often honestly underestimate the effort required to update knowledge while teaching a course. Moreover, even in the best of circumstances, delineating what is actually beyond the limits of a person's competency is a judgment call about which ethical and responsible people may disagree. The question about the exact point at which a professional's knowledge becomes outdated or limited is never easily answered. However, there are several practical guidelines administrators can use in making this judgment:

- Does the person's graduate transcript or *curriculum vitae* show formal training, continuing education, or research involvement directly related to the content of the course(s) to be taught?
- Is there evidence (either from written materials or personal interviews) that the candidate has kept current with the theory and research relevant to the course?
- Are there other faculty and/or administrators in the institution available for consultation about a candidate's knowledge-base when competency is in doubt?
- Can the prospective adjunct faculty member produce a syllabus or reading list for the course that shows current expertise?
- In interviews, is the candidate able to provide a realistic assessment of both strengths and weaknesses of his or her competence in a given area? (Extreme levels of confidence in the absence of actual experience teaching the course in question is a reason for caution in many cases).
- Is the candidate open to supervision and consultation activities while teaching a course for the first time?
- Does the candidate exhibit a diligent attitude toward teaching this content and is he or she able to describe the steps to be taken to ensure that this diligent attitude is maintained until the completion of the course?

When still in doubt about competency, an administrator or faculty member can turn to the more fundamental ethical principles that underlie the duty to competence. These are the principles of *fidelity* and *beneficence* (Beauchamp & Childress, 1989). Fidelity means that a person who makes promises to others (either explicit or implicit) has a duty to keep those promises, barring unforeseen developments. Another way to conceptualize the duty to fidelity is as a loyalty obligation. When in doubt about competence, administrators and adjuncts should evaluate each of the potential courses of action in terms of their compliance with the promises they have made or implied.

The principle of beneficence applies to both education and human service professions, because both exist to "do good for others or help them"—the very meaning of the term. Other types of organizations do not necessarily have a duty to do "good." Furniture manufacturers, for example, have no such duty, because they do not hold themselves out to the public as professional helpers or "do-gooders." Consequently, their only ethical obligations are to avoid harm to the people who buy their products (termed non-maleficence by ethicists) and to be faithful to their promises. So, when wrestling with a particularly confusing or complex ethical question, faculty and administrators may find the beneficence of their alternatives useful. In other words, they may come closer to a resolution by asking of each possible alternative, "Does this provide the benefit (i.e., the learning) that we have promised?"

Needless to say, even an adjunct faculty member who is at the cutting edge of his or her field cannot be considered competent unless capable of communicating that knowledge in a fashion that promotes student learning. To promote student learning competent, faculty are able to:

- identify their philosophy of teaching and the teaching methods appropriate to a particular content;
- create clear and complete syllabi and records of student performance;
- develop explicit, objective grading and evaluation policies;
- adapt instructional methods to the needs of varied learning styles;
- encourage students to develop an attitude of inquiry toward the course content;
- foster student-to-student interactions that promote learning;
- handle classroom management issues appropriately (including dealing with uninvolved or disruptive students, late or missed assignments, or students experiencing personal crises that interfere with their performance in class); and

- be able to respond to suggestions for improvement of teaching from managers or student course evaluations.

On a final note, competence to teach must be distinguished from exceptional teaching. The ethical standard here is not one of exceptionality. Rather, these guidelines are meant to clarify the minimum or threshold levels of performance needed for the task at hand. Those who supervise adjunct faculty also have an obligation to help those at the threshold level of competence to develop further and enhance the quality of the teaching they provide to students.

Responsible use of power

Faculty hold power over students' academic success and influence their post-college plans through the content of their letters of reference. Their power is enhanced by the autonomy most institutions give faculty in organizing, conducting and evaluating student performance. Administrators have control over who gets hired, rehired or fired and what they get paid for their work. For both groups then, the abuse of power is always a possibility. Adjuncts and administrators need to strive then to avoid such abuses and use their power responsibly.

Specifically, faculty need to be as fair and objective as possible in the ways they evaluate students' academic performance. Although complete objectivity is impossible, faculty should seek to make judgments upon criteria that are explicit and relevant. Criteria are explicit when they are known to both faculty and students in advance of the assignment, capable of close replication by other competent faculty in the field, and implemented consistently. Criteria are relevant when they are based on students' performance of the task at hand rather than extraneous factors such as students' race, gender or attractiveness.

Relevancy is also determined by the degree to which the evaluation tool is connected to the major goals of the course. Faculty are using their power over students' grades responsibly when the tests and assignments given are clearly related to the major goals of the course, including the important skills or content students need to learn. Evaluation tasks that attend only to minor details or tangential material are not consistent with this standard. Students have a right to expect that they will be evaluated on the major topics in the course. This is not to imply that evaluations need to be easy or that stringent standards are inappropriate. Comprehensive tests and assignments that challenge students to work at their full potential are fully consistent not only with this standard but also with the ethical principle of beneficence. When "class participation" or other less tangible forms of evaluation are used faculty should aim for as much explicitness as possible so that their relevance to the course is obvious to the objective observer.

In parallel fashion, when students have the opportunity to evaluate the quality of their instruction, faculty members should strive to design instruments that give a full and fair picture of the course and provide students with opportunities to suggest possible improvements in future classes. Adjunct faculty and their managers should also make arrangements so that students can submit such evaluations anonymously and without fear of their comments having an impact on their grades. Recent research by Braxton and Bayer (1999) suggests that objective evaluation and opportunities for confidential course evaluations are central ethical values of faculties in institutions of higher education. They also note that violations of these ethical norms occur across all kinds of campuses and that they seriously erode student confidence in the educational process. Faculty from a variety of institutions in their national study placed "particularistic grading" in the category of offenses that deserve the most severe penalties (along with behaviors such as moral turpitude and condescending negativism).

In sum, criteria for judging whether faculty are meeting this ethical standard for evaluation include:

- Are student assignments and examinations clearly related to the goals and content of the course?
- Are criteria for grading explicitly stated along with the grading scheme?
- If "class participation" and other less objective criteria are used, has the faculty member reduced the possibility of bias in this evaluation as much as possible?

- Are comments in letters of reference based on course performance or other evidence of student capabilities?
- Are student course evaluations conducted so that students are assured anonymity and freedom of expression and do the evaluation questions allow for fair comments by students?

Responsible use of power entails more than fair grading. Faculty are obligated both by ethics and by law to act in non-discriminatory ways with students and colleagues. Avoiding sexual harassment and inappropriate sexual relationships with students is one crucial aspect of non-discrimination, given the abundant evidence that these violations occur frequently on college campuses and the notorious nature of some of this misconduct (Lott & Reilly, 1996). While there are clearly some faculty members who engage in willful and self-interested violations of this standard, many faculty members blunder into harassing conduct. Frequently, they fail to think through the implications of their words or actions or they lose sight of the boundaries that must exist between them and their students. In the latter instance, because the students enrolled in their classes are young adults with whom they may share some interests, they begin to establish personal relationships with them. Personal relationships with students while they are enrolled in one's courses are ethically problematic because they compromise the objectivity that is essential for fair evaluation. They also overlook the influence of their power and status as a possible factor in the student's interest in a friendship with them in the first place. Thus, the consensus among scholars is that faculty ought to avoid personal relationships with students while they are also responsible for evaluating their performance.

Psychologists and physicians refer to this as "avoiding dual relationships" (Welfel, 1998) and advise that attempting to carry out a second role with a student while in the midst of an evaluative one carries with it a high risk of abuse of power. The student may not get a fair evaluation and the other students in the class may feel they were at a disadvantage because they did not have a friendship with the professor. Moreover, if the friendship sours during the course, the classroom may become a tense and uncomfortable environment.

Ethicists also view dual relationships as problematic because they place students at significant risk for harm and avoiding risk of harm is what ethicists call the most fundamental ethical principle (Beauchamp & Childress, 1989).

Sexual relationships with students are not the only type of dual relationship that risks harming students. Any kind of secondary relationship with students that makes it difficult for them to fully benefit from instruction or that lessens faculty objectivity is ethically problematic. For that reason, entering into business relationships with current students or establishing non-sexual personal relationships with them may prove as harmful as romantic connections.

It is important to distinguish between personal relationships and professional mentoring, however. Becoming a mentor to a student is clearly a desirable role for faculty, one that they ought not to shun because of fears of a problematic dual relationship. To evaluate whether a mentoring relationship falls within acceptable boundaries, faculty should ask themselves the following questions:

- Is the nature of the relationship with the student primarily professional, focusing primarily on the student's career and educational development and not on personal issues for either party?
- Is the relationship not complicated by sexual attraction on the part of either party?
- Is the faculty member comfortable with other members of the department knowing about the mentoring relationship? If not, perhaps it ought to be re-evaluated. Haas and Malouf (1995) refer to this as the "clean, well-lit room standard." In other words, if a professional feels at ease in a open and frank discussion of the situation with peers, then it is probably an ethically acceptable situation.
- Is the faculty member capable of putting the educational and career development of the student ahead of any personal gain?

Another way to conceptualize the responsible use of power is as the avoidance of conflicts of interest. The only interest or investment of a faculty member or administrator should be the educational growth of the students and the advancement of knowledge in the field of study. Consequently, an adjunct faculty member who accepts a teaching appointment for the sole purpose of gaining clients or referrals for his or her business or selling more copies of a newly published book is abusing power. In those instances, students have become a means to another end rather than an end in themselves. Students are also being deceived about the purpose of their enrollment in the course. They register with the belief that the instructor's purpose is to help them learn; without any implied deceit about the instructor's motivation, they would elect to take another instructor.

Obviously, the motives of any flesh-and-blood faculty member cannot be fully selfless. Few would work without compensation, for example, and many assign their own texts in their classes. Such behaviors become ethically problematic when the primary benefit of such actions falls not to the students but to the faculty member. As long as there is a clear educational benefit to students from the faculty member's action and as long as the faculty member would choose another action if he or she saw more benefit to the student in that action, no conflict of interest exists. Using this reasoning, an adjunct faculty member is free to use in class an example from his or her private practice or business if relevant to the objectives of the course or to disclose his or her business during the initial class introductions. Passing out business cards, free products, or assigning students to visit the faculty member's business web site are unlikely to be ethical, both because their benefits to students are questionable and because the students are likely to perceive such actions as primarily self-interested even if there is potential educational value. Faculty and administrators ought to avoid engaging in actions that are vulnerable to perceptions of a conflict of interest whenever possible because it erodes trust and compromises a student's engagement in the course.

Respectful Relationships with Coworkers and Students

The third primary ethical responsibility of all faculty is to respect the autonomy, dignity and privacy of all participants at the institution. They also have a duty to respect the professional credentials and diverse points of view of colleagues. Freedom of thought and expression are core values of a college or university. In practical terms, these values mean:

- Recognizing that the search for knowledge often engenders honest scholarly disagreement and that progress depends not on advocating one view and disparaging others, but rather on the calm, rational analysis of evidence.
- Differentiating between energetic debate about a controversial or unresolved issue and personal attacks on the character or intelligence of colleagues with opposing views.
- Encouraging students to develop their own thinking even when they align themselves with a different or novel theory or approach. Of course, when their theories are illogical or inconsistent with evidence, faculty ought to point out those inconsistencies and encourage students to think further on the issue.

Respect for students also includes honoring their rights to privacy. In the course of interactions in the classroom students occasionally reveal personal information that they have shared with few people. Students might disclose for example, a family member's struggle with mental illness in psychology course or a humiliating experience of discrimination in a sociology course. At other times, personal information is disclosed when students need to explain why assignments are late, classes missed, or accommodations in evaluation procedures are needed. In each case students typically expect faculty members to handle that information discreetly. Faculty members, therefore, need to be aware of their obligations to protect the privacy and dignity of the student in the way they treat such information. Specifically, they ought to:

- Avoid sharing those disclosures with others without student permission unless there is a clear and compelling reason to do so. As mentioned earlier, comments that reveal a serious risk of suicide fall into the latter category. Disclosures of child abuse and neglect also need to be reported rather than kept private.
- In a course in which disclosure of personal information is relevant or even encouraged, the guidelines for confidentiality and its limits should be explicitly discussed with students at the initiation of the course.

- Similarly, disclosures from co-workers ought to be treated with the same respect and kept confidential. This guideline applies to those supervising adjunct faculty as well as co-workers. Personal data that managers obtain in the course of hiring or supervising adjuncts can only be revealed if directly related to promoting the well-being of students or the adjunct faculty member in question.

In cases in which the interest of the student or co-worker in privacy is unclear, the faculty member is bound to keep that material private until he or she can clarify the student's wishes in regard to confidentiality of the disclosed material.

The research of Braxton and Bayer (1999) supports the importance with which faculty should regard this ethical obligation. They found "personal disregard for the rights of others" in the category of the most serious ethical violations of faculty.

Occasionally, adjunct faculty become aware of instances of misconduct by their colleagues. In such situations loyalty and respect for the rights of colleagues may conflict with the adjunct faculty member's duty to the students and the institution. Depending upon the potential seriousness of the offense, an adjunct faculty member may need to breach confidentiality in order to get the damage of the misconduct redressed. AAUP considers collegial misconduct such an important topic that the association issued a statement on it in 1998. This document provides faculty, faced with this difficult situation, some guidance in responding to the misconduct in a way that honors the rights of the colleague to the fullest degree possible while also protecting the students and the institution.

Guidelines for Managers to Foster Ethical Practice

One of the major ethical responsibilities of managers of adjunct faculty is to put into place mechanisms to foster ethical practice and reduce the incidence of misconduct. Many adjunct faculty have not been fully acculturated into the norms and values of academia and so a substantial portion of the unethical practices in which they engage may be the result of ignorance or misguidance about these duties. The data that suggests that adjuncts are less closely supervised than tenure-track faculty also means that they often do not have the same fear of repercussions for violations that may motivate some full-time colleagues to avoid misconduct (AAUP, 1997a,b). Managers who seek to promote responsible teaching by adjuncts are advised to adapt the following guidelines to their institutions:

- Share copies of the institution's ethical standards or the standards of the AAUP with all incoming adjunct faculty so that they have a understanding of the broad parameters of responsible teaching;
- Include a discussion of the ethical responsibilities of adjunct faculty in all orientation meetings;
- Establish regular meetings with adjunct faculty, especially those new to the position so that a dialogue about teaching effectiveness and ethical responsibilities can occur;
- Encourage consultation between adjunct and full-time faculty about teaching so that adjunct faculty feel they have other resources in the institution besides the supervisor with whom they can discuss these issues;
- Mandate anonymous and confidential course evaluation procedures for adjunct faculty;
- Make clear the penalties for violation of these responsibilities;
- Develop a method of acknowledging exemplary adjunct faculty behavior;
- Avoid practices that communicate to adjunct faculty that they are "second-class citizens" in academia; such practices undermine the message that their ethical responsibilities are as important as any other faculty member's; and
- Recognize that managers must provide ethical leadership for their programs and that they must be vigilant about their own compliance with ethical guidelines and standards.

Managers who are committed to following these guidelines will have taken a crucial first step in assisting both adjunct faculty and their students in creating a the kind of learning environment college catalogues promise prospective students.

References

American Association of University Professors. (1987). *Statement on professional ethics*. Washington, DC: Author.

American Association of University Professors. (1993). *The status of non tenure-track faculty*. Washington, DC: Author.

American Association of University Professors. (1997a). *Guidelines for good practice: Part-time and non tenure-track faculty*. Washington, DC: Author.

American Association of University Professors. (1997b). *Statement from the conference on the growing use of part-time and adjunct faculty*. Washington, DC: Author.

American Association of University Professors. (1998). Collegial misconduct. *Academe, 84,* 58.

Beauchamp, T.L., & Childress, J.F. (1989). *Principles of biomedical ethics.* (3rd ed.). Oxford, England: Oxford University Press.

Braxton, J.M., & Bayer, A.E. (1999). *Faculty misconduct in collegiate teaching.* Baltimore: Johns Hopkins University Press.

Clery, S. (1998). Faculty in academe. *NEA Higher Education Research Center Update, 4* (4), 8-16.

Gappa, J.M., & Leslie, D.W. (1993). *The invisible faculty: Improving the status of part-timers in higher education.* San Francisco: Jossey-Bass.

Haas, L.J., & Malouf, J.L. (1995). *Keeping up the good work: A practitioner's guide to mental health ethics.* (2nd ed.). Sarasota, FL: Professional Resource Exchange.

Lott, B., & Reilly, M.S. (1996). *Combating sexual harassment in higher education.* Washington, DC: National Education Association.

Robinson, G.M., & Moulton, J. (1985). *Ethical problems in higher education.* Englewood Cliffs, NJ: Prentice-Hall.

Welfel, E.R. (1998). *Ethics in counseling and psychotherapy: Standards, research and emerging issues.* Pacific Grove, CA: Brooks/Cole.

Dr. Elizabeth Reynolds Welfel is currently a Professor and Coordinator of the Counselor Education Program at Cleveland State University.

6

Legal Issues Concerning Adjunct Faculty and Their Managers

By William Murphy, Esq.

Overview

This chapter will give adjunct faculty and their managers general information concerning the following legal issues:

- Legal rights of adjuncts based on institutional types and common law;
- Adjuncts' employment relationships;
- Constitutional rights of adjuncts, including due process;
- Forms of adjunct faculty liability including general and tort liability, as well as negligence;
- Protections against discrimination including sexual harassment; and
- Issues of academic freedom as outlined by AAUP Guidelines.

Introduction

In today's litigious society, all individuals working in an educational institution need to understand the potential for lawsuits against the institution and against them personally. The purpose of this chapter is to provide adjunct faculty and managers with an increased awareness of some of the legal issues that directly relate to adjunct faculty.

This chapter provides certain basic general information concerning relevant federal and state statutes as well as case law and how these laws may apply to adjunct faculty and others who work in institutions of higher education. It is designed to be used as a resource when legal issues arise concerning employment, due process, academic freedom, constitutional rights, sexual harassment under Title II and Title IX, and the tort liability of adjunct faculty. It is also intended to increase knowledge of relevant legal matters in the area of higher education law and to help decrease the volume of litigation filed against institutions of higher education and their administrators and faculty.

The material presented here is not intended as a substitute for professional services in specific situations or to furnish legal or professional advice, but to present the sources of law related to these issues and their implications for adjunct faculty managers.

Legal Rights of Adjunct Faculty
Sources of Law

The legal rights of adjunct faculty can only be determined by reviewing the sources of law applicable to post-secondary education and the types of institutions that the adjunct faculty member works in, i.e., public or private.

If adjunct faculty teach in a public institution, their basic legal rights will be determined by the protections provided by the United States Constitution; the applicable state constitution; relevant federal, state and local statutes or ordinances; as well as the applicable administrative rules of any governing state or federal agency. Adjunct faculty may also have rights provided by the internal policies and procedures or rules of the institution. In most cases, they will have contracts with the institution that identify the terms and conditions of their employment relationship with the institution.

There may also be certain long-standing and widely accepted academic customs at the institution that may provide certain rights in established practices or understanding in certain situations. This source is sometimes referred to as Campus Common Law (Kaplin & Lee, 1995).

For adjunct faculty who teach in private institutions, the constitutional protections would not be available, but the other sources of law including certain federal and state statutes, a well as the rules and regulations of the federal and state administrative agencies and of the institution and their contract would provide a basis for establishing their rights.

In some institutions adjunct faculty may be included in a collective bargaining agreement which would then provide them with the rights that were negotiated into the agreement for adjunct faculty. However, in an institution in which they are not included as members of a collective bargaining agreement or in an institution where there is no collective bargaining agreement for faculty, they must rely on the sources of law which have been cited above to determine the rights that may be applicable to them.

Finally, the common law must be reviewed to determine if there are any case precedents applicable to the rights of adjunct faculty. Common law is case law consisting of a large body of principles, rules, and concepts which is not based on written (statutory) law; however, many of the basic concepts of common law have been incorporated into the written law through usage and custom. When a court decides a case and records its decision in a written opinion, that opinion, known as a case, becomes a precedent. That is, the principles on which the case was decided may be used to decide future cases with similar factual situations.

Common law provides a method called "synthesis of decisions", whereby the principle of a case can be applied to different fact patterns. This method involves the formulation of principles for general application, coupled with the extension of those principles through logic to meet new fact patterns. The impact of the case's precedent depends on the court in which it is decided. A higher court is not bound to follow the precedents established by the lower courts in its jurisdiction. Lower courts, however, are bound to follow the precedents of the higher courts having jurisdiction over them. Courts of equal rank may use each other other's precedents, just as the courts of one state may borrow from the precedents of another state or federal court. Courts often use the precedents of equal or lower courts, the courts of other states, and the federal courts when such precedents are well reasoned or address new problems. (Ohio State Bar Foundation, 1998).

Public vs. Private Institution's Legal Distinctions

The law provides that public institutions and their officers are fully subject to the constraints of the United States Constitution, whereas private institutions and their officers are not. This is because the United States Constitution is intended to limit only the exercise of government power and does not prohibit private individuals or corporations from impinging on such freedoms as free speech, freedom of association, and due process. Thus, adjunct faculty teaching in private institutions do not share the protections of the United States Constitution as their counterparts do who are teaching at public colleges and universities (Beckham, 1986).

At private institutions the contractual relationship between the faculty member and the institution provides the basis for the rights of adjunct faculty. Private institutions may be subject to federal and state regulation in specific circumstances but they are not prohibited from restricting freedoms such as free speech, association, equal protection and due process.

Employment Relationships Between Adjunct Faculty and the Institution

Employment Relationship

Adjunct faculty may have several different types of employment relationships with the institutions where they teach. They may have a written appointment letter from the institution or a written contract of employment for a definite term. In the absence of a term employment contract or written appointment letter, they would have employment at-will status.

At-Will Status

An employee hired for an indefinite term without a written contract of employment is generally regarded as being subject to termination for any cause at any time. At-will employees have no property interest in continued employment. However, at-will public employees generally can not be terminated in retaliation for the exercise of a constitutional right or for an impermissible reason (race or sex discrimination).

In reviewing at-will cases, courts will attempt to ascertain the intent of the parties and the existence of implied or expressed contractual provisions which may alter the terms of any termination. Courts have recognized employee handbooks, institutional policy, and oral representations in some situations as providing evidence of an employment contract (Siegel & Stephen, 1991).

Term Contract

However, most adjunct faculty will generally be employed under a written contract of employment with the institution which will, at a minimum, specify a definite term of employment, course or courses to be taught, and the compensation to be paid during the employment term.

A requirement of cause to terminate would apply to a term contract for a public employee if the institution sought to dismiss the adjunct faculty member prior to the effective date of contract termination. A public employee dismissed during the term of a contract and in breach of its provisions has a legitimate claim of a entitlement and a property interest in continued employment subject to due process protection.

The general rule in higher education is that all limited or term contracts can be non-renewed. That is, at the end of the term for which they are written, there is no expectancy of re-employment on the part of the adjunct faculty member. Thus, when the contract comes to an end, there is no right to a notice of non-reappointment, no right to a hearing, and no right to reasons for non-reappointment.

However, during the term of a contract, an adjunct faculty member in a public institution would be entitled to the same constitutional due process protections as any public employee with a contract. These rights flow from the Fourteenth Amendment to the United States Constitution and decisions of the United States Supreme Court.

Constitutional Due Process Protection

In the landmark case of *Board of Regents of State Colleges v. Roth* (1972), the U.S. Supreme Court held that any right to procedural due process for a public employee requires that a "liberty" or "property" interest be implicated.

A "liberty" interest applies if the employee's "good name, reputation, honor or integrity is at stake" or if "a stigma or other disability has foreclosed his freedom to take advantage of other employment opportunities". There is no liberty interest in the continuation of employment itself, and the mere non-renewal of a contract does not constitute a deprivation of liberty. To implicate a liberty interest, one must establish that the employer made a stigmatizing charge to the public that resulted in dismissal.

A "property" interest may also be implicated in the dismissal of non-tenured employees. *Roth* held that an assistant professor had no property interest sufficient to require university authorities to give him a hearing on the non-renewal of his contract.

However, in a companion case, *Perry v. Sindermann* (1972), the Court found that a non-tenured teacher could state a claim to continuing employment if there were rules or understandings that could give rise to "implied" tenure. If one can show a "common law of re-employment" or a "de facto tenure policy" that has expectation of renewal, reasons for the non-renewal and a hearing are required.

Adjunct faculty and managers should become familiar with the policies and procedures of the institution directly related to the appointment and non-reappointment of adjunct faculty. Managers of adjunct faculty in public institutions should also be aware of the property interest the adjunct faculty member has because of the written contract. That property interest protects them from arbitrary dismissal during the term of their contract.

Managers should also be careful, during the course of a non-renewal, not to make charges against adjunct faculty which could damage their reputation, standing, or associations in the community or to make the charges public. These statements could form the basis of a liberty interest and entitle the adjunct faculty member to a procedural due process hearing.

Adjunct Faculty's Legal Responsibilities
General Liability

Both public and private institutions can be held liable for injury, death, or loss resulting from the negligence of the institution and/or its employees. Each state may have laws providing some form of sovereign, governmental, or charitable immunity which may apply to the institution and/or to the employees of the institution.

While some courts have held that colleges sponsored by private organizations are not liable as a charitable institution, the doctrine of charitable immunity has been abrogated in most jurisdictions, and charitable institutions, including private colleges, are being held liable for their negligence (*Moore v. Mayle*, 1950).

Adjunct faculty may be held personally liable for damages that they cause due to their negligence. In some states, adjunct faculty may have immunity from liability unless their acts or omission were manifestly outside the scope of their employment or official responsibilities, involved malice or bad faith, or were made in a wanton or reckless manner.

In some cases, state law may provide that the institution has a duty to defend and indemnify its employees for their acts or omissions which result in injury to others and which occur within the scope of their employment.

Adjunct faculty may also be personally liable for constitutional violations if their actions are alleged to have caused the deprivation of any person's rights, privileges, or immunities secured by the Constitution and laws of the United States.

In most cases, institutions in both the public and private sectors will carry insurance and/or provide some form of indemnification for adjunct faculty.

Tort Liability

A significant amount of litigation against institutions of higher education falls under the classification of tort liability.

A tort is a civil wrong other than a breach of contract. The field of torts concentrates upon the compensation of individuals for losses that they have suffered in respect to their legally recognized interest. The compensation is provided by the tortfeasor (wrongdoer). Generally, liability is based upon the unreasonable interest of others, however, what is unreasonable is subject to much interpretation. The field of tort liability can be divided into three categories:

1. Intentional acts to harm,
2. Unintentional acts which harm, and
3. Strict liability or liability without proof of fault. (Van Der Smissen, 1990, Sec. 1.4, p.47).

Intentional torts are those in which the tortfeasor intends to cause injury. Some examples of these are defamation, libel, slander, invasion of privacy, misrepresentation, false imprisonment, and assault and battery.

Unintentional acts which harm individuals are classified as negligence. Negligence can be defined as an "unintentional breach of a legal duty causing damage reasonably foreseeable without which breach the damage would not have occurred" (Van Der Smissen, 1990, Sec. 1.42, p.65).

Strict liability is liability without fault or absolute liability. It is designed for the protection of society and the standard of conduct is absolute. It is intended to focus on the danger of the activity or product rather than on the conduct or intent of the tortfeasor.

Elements of Negligence

Most tort cases filed against institutions of higher education are based on the theory of negligence. In order to establish a claim for negligence, one must prove four elements:

1. A duty which is an obligation recognized by the law requiring a person to conform to a certain standard of conduct for the protection of others against unreasonable risks,
2. An act, which is a failure on the part of such person to conform to the

standard required,

3. Proximate cause, which is a reasonably close causal connection between the conduct (failure to conform to appropriate standard) and the resulting injury, and

4. Damages, which consist of the actual loss or damage to the interest of another. (Van Der Smissen, 1990, Sec. 2.1, p. 2).

Duty of Teachers

In cases involving educational institutions and teachers, the existence of the duty to conform to a certain standard of conduct is inherent in nearly every situation that involves teaching or supervising students. The most common duties of teachers are to provide adequate instruction, to warn of dangers, to provide adequate supervision, and to maintain equipment and facilities in good repair.

Duty as an element of negligence refers to the responsibility toward others to protect them from unreasonable risk of injury arising from the relationship between the parties. Teachers have a duty to act as reasonably prudent persons under all circumstances.

The duty to provide adequate instruction includes two aspects. One is the actual instruction of skill, technique, and strategies including methodology of teaching. The second aspect focuses on safety, including rules and regulations of the game. One court has defined proper instruction as "an explanation of basic rules and procedures, suggestions for proper performances, and identification of risks" (*Green v. Orleans Parish School Board,* 1978).

In physical education classes and athletic activities, courts have held that teachers have an affirmative duty to instruct students on reasonable safety precautions to be observed while engaged in class activities (*Darrow v. W. Genessee Central School District,* 1973).

The duty to provide safe equipment and facilities can include, in some cases, providing safety devices and protective equipment. It is not always sufficient to warn of dangers and activities, if safety devices and protective equipment are essential for the protection of students (Van Der Smissen, 1990, Sec. 19.231, p. 229).

Lack of supervision is one of the most common allegations of negligence against teachers. Adjunct faculty are responsible for providing adequate supervision for activities of students in their class or in activities assigned to the adjunct faculty member.

Areas that require special attention include, but are not limited to, laboratories where chemicals are being used, clinical areas—particularly where patients are being treated, physical education classes, shops, intercollegiate and intramural sports, student activities, and field trips.

In those activities which carry more risk of injury, the adjunct faculty member should be made aware of any institutional policies or procedures relating to these activities and should realize the importance of providing safety instructions and warnings of dangers, as well as providing safe equipment. If equipment is not in good repair, it should not be used. The notice of detective equipment should be reported to the administration.

Nondiscriminatory Employment Protection for Adjunct Faculty

Title VII of Civil Rights Act of 1964

Adjunct faculty working in public and/or private institutions are protected by the provisions of Title VII of the Civil Rights Act of 1964, 42 U.S.C.A. § 2000e *et seq.* Title VII is the most significant of the modem federal statutes prohibiting employment discrimination. It provides that an employer shall not discriminate against an employee or job applicant in any of the terms or conditions of employment because of such individual's race, color, religion, sex, or national origin (42 U.S.C.A. § 2000e-2). It further prohibits retaliation against any individual who opposes unlawful employment practices or participates in investigations and enforcement proceedings under Title VII (42 U.S.C.A. § 2000e-3).

Title VII is enforced by the Equal Employment Opportunity Commission. The Commission has the responsibility for investigating any charge filed with it and to determine whether there is reasonable cause to believe the charge is true.

If the Commission determines there is reasonable cause to believe the charge, it must attempt to conciliate the charge. If the Commission finds no reasonable cause, or it finds reasonable cause but is unsuccessful in concil-iation, or if the Commission fails to complete its investigation within 180 days of the filing of the charge, the Commission may issue a letter inform-ing the complainant that he or she can file suit within 90 days of receipt of the notice. The suit can be filed in federal or state courts.

Many states have also adopted legislation to set up their own state civil rights commission, which then allows the Equal Employment Opportunity Commission to defer the charge to the state commission for investigation and enforcement.

There is a substantial number of charges filed against institutions of higher education under this law. Adjunct faculty as well as other employees in the institution can file charges of discrimination against the institution and those charges must be investigated and a determination made by the federal or state agency.

Age Discrimination in Employment Act

Adjunct faculty are also protected by the federal Age Discrimination in Employment Act (ADEA) which prohibits discrimination on the basis of age. It protects persons age 40 and over and provides for a civil suit in feder-al court. (29 U.S.C.A. § 626, 20 U.S.C.A. § 631 [A]).

Equal Pay Act of 1963

The Equal Pay Act of 1963 (29 U.S.C.A. § 206 [D]) also protects all employ-ees. It prohibits paying female employees a lower wage than male employ-ees for performing work which is equal in skill, effort and responsibility, and is performed under similar work conditions, unless the wage differential is based on a seniority system, a merit system, or system measuring quantity and quality of production, or some factor other than sex. Many states also have adopted their own state laws to prohibit wage-rate sex discrimination.

Sexual Harassment

Adjunct faculty are also protected from sexual harassment. However, they also may find themselves the subject of a sexual harassment complaint. The Equal Employment Opportunity Commission has promulgated specific guidelines under Title VII of the Civil Rights Act of 1964 prohibiting sexual harassment, which is defines as "unwelcome sexual advances, requests for sexual favors, and other verbal or physical conduct of a sexual nature" when:

1. Submission to such conduct is made either explicitly or implicitly a term or condition of employment;
2. Submission to a rejection of such conduct by an individual is used as the basis for employment decisions affecting the individual; or
3. Such conduct has the purpose or effect of substantially interfering with an individual's work performance or creating an intimidating, hostile, or offensive working environment. (29 C.F.R. § 1604.11[a]).

Relief for sexual harassment may be premised on one or both of two theories: (1) *quid pro quo* harassment (conditioning a tangible employment benefit on sexual favors), and/or (2) harassment t that gives rise to a hostile or abusive work environment.

The U.S. Supreme Court approved the Equal Employment Opportunity Commission Guidelines in holding that Title VII is not limited to *quid pro quo* harassment but that unwelcome sexual advances by a supervisor could also create a hostile work environment claim (*Meritor Savings Bank, FSB v. Vinson*, 1986).

In order to establish liability, a sexually hostile environment must be both objectively and subjectively offensive, one that a reasonable person would find hostile or abusive, and one that the victim, in fact, did perceive to be so. Courts must examine all the facts and circumstances; including the frequency of the discriminatory conduct, its severity, whether it is physically threatening or humiliating or a mere off-hand remark and whether it interferes with the employee's work performance.

However, simple teasing, off-hand comments, and isolated incidents (unless extremely serious) will not be considered to be a discriminatory change in the terms and conditions of employment (*Harris v. Forklift Sys. Inc.*, 1993).

Employers are now liable for the sexually harassing conduct of supervisors with immediate authority over the employee. In *Burlington Industries, Inc. v. Ellerth* (1998), the U.S. Supreme Court held that if a tangible employment action is taken against the employee, such as discharge, demotion, or an undesirable reassignment, the employer will be automatically held liable for sexual harassment. If no tangible employment action is taken against the employee, an employer may assert an affirmative defense to liability by showing (a) that the employer exercised reasonable care to prevent and correct promptly any sexually harassing behavior, and (b) that the employee unreasonably failed to take advantage of any preventive or corrective opportunities provided by the employer or to otherwise avoid harm. Proof that the employer had promulgated an anti-harassment policy with a complaint procedure, along with proof that the employee did not take advantage of the policy, will generally be enough to establish the affirmative defense.

If the harassment is done by a non-supervisory co-worker, most courts base liability on the question of whether the employer through its supervisory personnel knew or should have known of the conduct and, if so, whether the employer took prompt and appropriate corrective action (*Kauffmann v. Allied Signal, Inc.*, 1992).

Under Equal Employment Opportunity Commission Guidelines, an employer may be liable for harassment by non-employees if the employer knows or should have known of the conduct and fails to take corrective action.

Section 504 and Americans with Disabilities Act

Adjunct faculty are also protected by Section 504 of the Rehabilitation Act of 1973 (29 U.S.C.A. § 784) which prohibits discrimination against individuals with disabilities by recipients of federal funding. The Americans with Disabilities Act of 1990 (42 U.S.C.A. § 12112) also prohibits discrimination on the basis of disability against a qualified individual with a disability with respect to all aspects of employment. An employer must make reasonable accommodations to the individual's known physical or mental limitations unless the employer can show accommodation would impose an undue hardship.

131

Title IX of the Education Amendments of 1972

Adjunct faculty must also become very familiar with the provisions of Title IX of the Education Amendments of 1972 (20 U.S.C. § 1681 *et seq.*) which provide that "no person in the United States shall, on the basis of sex, be excluded from participation in, be denied the benefits of, or be subjected to discrimination under any education program or activity receiving federal financial assistance".

In *Franklin v. Gwinnett County Public Schools* (1992), the U.S. Supreme Court determined that a student could sue a school district for money damages under Title IX for a teacher's alleged sexual harassment of that student. This decision is applicable to all public and private institutions of higher education.

In *Gebser v. Lago Vista Independent School District* (1998), the U.S. Supreme Court determined that a school district may be held liable in damages under Title IX for a teacher's sexual harassment of a student. The court held that students may recover damages from a school district under Title IX for teacher/student sexual harassment if an official of the school district who had at a minimum the authority to institute corrective measures on the district's behalf has actual notice of and is deliberately indifferent to the teacher's misconduct.

The U.S. Supreme Court also held in *Davis v. Monroe County Board of Education* (1999) that schools that receive federal financial funds may be held liable under Title IX when a student sexually harasses a peer. To be held liable, the school must exhibit deliberate indifference to known sexual harassment that is "so severe, pervasive, and objectively offensive that it effectively bars the victim's access to an educational opportunity or benefit."

The court stated that plaintiffs need not show that the harassment physically excluded the victim from access to school resources. Rather, plaintiffs "must establish sexual harassment of students that is so severe, pervasive, and objectively offensive, and that so undermines and detracts from the victims' education experience that the victims/students are effectively denied equal access to an institution's resources and opportunities." The latter effect must be "systematic," making it theoretically possible, but unlikely, that single instances of harassment would qualify.

Adjunct faculty need to be aware of these decisions and their academic managers should provide a copy of the institution's sexual harassment policy and procedure to all adjunct faculty. It is also important to attend training workshops on the topic of sexual harassment and to report any observed instance of student-on-student sexual harassment to the proper authorities.

Academic Freedom Protections for Adjunct Faculty
Academic Freedom

The primary policy statement on Academic Freedom can be found in the American Association of University Professors (AAUP) 1940 Statement of Principles on Academic Freedom and Tenure and the 1970 Interpretive Comments (60 AAUP Bulletin [1974]) and the AAUP's 1976 Recommended Institutional Regulations on Academic Freedom and Tenure (62 AAUP Bulletin 184 [1976]). These documents are sometimes referred to as the prevailing policy statements on academic freedom.

The AAUP defines academic freedom as follows:

- The teacher is entitled to full freedom in research and in the publication of the results, subject to the adequate performance of his other academic duties; but research for monetary return should be based upon an understanding with the authorities of the institution.

- The teacher is entitled to freedom in the classroom in discussing his subject, but he should be careful not to introduce into his teaching controversial matter which has no relation to his subject.

- The college or university teacher is a citizen, a member of a learned profession, and an officer of an educational institution. When he speaks or writes as a citizen, he should be free from institutional censorship or discipline but his special position in the community imposes special obligations. As a man of learning and an educational officer, he should remember that the public may judge his profession and his institution by his utterances. Hence he should at all times be accurate, should exercise appropriate restraint, should show respect for the opinions of others, and should make every effort to indicate that he is not an institutional spokesman (AAUP, 1969, pp. 33-36).

Those institutions that have collective bargaining agreements with AAUP Chapters may have some form of the above-cited language concerning academic freedom incorporated into their faculty contract. If there is no faculty collective bargaining agreement, it is possible that the AAUP policy statements have been approved by the institution or may appear in faculty handbooks. If the statements have not been approved by the institution and are not incorporated in a faculty handbook then the statements generally would not apply to that institution.

However, courts of the United States, including the U.S. Supreme Court, have dealt with the concept of academic freedom. In some cases, courts have given it constitutional status under the First Amendment freedoms of speech and association, the Fifth Amendment against self-incrimination, and the Fourteenth Amendment guarantee of due process even though the U.S. Constitution does not specifically mention academic freedom.

Constitutional Status of Academic Freedom

One of the most important cases relative to establishing the constitutional status of academic freedom is *Sweezy v. New Hampshire*, (1957). In this case, the U.S. Supreme Court reversed a contempt judgment against a professor who had refused to answer questions concerning the contents of a college lecture delivered at the state university. The opinion of the court included the following observation:

> Scholarship cannot flourish in an atmosphere of suspicion and distrust. Teachers and students must always remain free to inquire, to study and to evaluate, to gain new maturity and understanding; otherwise our civilization will stagnate and die.

In a similar case in 1960, *Shelton v. Tucker* (1960), the U.S. Supreme Court struck down a state statute which required public school and college teachers to reveal all organizational affiliations or contributions for the previous five years. In this case, the Court made the following comments:

> But, in view of the nature of the teacher's relation to the effective exercise of the rights which are safeguarded by the Bill of Rights and by the Fourteenth Amendment, any prohibition of freedom of

thought, and of action upon thought, in the case of teachers brings the safeguards of those amendments vividly into operation. Such unwarranted intrusion upon the free spirit of teachers has an unmistakable tendency to chill that free play of the spirit which all teachers ought especially to cultivate and practice; it makes for caution and timidity in their associations by potential teachers.

The U.S. Supreme Court again upheld the concept of academic freedom in *Keyishian V. Board of Regents* (1967). In this case, several State University of New York faculty members refused to sign a certificate stating they were not and never had been communists. As a result, they lost their jobs and brought an action against the state on the grounds that their First Amendment Rights were violated. In that case, the court stated,

> Our Nation is deeply committed to safeguarding academic freedom... That freedom is therefore a special concern of the First Amendment, which does not tolerate laws that cast a pall of orthodoxy over the classroom ... The classroom is peculiarly the "marketplace of ideas." The Nation's future depends upon leaders trained through wide exposure to that robust exchange of ideas, which discovers truth "out of a multitude of tongues, rather than through any kind of authoritative selection."

In the *Keyishian* case, the court held that the faculty members' First Amendment freedom of association had been violated by the existence and application of a series of laws and rules that were both vague and excessive.

In 1968 a new type of academic freedom case was decided by the U.S. Supreme Court in *Pickering v. Board of Education* (1968). In this case a high school teacher had been dismissed for writing a letter to a local newspaper highly critical of the board of education's financial plans for the high schools. He brought suit alleging that his dismissal violated his First Amendment freedom of speech. The board argued that the dismissal was justified because the letter damaged the professional reputations of school board members and school administrators, would be disruptive of faculty discipline, and would tend to foment controversy, conflict, and dissension among teachers, administrators, the board, and the residents.

The court applied a test to balance the teacher's freedom of speech against the state's interest in maintaining an efficient education system. It identified five factors to assist it in applying the balance test:

1. Is there a close working relationship between the teacher and those he criticized?
2. Is the substance of the letter a matter of legitimate public concern?
3. Did the letter have a detrimental impact on the administration of the educational system?
4. Was the teacher's performance of his daily duties impeded?
5. Was the teacher writing in his professional capacity or as a private citizen?

In this case, the court found that the teacher had no working relationship with the board, that the letter dealt with a matter of public concern; that the letter was greeted with public apathy and, therefore, had no detrimental effect on the schools; that his performance as a teacher was not hindered by the letter; and that he wrote it as a citizen not as a teacher.

The court concluded from these facts that the interest of the school administration in limiting teachers' opportunities to contribute to the public debate was not significantly greater than its interest in limiting a similar contribution by any member of the general public and "that in a case such as this, absent proof of false statements knowingly or recklessly made by him, a teacher's exercise of his right to speak on issues of public importance may not furnish the basis for his dismissal from public employment."

There are four primary settings in which academic freedom issues generally arise. They are in:

1. Classroom activities;
2. Research and publication;
3. Institutional affairs; and
4. Private personal life (Kaplin & Lee, 1995, pp.299-324).

Classroom Activities

In classroom activities, courts generally defer to administrators and educators in matters dealing with disputes over course content, teaching methods, grading, and classroom behavior (Kaplin & Lee, 1995, p. 306).

In *Lovelace v. Southeastern Massachusetts University* (1986), the court rejected the free speech claim of a faculty member whose contract was not renewed after he had rejected administration requests to lower the academic standards he applied to his students. The court concluded that universities must themselves have the freedom to set their own standards on "matters such as course content, homework load, and grading policy" and "that the first amendment does not require that each non-tenured professor be made a sovereign unto himself."

Research and Publication and Institutional Matters

In cases involving research and publication as well as the freedom of faculty to speak on institutional matters outside the classroom, courts have generally been supportive of the faculty member. In these kinds of case, faculty generally have fared better with the courts than in classroom cases (Kaplin & Lee, 1995, p. 315).

In *Smith v. Losee* (1973), a non-tenured faculty member addressed a meeting of the faculty association in his capacity as president. His speech criticized the college administration. Subsequently, he was dismissed, and he brought suit asserting his First Amendment right to free speech. The court stated that even though he was speaking in his capacity as president of the faculty association, he was entitled to criticize the administration in such a manner without fear of being dismissed. The court said that having proved that his dismissal was grounded upon his exercise of First Amendment rights, the burden then shifted to the defendant college to show by clear and convincing evidence that the plaintiff's activities and speech "materially and substantially interfered with the requirements of appropriate discipline in the operation" of the college.

Since the college could not do that, the court concluded that the faculty member's interest in free speech far outweighed the interests of the defendants in promoting the efficiency and harmony of Dixie College.

Private Life

Faculty members' activities have the most protection from state or institutional regulation in their private lives. In *Hander v. San Jacinto Junior College* (1975), a state college attempted to enforce faculty grooming regulations. A professor was dismissed when he refused to shave his beard. The court stated that:

> school authorities may regulate teachers' appearance and activities only when the regulation has some relevance to legitimate administrative or educational functions. The mere subjective belief in a particular idea by public employers is, however, an undeniably insufficient justification for the infringement of a constitutionally guaranteed right. It is illogical to conclude that a teacher's bearded appearance would jeopardize his reputation or pedagogical effectiveness with college students.

These cases demonstrate that it is difficult to know when the concept of academic freedom will be enforced by the courts. Almost all the major cases are based on the U.S. Constitution and are applicable only to those who work in public institutions.

Adjunct faculty and managers should review the policies and procedures of their institution to determine if the AAUP policy statements have been approved in any manner by their institution.

Conclusion

Litigation against institutions of higher education, their managers and faculty continues to grow each year. The best course of action for institutions to take to reduce the potential for litigation is to exercise preventive law. In order to accomplish this, managers and adjunct faculty should develop a better understanding of their rights and responsibilities under the law.

It is essential that they attend legal training sessions on major legal topics, particularly on sexual harassment as it applies to both teacher/student harassment and student-on-student harassment. The courts have placed more responsibility upon institutions and their faculty and managers to be able to identify sexual harassment and to take the necessary steps to investigate and to implement corrective action when necessary.

The information is this chapter provides only the tip of the iceberg in identifying the law as it applies to institutions of higher education. It is suggested that the readers consider the information in this chapter to be a point from which they will take actions to become more informed about the law and how it applies to institutions of higher education.

References

29 C.F.R. 1604.11(a).

Age Discrimination in Employment Act of 1967, 29 U.S.C.A. § 626, 20 U.S.C.A. § 631 (A). (West, 1993).

American Association of University Professors. (1969). *Academic Freedom and Tenure*. Lanham, MD: University Press of America.

American with Disabilities Act of 1990, 42 U.S.C.A. § 12112. (West, 1993).

American with Disabilities Act of 1990, 42 U.S.C.A. § 12111 (10). (West, 1993).

Beckham, J.C. (1986). *Faculty/Staff Nonrenewal and Dismissal for Cause in Institutions of Higher Education, 8*, Asheville, NC: College Administration Publications.

Board of Regents of State Colleges v. Roth, 408 US 564, 573 (1972).

Burlington Industries, Inc. v. Ellerth, U.S. 118 S.Ct. 2257 (1998).

Darrow v. W. Genesse Central School District, 41 AD 2d 897 (1973).

Davis v. Monroe County Board of Education, US No. 97-843 (U.S. filed May 24, 1999).

Equal Pay Act of 1963, 29 U.S.C.A. § 206 (D). (West 1993).

Farragher v. City of Boca Raton, U.S. 118, S.Ct. 2275 (1998).

Franklin v. Gwinnett County Public Schools, 503 U.S. 60 (1992).

Gebser v. Lago Vista Independent School District, 524 U.S. 274, (1998).

Green v. Orleans Parish School Board, 365 So. 2d 834 (LA App. 1978).

Hander v. San Jacinto Junior College, 519 F. 2d. 273 (5th Cir. 1975.)

Harris v. Forklift Sys. Inc., 510 O.S. 17 (1993).

Kaplin, W.A., & Lee, B.A. (1995).*The Law of Higher Education, 17*, (3rd ed.). San Francisco: Jossey-Bass.

Kauffmann v. Allied Signal Inc., 970 F(2d) 178 (1992).

Keyishian v. Board of Regents, 385 U.S. 589 (1967).

Lovelace v. Southeastern Massachusetts University, 793 F. 2d 419 (1st Cir. 1986).

Meritor Savings Bank, FSB v. Vinson, 477 U.S. 57 (1986).

Moore v. Mayle, 405 ILL. 555, 92 N.E., 2d 81 (1950).

Ohio State Bar Foundation and Ohio State Bar Association. (1998). *The Law & You: A Handbook of General and Everyday Law Affecting Ohio Citizens, 4,* (11th ed.). Columbus, OH: Author.

Perry v. Sindermann, 408 US, 593 (1972).

Pickering v. Board of Education, 391 U.S. 563 (1968).

Section 504, Rehabilitation Act of 1973, 29 U.S.C.A. § 794. (West, 1993).

Shelton v. Tucker, 364 U.S. 479 (1960).

Siegel, B.N., & Stephen, J.M. (1991). *Ohio Employment Practices Law.* Cleveland, OH: Banks-Baldwin Law Publishing.

Smith v. Losee, 485 F. 2d 334 (10th Cir. 1973).

Sweezy v. New Hampshire, 354 U.S. 234 (1957).

Title VII, Civil Rights Act of 1964, 42 U.S.C.A. § 2000e-2. (West 1993).

Title VII, Civil Rights Act of 1964, 42 U.S.C.A. § 2000e-3. (West 1993).

Title IX, Education Amendments of 1972, 20 U.S.C. § 1681 et seq. (West, 1993.)

Van Der Smissen, B. (1990). Legal Liability and Risk Management for Public and Private Entities. Cincinnati, OH: Anderson Publishing.

William Murphy, Esq., is currently General Counsel-Assistant Attorney General for Cuyahoga Community College, Ohio.

The Academic Manager: Five Steps to Parity

By Michael H. Parsons

Overview

This chapter covers five areas in which adjunct faculty can reach parity with full-time faculty:

- Recruitment/Integration: Sources and Strategies;
- Orientation/Assimilation: Individual and Group Opportunities;
- Instructional Support: Contractual, Personal, and Technical;
- Evaluation: Substance and Structure; and
- The Parallax Progression: Identification, Professional Development, and Civic Value.

Introduction

The integration of adjunct faculty into the delivery of instruction is not a new phenomenon. In preparation for the 21st century, however, all aspects of the academic institution's instructional mission are undergoing comprehensive analysis. Miller (1997, p.90) conducted an ERIC review of models useful in preparing community college faculty for the new millennium. His synthesis provides a useful starting point for designing a process for managing adjunct faculty. "Community college teaching has emerged as a distinct profession. It requires a preparatory program that will instill the knowledge and skills needed for [effectiveness] and provide the philosophical grounding and socialization required for a role that has become ever more complex." The results of the review are equally applicable to part-time faculty. In another ERIC review, Leider (1998, p.1) focuses on part-time faculty. He reports that "part-time faculty continue to play an important role in community colleges. [In] 1993, the National Study of Post-secondary Faculty found that 53.4% of public two-year college faculty were teaching part-time as . . . that [which] follows explains, things haven't changed much." As the number of adjuncts remains constant and in certain areas, increases, the need for a management strategy becomes increasingly great. Is there a perspective available that provides insight?

In mid-1998, twenty senior educators from Europe and the United States met in Glion, Switzerland to develop a vision for engaging the concerns of the new century. The Glion declaration provides a point of view that is helpful in designing a management process. "The essential key ... to human well-being in this daunting new world is knowledge ... Those things on which the future of humankind will chiefly [rely] ... will depend increasingly on knowledge: knowledge discovered, knowledge gained, knowledge tested, knowledge shared, knowledge applied. And these things, in turn, will require wisdom: the way in which knowledge is weighed and used" (Rhodes, 1998, p.27-28). Knowledge, therefore, is the key to full integration of adjunct faculty into the culture of the community college. There are five steps that lead to parity of knowledge development between full-time and adjunct faculty. Their integration into a management strategy will assist institutions in allowing all of their personnel to engage the opportunities of the 21st century.

Recruitment/Integration: Sources and Strategies

While the number of adjunct faculty remains constant and in some specific areas increases, recruiting them continues to be a challenge. There are numerous sources that remain viable and several strategies that assist with recruitment.

It is essential that managers of adjunct faculty establish and cultivate access to primary personnel sources. The institution's instructional team needs to make contact with school district personnel who have responsibility for teacher selection and supervision. Secondary education faculty can provide subject matter knowledge as well as pedagogical expertise. Many of them consider adjunct teaching in the post-secondary environment as a personally enriching experience. Further, they serve as a contact point for student recruitment. It is useful to involve supervisory personnel in the formative quality control process. Further, the number of extracurricular activities required of teachers today makes collaboration essential so that good relations are maintained with the school district.

An equally important personnel source is the local chamber of commerce. Most of these organizations are structured around delivery systems that are useful to college instructional teams. Such committees as marketing, small business, international trade, manufacturing, and business/education partnerships allow for targeted recruitment. The members of the various committees are usually aware of the expertise that exists in the employer community served by the college. Further, they can often provide a point of contact that expedites access.

A third useful source links to the public service sector. United Way organizations provide access to potential adjuncts with specialization in human and community services. Again, these agencies integrate sources of teachers and sources of students.

A fourth agency that provides specialized expertise is the Service Corps of Retired Executives. Members of this group have a proven record of achievement in a wide range of fields. Further, they are interested in sharing their expertise and experience without a significant concern over remuneration. The college also benefits from the reputation of these individuals as former business, industry, or agency leaders.

Finally, there are several strategies that use adjunct faculty as the catalyst for creating synergy between the college and those seeking educational opportunities. Frequently, business and industry have personnel with specific expertise. They are often willing to work with community colleges in establishing a training/certification process. Their employees become subject matter expert adjuncts. The college assists them with course design, delivery, and certification. Usually the classes are heterogeneously grouped with students drawn from the sponsoring business or industry as well as from the college's general student body. Citicorp, the Credit Card Division of Citigroup/Travelers, designed a certificate program in financial services in collaboration with Hagerstown Community College (HCC). Citicorp Financial Services specialists serve as adjunct faculty. Several other financial agencies in the HCC service area enrolled students in the courses. The certificate became a critical element in Citicorp's personnel development program (Parsons, 1998, *National Council*, p.4).

Another example is the donation of adjunct faculty by small businesses or agencies that need educational services but don't have the resources to take advantage of the college's regular offerings. The Washington County (Maryland) Health Department provides adjuncts that volunteer to teach courses in the HCC Human Services Associate Degree program. The funds that would have been paid to them are used to provide partial scholarships to agency personnel who are enrolled in the courses (Parsons, 1998, *Memorandum*, p.1).

The essence of the recruitment/integration step is knowledge access. It is broad based and available if the college instructional team establishes a process to identify and takes advantage of it. The only limitation is the imagination of college personnel and service area representatives working together. Roueche, Roueche, and Milliron summarize the importance of the synergy:

Research on instruction has long shown the importance of demonstrating the application and relevance of knowledge for quality instruction. Part-time faculty can provide community college students with "real world" linkages that bring learning to life ... With part-time faculty, students experience an important professional and community resource that can enhance learning, inspire career choices, and connect students with professions and the community through outside affiliations (Roueche, J.E., et al., 1995, p.12).

It is the responsibility of the community college instructional team to make that potential a reality.

Orientation/Assimilation: Individual and Group Opportunities

The second step toward parity is to integrate the adjunct faculty member into the culture of the college. The process of orientation/assimilation is designed to begin as early as possible in the new adjunct's affiliation with the college. Two national studies conducted in the 1990s revealed that both two- and four-year colleges do a poor job of assimilating adjunct faculty (Gappa, 1993, p.213, Roueche, 1995, p.29). There is, however, a common thread that runs through the ideal programs described in these studies. Some colleges recognize that adjuncts will come to personify the institution to the students through their continued association with the institution. Attention must be given to making them excel in carrying out this role. Most of the models reflect a multi-dimensional approach.

The first dimension is an interpersonal one. The recommended process begins with the first level of the instructional team—department or division chairperson. One successful format used to ensure the orientation of new adjuncts is the Interview Checklist (Appendix 7.1). The new adjunct is assimilated through a process of awareness building. The chair provides the new instructor with the necessary tools to effectively implement the role of institutional representative. All of the items detailed in the Interview Checklist require explanation even if the new adjunct is already an experienced teacher. The differences in procedure from institution to institution make discussion essential. Further, the orientation should not be a static

147

process. Where possible, a walking tour of the instructional area is valuable. Familiarity with the classroom, sources of instructional support materials, access to telephone, fax, and computer support all assuage the new adjunct's performance anxiety.

Two other areas deserve special mention. Each institution has idiosyncratic expectations for a course syllabus. When discussing the syllabus document, a model should be provided. If possible, one for the course being taught should be selected. While the new adjunct is usually not bound to use every detail of the model, the example will ensure that all the expected/required content is included.

The second area is the text and supporting materials to be used in the course. If the new adjunct is given them at the time of the orientation, questions regarding their implementation can be answered. Further, the new adjunct will be able to begin planning immediately rather than waiting for the materials to arrive.

The second dimension is the institutional/legal aspect. To ensure that consistency is maintained, phase two should be the responsibility of the chief instructional officer (dean, vice president, or their designee). Some elements of the process that can be used are detailed in the Part-Time Faculty Interview Checklist (Appendix 7.2). While the list is short, it is an essential part of orientation process.

Most regional accrediting agencies are sensitive to the use of adjuncts (Parsons, *How*, 1998, p.1-2). An area of particular concern is the credentials of the adjuncts. It is essential that adjunct faculty records become a part of the permanent personnel file.

The Immigration and Naturalization Service requires proof that employees are eligible for work in the United States. An accurately completed I-9 form is the simplest way to avoid problems for employees and the college.

Finally, as campus security grows in importance, personal identification becomes essential. It is recommended that photo identification cards be provided to new adjuncts as soon as possible. The result will be easier integration for them into the college environment.

With these functions completed, the new adjunct is ready to join the staff of the college. However, they are still "strangers in a strange land." Is it possible to increase their comfort level and simultaneously improve their role as representatives of the college?

Several model programs present an integrating activity designed to meet these challenges. In large institutions it may be within a school, department or division; in smaller ones it may be institution wide. The first activity is a gathering to which all full-time and adjunct faculty are invited. From the perspective of the institution, the activity is composed of two parts.

In the first part, issues are presented that are of common concern to all academics. Announcements, discussion, and presentations must be precise and focused. Time is of the essence and, where possible, detail should be presented in writing and only the highlights reviewed.

The second part is the most important. This activity should be structured at the department or divisional level and its main purposes are to:

- create a partnership for excellence between the faculty,
- emphasize strategies for improving the quality of the teaching/learning process,
- establish a mechanism for solving the day-to-day teaching concerns of adjunct teachers,
- maintain enthusiasm for teaching among both full- and part-time teachers, and
- rekindle a sense of commitment to the college's mission among the adjunct (Johns, 1998, p.3-5).

Further, the departmental/divisional component allows the new adjuncts to become acquainted with the full-time faculty and other adjuncts with which they are likely to come in contact during their teaching. The result is twofold. First, they feel less "at sea" within the college; there are some familiar faces. Second, they have a point of contact beyond the chair or dean, offering another person to go to for answers and assistance.

The departmental/divisional component can also be characterized as knowledge transference. The operational procedures and regulations are "second nature" to veteran full-time and adjunct personnel. Only through a systematic, multi-dimensional process can the new adjunct become aware of and comfortable with the operational aspects of the college's culture.

Instructional Support: Contractual, Personal, and Technical

A common theme that pervades all national studies of adjunct faculty is that they should not function in isolation. While structure is important to assimilation, functional considerations are equally vital to new adjuncts. The two most important elements are the adjunct contract and the adjunct/part-time faculty handbook.

The contract or memorandum of agreement (Appendix 7.3) makes formal what has been discussed in both the individual and group orientation. The new adjunct has as a ready reference information such as length of service, courses to be taught, number of credits or equivalent, and salary. Since in most institutions there is a required minimum enrollment, that figure should also be included. Further, the issue of contractual responsibilities to full-time staff should be covered by the clause that allows the college to reassign section(s) as needed.

The relationship of the adjunct to the institution's fringe benefit package should be detailed since participation is typically not offered nor is the time taught counted toward tenure.

Finally, the performance issue requires attention. Evaluation should be referenced and the process of termination reviewed. These issues are essential in an era of ever-increasing accountability.

The adjunct's signature is required. The purpose is to assure that a legal awareness of the conditions of employment exists. Another useful element of the document should be the placement of pay dates in the lower right corner. Adding this information saves answering what is typically the most frequently asked question by adjuncts.

The second structural element is the part-time/adjunct handbook which can follow a similar format as outlined in the sample table of contents in Appendix 7.4. The publication has two purposes. First, it provides a ready reference to the most frequently asked student questions. Experienced adjuncts report that the handbook accompanies them to every class meeting. The second purpose is to provide examples of the most commonly used college forms. Via these forms, adjuncts can check a range of procedures that vary from permission to enter a closed class to material reproduction requests. The purpose is to save time – both that of the adjuncts and that of the staff who serve them.

The recognition that adjuncts are "the college" for many part-time students has been raised earlier. Assisting them in fulfilling this representative role requires access to institutional support personnel. How will the adjuncts get material prepared? Whom do they call if they are going to be late for class or are ill? Where do they get instructional media? These and other specific questions unique to each institution and/or teaching area require a personal communication system. Ideally, there will be division or department secretaries who have a list of adjuncts assigned to the area. They should be introduced to new adjuncts at the time of orientation. Further, there needs to be a media location within each teaching area. Adjuncts should be made aware of the location and access procedures at the time of hire. If the department/division or library have media support materials, adjuncts should be provided with lists of these teaching tools at the time of orientation.

Special services tend to be idiosyncratic to each institution. However, several are worthy of consideration. First, since over half of the adjuncts are reported to teach in the late afternoon/evening, support services such as an evening secretary, switchboard operator, media staff, and a make-up testing location make adjuncts feel a part of the college culture.

Second, technical support need not be highly sophisticated to be effective. Is there a copier or other duplicating machine available? Where do adjuncts go to make a phone call? Is there a private area where they can conference with a student or students when needed? Finally, is there a computer equipped with word processing/printing capability and Internet access available to them? These technical services and equipment are not given a second thought by full-time staff; adjuncts should have the same support.

Roueche, Roueche, and Milliron (1995, p. 120) summarize the support issue concisely. "[Adjunct faculty are] increasingly important players in the teaching and learning process. [It is] in the [college's] interest of appreciating the investment value of [them], and ultimately in the interest of establishing and maintaining the college's reputation for teaching excellence." The issue is essentially one of knowledge sharing. The adjuncts bring subject matter expertise to the college. In return, college personnel must provide them with sufficient structural knowledge to realize their potential.

Evaluation: Substance and Structure

One rapidly emerging trend of the 21st century is characterized by an emphasis on accountability. All of higher education is being required to provide data on the effectiveness of its practices. Since adjunct faculty teach 25-33% of the credit hours generated by community colleges (Roueche, 1995, p.30), it is expected that they will participate in a faculty evaluation process.

There are several systems available for adjunct evaluation. Ideally, every class taught should be evaluated. For numerous small institutions, however, the personnel are not available to do so. In this case, a sampling evaluation system can be used. The sampling system requires a series of components:

- evaluations by students and a supervisor;
- anonymity of student evaluations until the course is completed;
- timing of the application so that maximum results are achieved;
- the opportunity for narrative as well as forced choice responses;
- formal feedback to adjuncts with a developmental focus (Behrendt, 1983, p.14).

The model in use at HCC is based on the foregoing principles. Adjunct faculty are evaluated the first time that they teach and every third time thereafter. In certain circumstances (military base courses and selected business contractual instruction), every class is evaluated. The student and supervisor evaluation instruments (Figure 7.1 and 7.2) are both required in an adjunct "sampling" evaluation.

Figure 7.1 — Student Evaluation Instrument

FACULTY EVALUATION

INSTRUCTOR _____ COURSE _____

DATE _____

Instructions for Completion:
Please use a #2 pencil. Make sure entire block is filled in. Give only one response per question. Erase response completely if changing your answer. Please make your decisions based on your expectations when you entered the course or your experience with other courses.

Responses A-E across the top apply to questions 1-19 only.

(write comments on back)

For questions 1-19 use the following:
A. always   B. usually   C. sometimes   D. rarely   E. not applicable

	A	B	C	D	E
1. The instructor makes clear to you what is expected in this course.	☐	☐	☐	☐	☐
2. The activities or the objectives specified in the course syllabus are being accomplished.	☐	☐	☐	☐	☐
3. So that you can adjust, sufficient notice is given if the instructor modifies the syllabus or the schedule of major assignments.	☐	☐	☐	☐	☐
4. The instructor is well prepared for class and well organized in his/her presentation.	☐	☐	☐	☐	☐
5. The instructor communicates clearly.	☐	☐	☐	☐	☐
6. The instructor clarifies material when needed.	☐	☐	☐	☐	☐
7. The instructor promotes independent thought about the subject.	☐	☐	☐	☐	☐
8. The instructor encourages questions, discussion, and expression of your viewpoints.	☐	☐	☐	☐	☐
9. The instructor responds to your questions satisfactorily.	☐	☐	☐	☐	☐
10. The instructor is enthusiastic about the subject.	☐	☐	☐	☐	☐
11. The instructor is available to you outside class, either during office hours or by appointment.	☐	☐	☐	☐	☐
12. The exams in this class are representative of the information covered.	☐	☐	☐	☐	☐
13. The instructor's grading practices are clear.	☐	☐	☐	☐	☐
14. The instructor's grading practices are fair.	☐	☐	☐	☐	☐
15. Graded work is returned in a reasonable time.	☐	☐	☐	☐	☐
16. The instructor makes comments (oral or written) about papers, projects, homework, or tests to help you understand your mistakes.	☐	☐	☐	☐	☐
17. The instructor demonstrates knowledge of the subject matter.	☐	☐	☐	☐	☐
18. The teaching materials (handouts, audiovisual materials, etc.) in this course are helpful in understanding the subject.	☐	☐	☐	☐	☐
19. The instructor begins and ends each class on time.	☐	☐	☐	☐	☐
20. Your overall evaluation of the instructor is: A. excellent B. above average C. average D. below average	☐	☐	☐	☐	☐
21. In comparison to other college courses you have had, your opinion of this course is: A. excellent B. above average C. average D. below average E. not applicable	☐	☐	☐	☐	☐
Questions 22-24 are for data collection and do not affect the instructor's evaluation.					
22. Compared to the other college courses you have taken, the effort you put into this course is: A. much more B. somewhat more C. about the same D. somewhat less E. much less	☐	☐	☐	☐	☐
23. The textbook selected for the course contributed to your understanding of the course content. A. always B. usually C. sometimes D. rarely E. not applicable	☐	☐	☐	☐	☐
24. Are you a full-time or part-time student? A. full-time B. part-time	☐	☐	☐	☐	☐

Figure 7.2 — Supervisory Evaluation Instrument

SUPERVISORY RATING SCALE

	(a) Superior	(b) Above Average	(c) Average	(d) Below Average
1. The course syllabus clearly stated				
A. Grading procedure				
B. Objectives & goals for the course				
C. Course Outline				
D. Legal disclaimer				
2. The instructor prepared the evaluator for class visit.				
Ex. Comments on nature of class handouts or excerpt from text, topics to be discussed.				
3. The instructor had command of the class.				
4. The instructor connected the day's work to previous class(es) or to the total course plan.				
5. The instructor's speech patterns and mannerisms facilitate learning.				
6. The instructor is responsive to student questions and viewpoints.				
7. The presentation of material is clear and well organized.				
8. A person with no expertise in the subject could have learned something from this presentation.				
9. The instructor creates an effective learning environment.				
10. The instructor aroused interest in the class.				

Note: On a separate sheet of paper describe what you observed while evaluating this class.

The student instrument assesses three categories. The first category (items 1-9) deals with instructor preparedness. The second (items 12-16) focuses on evaluation practices. The third (items 10, 11, 17-19) describes practices that contribute to a positive learning environment. Items 20-21 are designed as controls on the preceding categories. Finally, data is gathered on demographic variables that impact on the teaching/learning process. Students are encouraged to make narrative comments that elucidate the classroom climate.

The supervisory instrument focuses on selected critical incidents that contribute to a positive teaching/learning environment. Supervisors are encouraged to make narrative comments that clarify or amplify their forced choices.

After the teaching period ends, adjuncts are provided with a statistical summary of the student forced-choice instrument, a typed copy of student narrative comments, and a copy of the supervisory checklist with comments. A cover letter prepared in the Dean of Instruction's office describes the relationship between the individual evaluation and the college's accountability system. The letter varies depending upon the quality of the evaluation. Since evaluations are processed soon after they are done, division chairs can follow up if immediate action is indicated.

What is the relationship between part-time evaluations, full-time evaluations, and college accountability? In 1994, Stovall reported on a study revealing "that part-time and full-time faculty are equally effective teachers from the perspective of student performance in the classroom"(p.1). However, there was a need to assess teacher behavior so that professional development for both full-time and adjunct faculty could be made more effective.

The assessment of the HCC database revealed that full-time and adjunct faculty behaved in a generally similar way in the classroom. The general assessment of both the instructor and the course did not differ statistically between full-time and adjunct faculty. However, variances were detected on several items. Adjunct faculty were reported to be less accessible than the full-time (item 11). Also, the teaching materials used by adjuncts were ranked as less helpful than those used by full-time faculty (item 18). The item analysis provides data to be used to increase parity between instruction delivered by full-time and adjunct faculty.

Quality of instruction as judged by the client is a critical component of HCC's accountability plan. The empirical results of the evaluation provide the college with a format for adjunct faculty development. The evaluation design selected focuses on improvement of instruction as perceived by the client.

The essence of the evaluation design is to test the knowledge possessed by adjunct faculty. The results validate their level of knowledge; it is up to college personnel to assist them in making it useful to the institution's clients.

The Parallax Progression: Identification, Professional Development, and Civic Value

For decades scientists have informed us that the perceived direction of an object depends upon the point from which it is viewed. This parallax perspective provides a useful progression for adjunct faculty development.

Adjuncts bring a broader, more diverse view of the community, the college, and the students than that possessed by full-time faculty (Roueche, 1995, p.6). Yet, the evaluation data indicate that they are not as effective in several critical areas as their full-time colleagues are. Is it possible to benefit from their perspective while improving their ability to implement the college's instructional mission? Experience suggests that a parallax perspective can be made positive. There are four components to making the process work.

1. **Mentoring has been described as a viable tool to improve adjunct performance. It has several aspects.** When an adjunct is teaching in a highly technical area, or is expected to deliver a specific component of instruction in a specific manner, or is preparing students for progression into a sequential course, a mentor model can be particularly useful. The process may include discussions, classroom visitations, syllabus review, or a video training tape. In general, the adjuncts welcome the opportunity and acclimate well to the institution's instructional environment when assigned a mentor.

2. **An environmental equity-training program** like the one developed at HCC focuses on diverse student characteristics and identifies instructional strategies that engage them. Full-time and adjunct faculty are teamed and then review instructional design, examine student learning

styles, observe in each other's classes, and discuss teaching strategies and their outcomes. After four years of environmental equity training, participants report that it has improved their teaching. Also, the evaluations of the participating adjuncts are generally above the college average. Finally, the perspective presented by the adjuncts enriches the teaching repertoire of the full-time faculty.

3. **Involvement of adjuncts in the group life of the college serves as a two-way outreach program.** They are informed of all instructional and cultural events presented by the college and are encouraged to participate. Further, an attempt is made to draw upon their expertise informally. The instructional team at the college conducts an open discussion between semesters. The topic is related to an institution-wide concern. All adjuncts are invited and many attend. Their perspective enriches the discussion and the outcome. Finally, the dean of instruction sponsors a structured forum during the spring semester. The presenters include an adjunct with expertise on the topic. All full-time and adjunct faculty along with students are invited. The discussion is lively with give-and-take among all. The formal presentations are published with copies provided to all full-time and adjunct faculty. Overall, a structured design to draw adjuncts into the college's culture has several positive benefits. First, adjuncts develop an increased identification with the college. Second, their expertise enriches the culture. Third, the formal and informal mentoring improves their pedagogy.

4. **Committee work creates a formal use of adjunct expertise.** Many of them serve on one of the college's program advisory committees. These bodies review curriculum, assess instructional technology, review student and employer evaluations of the programs, and introduce a variety of strategies for program improvement. The participation is synergistic, the college benefits from their expertise and, in turn, the adjuncts develop a more comprehensive understanding of the college's instructional mission. Further, with an increasing sense of participation in the group life of the college and a heightened awareness of the instructional mission, adjuncts often become community agents for the

college. They help spread the word regarding the value of and the services available through the college. In effect, they develop a civic value beyond their teaching responsibility.

In addition to the Parallax Progression, another strategy is the focus group analysis. The technique can be broad-based or issue-specific. Heterogeneous groups of adjuncts are convened to review instructional strategies, core values, and the college's revised mission statement. The result is a broader database for the institution, an improved sense of identification for the adjuncts, as well as a heightened awareness that their insights are valued.

Much more could be said about adjunct development but the topic is covered in detail elsewhere; this synthesis is based on applied knowledge. The college provides a knowledge-base regarding teaching and student development for application by adjuncts. Adjuncts provide a diverse core of knowledge based on their individual expertise. The college integrates the rich diversity into its instructional mission. All stakeholders—faculty, staff, and students—are the beneficiaries.

Conclusion: Toward a Synthesis of Equality

In January 1998, the senior research analyst with the U.S. Department of Education, Clifford Adelman, presented an assessment of the nation's higher education system. He was somewhat pessimistic. "The bottom line is that we are making a lot of promises to future students that we cannot fulfill… We do not have the capacity for two million new traditional students, let alone for all the other populations that seek the doorways to learning" (Adelman, 1999, p.27). There is another view possible.

In September 1997, the Sloan Foundation sponsored a national conference on the growing use of part-time and adjunct faculty. Their synthesis statement is more optimistic.

Is the increasing use of part-time and temporary faculty a cause or a symptom of profound changes buffeting American colleges and universities? … If society wants and needs just-in-time preparation for new careers at different stages in life without regard to physical location and at reasonable prices, then perhaps a more nimble and adaptable kind of institution is needed—one in which the faculty may or may not hold traditional doctorates, may or may not be full-time employees of one institution, may or may not even be physically present in a particular place at a particular time (Leslie, 1998, p.27).

The foregoing statement describes the challenges facing academic institutions at the dawn of the 21st century. Adjunct faculty will play an increasingly important role in implementing the instructional mission of "the peoples' college." Is it possible to be agile and accountable at the same time? If the five steps to parity are followed and the suggestions contained in the other sections of this manual are heeded, the answer is yes.

References

Adelman, C. (1999). Crosscurrents and riptides: Asking about the capacity of the higher education system. *Change: The Magazine of Higher Learning, 31*(1), 20-27.

Behrendt, R. L. & Parsons, M. H. (1983). Evaluation of part-time faculty. In Albert B. Smith (ed.), *Evaluating Faculty and Staff. New Directions for Community Colleges #41*, San Francisco: Jossey-Bass.

Gappa, J. M., & Leslie, D. W. (1993). *The invisible faculty: Improving the status of part-timers in higher education*. San Francisco: Jossey-Bass.

Hersch, W. & Weber, L. (1998). The Glion Declaration: The University at the Millennium. *The Presidency*, 1(2), 26-31.

Johns, R. M., & Parsons, M. H. (1992). Decentralizing staff development for part-time Faculty: An emphasis on quality. *Adjunct Info: A Journal for Managers of Adjunct and Part-Time Faculty, 1*(1), 1.

Leider, S. (1998). *Part-Time Faculty: Information Bulletin*. Los Angeles: ERIC Clearinghouse for Community Colleges.

Leslie, D.W. (1998). *Part-time, adjunct, and temporary faculty: The new majority?* Report of the Sloan Conference on Part-Time and Adjunct Faculty. New York: The Sloan Foundation.

Miller, A. A. (1997). ERIC Review—Back to the future: Preparing community college faculty for the new millennium. *Community College Review,*

24(4), 83-92.

Parsons, M. H. (1998, April). *How the other 2/3 live: Institutional initiatives for part-time faculty Assimilation in America's two-year colleges*. Paper presented at the 78th Annual Convention of the American Association of Community Colleges, Miami Beach, Florida.

Parsons, M. H. (1998, October). *Unpublished paper*. Paper presented at the National Council for Occupational Education 24th Annual Conference, Daytona Beach, Florida.

Parsons, M. H. (1998, November). *Memorandum of Agreement*, Washington County Health Department, Maryland.

Roueche, J. E., Roueche, S. D., & Milliron, M. D. (1995). *Strangers in their own land: Part-time faculty in America's community colleges*. Washington, DC: Community College Press.

Stovall, R. H. (1994). Student performance in classes taught by adjunct vs. full-time faculty. *Adjunct Info: A Journal for Managers of Adjunct and Part-Time Faculty, 2*(3), 1.

Dr. Michael H. Parsons *is currently the Dean of Instruction at Hagerstown Community College, Maryland.*

Chapter 7 Appendices

Appendix 7.1

Hagerstown Community College

PART-TIME FACULTY INTERVIEW CHECKLIST

Part 1:   During the interview with the division chairperson:

_____   Receive college catalog, Handbook for Part-Time Faculty, and Student Handbook

_____   Review location of the following:
_____ classroom(s)	_____	Library/Learning Resources Center/
_____ conference areas		Teaching-Learning Center
_____ emergency telephone	_____	Reprographics/Faculty Secretaries
_____ cafeteria	_____	Bookstore (parking sticker)
_____ audiovisual equipment/		(Order textbook from publisher
materials		if time permits)

_____   Discuss procedure for receiving mail from the college
Is a mailbox requested? _____ yes   _____ no

_____   Discuss beginning and ending dates of class(es)

_____   Discuss Honor Code (see Student Handbook)

_____   Discuss class roster(s)   ) Discuss importance
) of READING memos &
_____   Discuss final examination requirement and schedule   ) returning forms
) **ON TIME** -- **Call** if
_____   Discuss mid-term deficiencies and final grades   ) it's a problem
) meeting a deadline
_____   Discuss course syllabus

_____   Discuss teaching evaluation

_____   Discuss salary: Set at $_____/credit; minimum enrollment of _____ for full pay;
          _____ will or _____ will not accept partial pay for _____ minimum enrollment

_____   _____
Instructor   Division Chairperson

_____   _____
Date   Date

Original (white):   Instructor
Copy (yellow):   Dean of Instruction

Appendix 7.2

Hagerstown Junior College

PART-TIME FACULTY INTERVIEW CHECKLIST

<u>Part 2:</u>   During the meeting with the Dean of Instruction:

_____   Review syllabus, evaluation, salary, and Part-Time Faculty Handbook

_____   Complete an I-9 form (**<u>must</u>** be done within three days of start date)

_____   Complete a W-4 form

_____   Make arrangements to get a Staff I.D. Card

_____   Have official transcript(s) sent to Dean of Instruction

_____   _____
Instructor   Dean of Instruction

_____   _____
Date   Date

Original (white):   Instructor
Copy (yellow):   Dean of Instruction

Appendix 7.3

 Office of the Dean of Instruction

Hagerstown Community College

11400 Robinwood Drive • Hagerstown, Maryland 21742-6590 • 301-790-2800 • Voice-TDD • www.hcc.cc.md.us

MEMORANDUM OF AGREEMENT
PART-TIME FACULTY

We are looking forward to your association as a part-time member of the instructional staff of Hagerstown Community College. Your assignment for the _____ semester includes the following:

_____	_____	_____ semester hours
_____	_____	_____ semester hours
_____	_____	_____ semester hours
_____	_____	_____ semester hours

Your total salary for the semester will be _____ and this amount will be divided into _____ payments of
_____. For FY _____ a course must have a minimum of _____ students enrolled to guarantee full pay for an instructor. Participation in the College's fringe benefit program is not available to part-time faculty.

A copy of the class schedule is enclosed for your information. Further obligations of your teaching responsibility are detailed in the Part-Time Faculty Handbook; your division chairperson will give you a copy. The College reserves the right to conduct an evaluation of your performance during the semester. If you are selected for evaluation, you will be informed by your division chairperson.

Further, the College reserves the right to terminate a part-time appointment at any time if, in the judgment of the Dean of Instruction after consultation with the division chairperson, the appointee's performance of professional and personal responsibilities is incompatible with the standards required by the College.

This offer of employment is contingent upon adequate student enrollment and the availability of full-time staff. It should also be noted that the time you spend as a part-time employee of HCC will not count toward tenure if you ever join the staff on a full-time basis.

To indicate your acceptance and understanding of this agreement, please sign and return the enclosed copy. Please retain the original for your own record. We hope that your assignment for this semester will prove to be a challenging one.

Sincerely,

Michael H. Parsons
Dean of Instruction

The conditions of employment for a part-time instructor as outlined in this memorandum are reasonable and acceptable to me. I understand that this contract is for the stated session only and does not obligate the College for future employment on either a full- or part-time basis.

Date _____   *Signature* _____

Appendix 7.4 — Table of Contents of HCCC Adjunct Faculty Handbook

TABLE OF CONTENTS

- i -

- ii -

- iii -

- iv -

Distance Education Technology: What the Adjunct Manager Needs to Know

By Tinnie A. Banks

Overview

This chapter is intended to discuss the following:

- The types of distance education technologies and the necessary support for each type,
- Selection and training of adjunct distance education faculty,
- Types of synchronous and asynchronous delivery systems along with the needed equipment,
- Development of programming for both delivery systems, and
- Discussion of Copyright and Fair Use issues related to distance education programs.

Introduction

According to the 1999 edition of Peterson's *Guide to Distance Learning Programs*, there are a total of 2,000 doctoral, graduate, undergraduate and certificate programs available from approximately 900 institutions delivering courses using distance education technology, including prestigious universities such as Duke, Stanford and Syracuse. Historically, distance education was considered an "alternative" form of education, now it is considered mainstream (Kearsley, 1998). Its rapid growth and subsequent entrance into the mainstream can be attributed to four interrelated phenomena: the emergence of lifelong learning, efforts to make instruction more learner-centered, a desire to provide access irrespective of where a student lives and the development of "knowledge media" (Merisotis, Phipps, & Wellman, 1998). The "desire to provide access irrespective of where a student lives" can be achieved with either synchronous or asynchronous distance education technology. A synchronous distance education course meets at a scheduled time but in multiple, predetermined locations. With an asynchronous course, the learners don't attend a formal class but can access instructional materials anytime and anyplace as long as a computer or television and videocassette recorder are available. Students and instructor interact primarily using computer-mediated technology such as desktop videoconferencing and text-based communication tools such as electronic mail and threaded discussions.

Learner flexibility, convenience and opportunity are all available with both asynchronous and synchronous distance education mediums in varying degrees. The synchronous distance education technologies (Interactive Video, Desktop Video Learning Systems, Instructional Television Fixed System) provide convenience and opportunity primarily based on the proximity of the class location to the learner. Courses designed to use these technologies are in essence, traditional courses bound by a predetermined class time that convenes in multiple locations with more advanced multimedia technology available to both learner and instructor. Face-to-face interaction between students and instructor remains an integral component with synchronous courses.

While the synchronous distance education technologies provide convenience and opportunity primarily based on the proximity of the class location to the learners, asynchronous distance education technologies (telecourse, Internet, CD-ROM), characterized by anytime, anyplace learning, provide the ultimate flexibility in both convenience and opportunity. This flexibility is available at the expense of face-to-face interaction with the instructor and fellow students during a scheduled class period. Even so, asynchronous courses provide a comparable learning experience as synchronous or traditional courses, especially for nontraditional students (Kearsley & Moore, 1998). One of the key characteristics of non-traditional higher education or distance education is the age of the students. Today, instead of the traditional undergraduate age range of 18 to 23, more than 45% of college students are over 25 years of age and this percentage will continue to increase (Cantelton, 1995). These nontraditional students are the most successful distance education students. Successful distance education students are older, seek further education voluntarily, have post-secondary education goals with expectations of higher grades and are highly motivated and self-disciplined (Trier, 1996).

Distance Education Programs and Courses

For some universities, the new digital environment suggests focusing resources on just a few unique or particularly outstanding programs and delivering them. For others it will mean organizing programs differently to take advantage of a combination of program strengths and for still others it will mean developing the right partnerships to shore up weaknesses in programs, delivery, service to students, or other areas important to offering quality programs (Hanna, 1998). The selection of programs or courses delivered using distance education technology can usually be traced to the college's mission, strategic priorities and technology plan.

A common theme for implementing multiple distance education delivery modes is the desire to serve students located beyond the institution's traditionally defined state or county boundary lines or to make available specialized programs to meet the educational needs for a regional profession. Synchronous and asynchronous delivery offers flexibility in both time and location for distant learners. Once these strategic priorities and the specific programs have been identified, the available instructional technology resources can focus their efforts on development of these targeted programs. Miami-Dade Community College's Master Plan for Technology lists the following distance education goals:

> The overriding goal of distance education is to provide our students the opportunity to access quality instruction anytime, anywhere such access is desired and to facilitate this barrier-free delivery of instruction through technology. The college will establish a distance education system that will:

- Provide quality curriculum appropriate to its diverse population of students, incorporating flexible modalities to match discipline content with learner needs;

- Incorporate a variety of delivery methodologies and technologies to provide flexibility in time and/or location;

- Provide and support diverse technologies to enable the varied methodologies used in distance learning;

- Provide an on-demand, seamless academic and student support system that is prompt, convenient, and effective, which provides the services necessary to support the educational mission of the college;

- Facilitate the design and implement of a framework of equipment and technological capability, support services, and training to provide faculty, staff, and students the communications, enhancements, and access to maximize and energize their education in both traditional and nontraditional courses and labs;

- Be based upon guidelines derived from market/consumer-based information, and

- Contribute to and support a network of partnerships and consortia in the academic, professional, and business areas (including the business community and Dade County Schools).

Miami-Dade's Virtual College provides centralized support of their distance education program that combines synchronous and asynchronous distance education technologies. The goal of the Virtual College is to offer complete Associates of Arts and Associates of Science degrees online. Each regional campus provides technical and administrative support (advisement, testing, library resources and technology-based assessments) on location and via e-mail by the campus distance education coordinators. An admissions form, course syllabi and learning forums are all available online for distance education students.

Supporting Distance Education Technology

Program managers and faculty will need instructional technology resources to effectively integrate the technology into the curriculum. Use of instructional technology is generally a behavior-modification process that requires three ingredients: access to resources that promote the desired behavior, convenience in adapting the desired behavior, and reward and recognition for the desired behavior (Rao & Rao, 1999). As of fall of 1998, more than three-fourths of the two- and four-year colleges had information technology support to assist faculty with instructional integration (Green, 1998).

Colleges in the early stages of implementing distance education technologies may have instructional technology resource personnel who are dispersed among instructional television, computer services and academic divisions. In these situations, a resource list of support personnel and their respective services would be beneficial and save time in initiating course development. The best-case scenario for assisting faculty in the integration of technology into the curriculum would be a centralized organization with resources dedicated to supporting the faculty with all of their instructional technology needs.

This model would facilitate a systems approach to instructional design, allowing the experts in their respective areas to contribute to the program and/or course design and development. Effective instruction begins and ends with quality of instructional design. Florini (1990) asserts that "whether intended for electronic delivery or for more traditional means, efficient and effective instruction depends on good instructional design.

Well-designed instruction intended for electronic delivery takes advantage of strengths of a particular technology and compensates for its weaknesses. No amount of planning nor any particular technology can compensate for poorly designed instruction."

To support the faculty of their distance education programs, the University of Pittsburgh established the Center for Instructional Development and Distance Education (CIDDE) to strengthen the instructional development and support services available to faculty and serve as the primary contact point for addressing instructional services needs. The CIDDE is comprised of Instructional Development, Instructional Technology, and Instructional Design departments. Each department is responsible for a different part of the support of distant learning faculty.

Instructional Development focuses on supporting instructor efforts to enhance the teaching and learning experience. These services include assisting instructors in the design, development, and revision of course activities and materials. Instructional Development also provides instructors with opportunities to learn more about the theory and practice of teaching. Instructional Development provides support in the following areas:
- Curriculum and instructional development assistance for the creation of new academic courses and programs or the enhancement of existing ones;
- Instructional material design using print, video, interactive television, computers and other media;
- Application of technology to enhance and improve instruction;
- Design and development of distance education courses and programs; and
- Assistance with selection and implementation of classroom teaching methods and strategies. Research to identify existing instructional materials in various media.

Instructional Technology provides technical support for the design and development of teaching materials that integrate instructional media and computer technology. Departments within the Instructional Technology provide professional graphic, photographic, video, engineering, electronic imaging, and audio/visual support to the University community. Instructional Technology staff design, develop, and support specialized instructional facilities, including the University's media-enhanced classrooms and interactive television (ITV) classrooms.

Instructional Design consults with faculty about aspects of curriculum development and instructional project management. They bring expertise and experience of learning theory, instructional design and technology, faculty development, and specialized student support. Their responsibilities include:

- Curriculum and course design consultation,
- Consultation for the design and evaluation of instructional materials using various media,
- Selection and implementation of classroom teaching methods and strategies,
- Research related to instructional resources and decision-making,
- Grant writing assistance for instructional development projects, and
- Faculty training for the instructional use of interactive television and other instructional technology.

Selection of Distance Education Faculty

Distance education administrators will usually recruit faculty from the institution's existing pool of instructors to teach using a distance education medium. Adjunct faculty can request or be asked to teach a distance education course especially if they have experience teaching the traditional version of the same course. Institutions vary on compensation for development of distance education courses and ownership rights. Some institutions have a "work for hire" policy. This means that any work done by a faculty member under contract belongs to the institution. Other institutions have policies about joint ownership and revenue sharing similar to patent agreements. At other times the faculty can negotiate to retain all copyrights—even of instructional materials (Boettcher, 1999). Cash, release time, hiring on-campus faculty on an overload basis are all possibilities. Becoming familiar with the current policy at the institution allows adjunct managers to discuss these issues when hiring faculty to develop and teach distance education courses.

The Guide to Managing a Telecourse/Distance Learning Program encourages institutions to establish instructional standards and requirements for the entire teaching and learning process that ensure a high quality distance learning program. Suggested criteria for the selection of distance learning faculty include:

- Faculty must meet the minimum qualifications required of the traditional classroom teacher,
- Faculty should be selected and recommended by the academic department of the specific discipline in consultation with the program director,
- Faculty who are respected by their colleagues and are already successful in teaching in a regular face-to-face classroom setting,
- Faculty must be interested in learning the concepts of distance instruction because the variety of distance instruction methods requires faculty to have skills beyond those expected of traditional faculty,
- Faculty will need to be open to innovative instructional approaches and learn how to implement them, and
- Faculty must be able to work with a more diverse student body. Distance learners are older than the traditional 18- to 22-year-old college students.

Orientation training sessions for new distance learning faculty should include sharing information about overall program goals as well as their specific responsibilities. Other discussion topics may include current trends and developments in the field as well as similarities and differences between distance learning instruction and traditional classroom teaching. Faculty should be encouraged to attend workshops or conferences on distance learning-related topics such as effective distance learning instructional techniques and delivery technologies.

Synchronous Distance Education Technology

Interactive Classrooms at Lorain County Community College

Commonly referred to as a virtual classroom or interactive classroom, these two-way video and audio classrooms facilitate the extension of the traditional single classroom location to include additional groups of learners at one or more remote sites. The transmission of the course originates from a college or host site and is made available to pre-selected remote sites such as college branch locations, community centers or area high schools. With two-way video and audio equipment, the instructor and students in each location are visible using a wide screen television and/or projection screen and unit. Each student has the capability to ask a question or make comments to the entire class by pressing an audio control panel that focuses the camera on the student. Able to take advantage of the remote site, the learner benefits from the convenience of both reduced commuting time and expense, allowing the college to extend enrollment of the course to more students. Kent State University, the Mississippi Community and Junior College System and the Western Illinois Educational Consortium use interactive television technology to deliver instruction to multiple remote sites.

Kent State University—Kent, Ohio

Videoconferencing enables Kent State University to reach place-bound students who frequently work full-time, enhancing its competitive position in attracting students. The University uses desktop videoconferencing and shared multimedia applications over a Wide Area Network that connects seven regional campuses, enhancing its competitive edge in attracting students. Internationally, Kent State University will use Digital Visual Communications to expand its offerings to students at its campus in Geneva, Switzerland, increasing their direct involvement with the Ohio faculty.

Kent State University became a partner with Lorain County Community College (LCCC) in Elyria, Ohio by offering bachelor's and master's degree programs in business administration as part of the LCCC University Partnership program. LCCC has 12 bachelor's and four master's degree programs available through Cleveland State University, Youngstown State University, University of Akron and Ashland University; all of which use interactive video technology to deliver instruction.

Mississippi Community and Junior College System

In a state characterized by its predominantly rural nature, with a landscape punctuated by both the urban and the isolated, Mississippi has faced a challenge in providing educational opportunities and meeting the diverse needs of residents. Thus, in 1994 the Mississippi Community College Network (CCN) was developed, based on a demonstrated need to educate a greater number of the state's health-care professionals with limited financial resources. In fact, fulfilling this need was considered crucial to meet the rural health-care needs in Mississippi. Initially, the CCN linked the 15 Mississippi community and junior colleges with each other, with the Mississippi Cooperative Extension Service, and with the University of Mississippi Medical Center.

Western Illinois Education Consortium (WIEC)

In 1992, the state of Illinois formed ten regional education consortia—affiliations of universities, community colleges and school districts, and government and business organizations charged with combining resources to meet citizens' diverse education and training needs. The largest of these affiliations, and arguably the most successful, is the Western Illinois Education Consortium (WIEC). WIEC received special recognition at the 1996 International Teleconferencing Association Conference for achievements in distance learning applications.

WIEC network has 21 members at 42 sites. The objectives of the WIEC network are to:

- create an instructional network that matches college curricula offerings with interested students;
- expand the reach of secondary and post-secondary education;
- enhance work force training through the participation of business and industry;
- promote collaboration; and
- reduce administrative travel expenses, using advanced technologies such as VTFL videoconferencing equipment to consolidate technologies into an integrated system supporting instruction.

Required Skills and Training

To teach effectively in a virtual classroom, the instructor will need to become familiar with the process for initiating the connection with any remote site and his or her responsibilities for operating the available presentation tools.

An instructional technology technician supports and troubleshoots the connection to the remote sites and will provide training on operating procedures in the interactive classroom including the multimedia equipment. Interactive classrooms have the capability to allow the instructor to control the multimedia equipment using a control panel. Depending on the facilities, the faculty may need to cue the technician to control the presentation tools. The interactive classroom includes access to multimedia presentation tools such as a large projection screen or television, personal computer, document camera, videocassette recorder and whiteboard, all of which can be selected using the control panel.

Because synchronous ITV classrooms provide extensive projection capabilities, instructional methods and materials like transparencies, handouts, movies, etc. that have been used in the traditional classroom can be reused in the multiple-site interactive classroom. However, with the availability of the multimedia equipment and the inevitability of remote students, the instructor will have the opportunity to enhance each learner's experience by incorporating techniques that integrate the technology into the curriculum. Given multiple site locations, the instructor can collaborate with the instructional technologists and designers to provide interactive activities that engage each site in the learning process. The possible uses of the personal computer, document camera and whiteboard in the ITV classroom are shown below:

Personal Computer:
- Microsoft PowerPoint™ presentations
- Any Windows application (Adobe Photoshop™, Microsoft Excel™)
- View video clips
- World Wide Web Virtual Tours
- World Wide Web Online Surveys or Quizzes
- World Wide Web sites with supplemental content

Document Camera
- Transparencies
- Objects projected in 3D Packaging
- Original documents

Whiteboard
- Exercise results at each site
- Critiques of other site's work from each site
- Project collaboration by student groups at each site

The aforementioned Center for Instructional Development and

Distance Education at the University of Pittsburgh provides the following five-step training process for faculty slated to provide instruction using interactive video technology:

1. **Orientation Video:** Faculty view a 15-minute video describing the technical and instructional components of ITV.
2. **Faculty Workshop:** Faculty scheduled to teach through ITV attend a two-hour workshop.
3. **Instructional Assistance (Pluming):** Faculty work individually with Instructional Designers to develop ITV courses.
4. **Rehearsal/Practice:** Faculty present a 15-minute lesson, receiving feedback from CIDDE support staff.
5. **Classroom Observation:** Faculty receive individual feedback and continued classroom support from Instructional Designers.

Figure 8.1 — Example Lesson Plan for an ITV History Class

Figure 8.2 — Example Lesson Plan for an ITV History Class

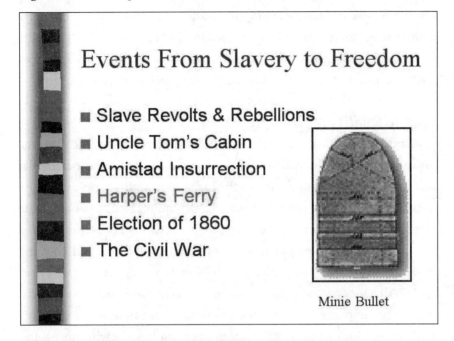

Events From Slavery to Freedom

- Slave Revolts & Rebellions
- Uncle Tom's Cabin
- Amistad Insurrection
- Harper's Ferry
- Election of 1860
- The Civil War

Minie Bullet

Instructional Television Fixed Service (ITFS)

A course delivered in an ITFS classroom is commonly referred to as an interactive television format. These courses have a scheduled meeting time and a live instructor that is broadcast on a local cable channel. The ITFS classroom provides one-way video and two-way audio capabilities for remote students. Students can either be in the live classroom at the host site, a group of learners at a remote location such as a high school or community center, or in the comfort of their own home. The students at the remote sites aren't visible to the instructor in the ITFS classroom. The remote students communicate with the class by simply making a phone call. Instruction is live and can be spontaneous but the course is designed using the traditional instructor-led lecture approach. Although the class is delivered in a live format, students have the option of recording the program using a video cassette recorder and viewing the lecture and class activities at their own convenience.

Required Skills and Training

Similar to other distance education technologies serving remote students, instructional strategies will need to be integrated into the curriculum that addresses their needs and ensures they are active participants during the class period. The Utah Educational Network requires faculty to participate in training prior to teaching over their satellite network. The Network offers an EDNET faculty development workshop called "Reaching and Teaching through Television". The primary goals of each one-day workshop are to explain distance learning technologies to system users and presenters, to prepare participants to convert teaching strategies and techniques from a regular classroom setting to a telecommunication-based environment, and to allow participants to practice on the system before they begin teaching. Key components of the faculty/presenter workshop are:

- Simulating the distance education classroom environment by actually using technologies available in Utah,
- Modeling and discussing effective distance learning instructional techniques,
- Giving participants an opportunity to discuss the distance education experience with faculty who have had a successful television teaching experience,
- Providing each participant with an opportunity to prepare and deliver a brief presentation using technology (the presentation is videotaped for the participant), and
- Providing each participant with an extensive training manual entitled "Reaching and Teaching through Television."

Desktop Videoconferencing Learning Systems

Interactive video course classrooms are fixed predetermined locations based on the technological infrastructure of the institution. Desktop videoconferencing capability and the Internet will expand the reach of a synchronous distance education course to include single students in their home or office.

LearnLinC™, ClassPoint™ and Symposium™ are instructor-controlled teaming systems that deliver synchronous (or even asynchronous) interactive courses in a classroom or via the Internet. Communication between the instructor and remote students is accomplished with both audio and desktop video conferencing capabilities. Additional features include synchronization of multimedia content, web sites and software applications on each student's computer, ability to recognize student participation and to enable students to singularly address the class.

The physical location of the instructor and students can be anywhere because each can join the class irrespective of their location. Common features among the aforementioned learning systems include floor control, audio conferencing, feedback, text chat, class agenda and content area.

- **Floor Control** provides classroom coordination and control between instructor and student, allowing all participants control of the course content, audio and video conferencing and classroom coordination.
- **Audio Conferencing** allows the instructor to speak to the entire class and to have a two-way conversation with any student who is given floor control.
- **Feedback** allows instructors to continuously poll students about the pace of instruction. Students select feedback answers such as Faster, Perfect, or Please Review. The instructor can see a percentage for each response. Instructors may also customize response sets or choose from several default feedback sets.

- **Text Chat** allows instructors and students to compose and exchange ideas and comments with everyone in the class. Students can also send private messages to the instructor that they might not offer in a public forum.
- **Class Agenda** allows instructors to list the learning components to be launched automatically on all student computers.
- **Content Area** contains the class's educational content in formats such as a PowerPoint™ presentation, Excel™ spreadsheet, Macromedia Authorware™, Asymetrix Toolbook™, or HTML. Individualized instruction can be integrated with the instructional materials, giving the added convenience of both self-pacing and anonymity as the student works through the curriculum.

Developing Instructional Materials

Desktop video learning systems are used in conjunction with interactive, self-paced instructional materials. These materials can be authored in PowerPoint™, Macromedia Authorware™ or Asymetrix Toolbook™. Both Authorware and Toolbook can produce interactive multimedia content. Instructors should solicit assistance and resources from their instructional technology personnel to design the instructional materials. Teams that includes full-time faculty members, multimedia developers, copyright specialists and instructional designers as well as the specific course's instructor would reduce overall development time and ensure the end product could be reused by other instructors. Adjunct faculty managers should provide information about the institution's compensation and intellectual property policies prior to hiring adjunct faculty to participate in the developmental efforts. The University of New Hampshire, Rensselaer Polytechnic Institute and Berean University have all developed desktop videoconferencing learning systems using LearnLinC™.

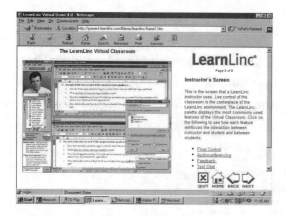

University of New Hampshire

UNH is piloting a live instructor-led online degree program in electrical engineering. Instructors and students use headsets, a computer and Internet connection to log on to a class in six separate locations, including students' homes. The instructional materials include higher quality video and graphics to convey information. Each completed class is archived and available for playback. Both instructor and students can ask questions and receive immediate feedback.

Rensselaer Polytechnic Institute & City University of Hong Kong

A joint program between Rensselaer Polytechnic Institute (NY) and the City University of Hong Kong has brought together students from opposite sides of the globe to take graduate-level courses using LearnLinC™. Rensselaer Professor Chun Ming Leung taught a course called "Survival Skills for Research Scientists" once a week to 20 City University students and 12 Rensselaer students, all logged into a LearnLinC session via the Internet. PictureTel room videoconferencing provided face-to-face communication while the LearnLinC Virtual Classroom allowed the instructor and students to share control of the course content.

Berean University

For the past 50 years, Berean University (KY) has been delivering quality distance education. Recognized as a leader in distance education Bible studies,

Berean University has trained thousands of people to be certified lay workers and licensed ministers.

One of Berean's goals was to increase the number of students completing their assigned distance learning studies and wanted to implement a method to bring students closer to the instructors in real time and increase the accountability factor. LearnLinC™ fit into their plans perfectly and they now see 90% completion rates for online courses.

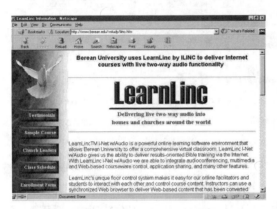

Asynchronous Distance Education Technology

Distance education originated with the asynchronous delivery of the correspondence or independent study course. These courses consisted primarily of printed materials, eventually including video or audiocassettes. The history of distance education has fallen short in the area of interaction. Without student interaction and greater access to information and other tools, the student is at a disadvantage compared to students in an on-campus educational model (Stewart, 1995). For students who are using text-based computer-mediated technologies, frequent and regular feedback is more important because they do not receive body language feedback as classroom students typically do (Cook, 1995). The challenge for asynchronous distance education technologies is to provide this interaction to ensure a comparable learning experience for distant students.

Telecourse

Delivery of a course using a standard television (telecourse or ITFS) began the revolution toward digital distance learning environments. Primarily available at community colleges, a telecourse is a self-paced learning system that consists of pre-produced videotaped instructional programs integrated with printed materials such as a syllabus, course outline, a study guide, textbooks and tests. The videotapes are broadcast on a public television or cable channel at a scheduled time. The student can watch the live broadcast or record it using a video cassette recorder. The telecourse provides limited face-to-face interaction with either the instructor or other students except during on-campus orientations and assessments.

The Public Broadcasting Service (PBS) serves as the national broker for the distribution of telecourses, whose centralized service reduced the cost of telecourse licenses to individual colleges and universities. Annenberg Corporation for Public Broadcasting has also made a major contribution to advancing telecourse delivery. Miller (1995) states "[t]he telecourse model has been advanced significantly by the Annenberg Corporation for Public Broadcasting (CPB) Project by funding the development and distribution of many highly used telecourse packages. The Project raised the video production standards for telecourse production and helped bring this end of independent study into the mainstream of community college life and into many four-year curricula." More recently, the Going the Distance Project (GTD) was launched in 1994 as a new PBS educational initiative comprised of 150 courses that are primarily video-based. The courses are offered at community colleges but are available to institutions nationwide for undergraduate course credit.

Brey (1991) reports that most institutions with distance learning programs use multiple technologies to provide students with flexible access to video materials. Community colleges typically select two or three of the following delivery systems: public television, low-power television, commercial television, cable educational access, national cable network, library viewing, tape check-out, videodiscs, CD-ROM, and CDI/DVI. Adjunct managers need to apprise new telecourse instructors of the institutional policies for selection of telecourses and distribution of course materials. GTD recommends faculty evaluate all courses for consistency of course objectives and content to existing curriculum prior its adoption into an existing program.

Cuyamaca College, CA has a general meeting of distance learning faculty each semester to share information about common tasks and objectives, address group-related questions and concerns, and share ideas or techniques to enhance learning. The general responsibilities of their telecourse instructors are as follows:

- Attend workshops for telecourse faculty,
- Develop Student Instructional Handbooks on established guidelines,
- Conduct student orientation sessions at beginning of semester,
- Conduct telecourse marketing survey during orientation,
- Conduct scheduled seminars on campus a minimum of five times per semester,
- Meet scheduled time lines on assigned tasks,
- Maintain office hours and answer student's questions by telephone, fax or e-mail,
- Evaluate courses offered at the end of each semester,
- Assist in the promotion of telecourses such as marketing and recruiting students,
- Communicate with Telecourse Program Office about problems and suggestions related to telecourse offerings, and
- Other duties as they occur.

Internet Courses

The emerging asynchronous distance education technology of choice for both educational institutions and distant learners is delivery via the World Wide Web. Due to the accessibility of the Internet, online programs are capable of serving new populations of students and provide the ultimate flexibility in both convenience and opportunity for distant learners. Online distance learning consortia are continually being formed such as Colorado Community College Online, South Regional Educational Consortium and Western Governors University. The consortia provide a centralized online catalog of courses offered by its member institutions. Information about admission policies, online registration and examples of syllabi is conveniently available at the catalog site. Learners can enroll at any participating college enabling the student to complete coursework toward earning a degree that time, money and convenience wouldn't allow with either a traditional or a synchronously delivered course.

While both traditional and synchronous courses provide face-to-face interaction, online course interaction is primarily text-based. Electronic mail, bulletin boards/discussion groups, and chat rooms facilitate text-based communication among distant learners and promote a sense of community. Integrated online courseware products such as (Appendix B: Wichita State online course review) WebCT, TopClass and CourseInfo have these communication tools integrated into the courseware and readily available to the instructor. Selecting an online course software package will reduce development time for non-technical faculty member because they include tools to facilitate the creation and presentation of the course content and homepage, have the ability to easily design a variety of assessment instruments, and provide student tracking.

Course Design

The assistance of available instructional technology professionals at the institution and/or resources in the academic department can provide faculty with an overview of the services available. They know about institutionally defined design standards, assessment policies, and online course software packages; and can provide an orientation to course design at the institution.

Teaching in an asynchronous learning mode requires advance preparation of course material, detailed attention to learner questions, facilitation of peer-to-peer interaction and continuous guidance to learners. One of the primary responsibilities of faculty is the development of the course syllabus. The course syllabus for a distance learning course will differ from its equivalent in the traditional format because it serves as a student instruction handbook, providing more detailed information regarding goals and objectives, assignments and expectations, evaluation methods, and techniques for studying that will optimize the learning experience. It should also provide a complete course schedule that will help students monitor their own progress as the academic term progresses. Major steps frequently used to create an online course:

1. Contact instructional technology resources for overview of the development process,
2. Create course home page,
3. Create syllabus,
4. Create weekly schedule of reading materials and assignments,
5. Design and create the modularized course contents or weekly "lecturettes",
6. Add computer conferencing, including discussion groups and a help desk,
7. Add testing and course management tools,
8. Provide both formative and summative evaluation such as surveys and performance evaluation.

Appearance and structure are important factors in determining successful online courses. The American History course at the University of Wisconsin has won numerous awards by meeting or exceeding the following criteria:

- Entertaining
- Integration of web sites using hyperlinks
- Consistent menus and navigational tools
- Accessibility through most web browsers, including text-only
- Opportunities for interaction
- Artistic value
- Course stability
- Instructor disclosure and credibility

The asynchronous form of an Internet course requires the modularization of instructional content. Modularized content is an instructional unit that is competency-based, activity-based, modularly constructed and workplace-verified. Instructors must determine the objectives of each module and have an exercise and/or forum discussion to reinforce learning and maintain student interaction. For each module or small group activity, the instructor should consider that each unit does the following:

- Carefully sets learning activities

- Communicates objectives to all in the group
- Assures the objectives are understood
- Designs instructional strategies to meet the objectives
- Implements the strategies
- Gathers data on progress towards meeting the learning objectives and make adjustments
- Emphasizes writing assignments/case studies/projects (with some for individual students and others for small groups of students)
- Links to integrate commercial or self-produced CD-ROMs
- Links to Internet sites with supplemental content, i.e., virtual tours

Facilitators of learning in a computer-mediated environment must recognize the importance of community development in instruction and use means to assist in its development (Cook, 1995). Building community can be accomplished by taking advantage of computer conferencing features to sustain student involvement and provide all forms of text-based interaction, i.e., instructor-class, student-class, student-group, instructor-student. Incorporating these forms of interaction into the course design can be easily done with online course software packages that have the ability to create multiple public and private forums. Additional interactivity tools available include a synchronous chat tool, online test creation and student tracking information. E-mail and forum interactivity tools can be used to provide the following functions:

ANNOUNCEMENT	The faculty member could describe the work to be done during the coming week and perhaps beyond, provide new administrative information and reinforce old information.
REINFORCEMENT	The faculty member could summarize substantive material previously covered, ask for questions about the material and post a public answer so all students could benefit from the answer.
TESTING	An examination could be provided, with answers sent privately from each student to the faculty member and results returned privately
EVALUATION	Assignments could be sent privately to the faculty member with corrections and an evaluation sent back to the individual student.

ADVISING/MENTORING	Students could privately ask the faculty member for general advice and receive a private response.
STUDENT WORK GROUP	Small subsets of the students in the course could work together: 1. providing mutual support and advice on a variety of topics, including test preparation and administrative matters; 2. providing a critique of each other's written work, such as a term paper; 3. developing a team presentation on a specific topic; and, 4. developing an analysis of a case study.

Table 8.1 - Interactivity Tools

Preparation of Instructional Materials for the Internet

For Internet delivery, all instructional materials need to be digitized. Textbook publishers now frequently provide course content on a CD-ROM formatted for online delivery complete with HTML files, PowerPoint presentations and video clips. Many also list supplementary Internet sites with additional course content in the textbook. They have also formed partnerships with Internet courseware companies such as TopClass, CourseInfo and WebCt to facilitate full-service online delivery of a course, negating the need for the instructor to convert the materials.

The Internet only recognizes text files of HTML (hypertext markup language) and .gif or .jpeg graphic files. These files are the most common types that you will find on the Web but are by no means an exhaustive list. Content that is not in one of the above "web ready" formats needs to be converted before it can be read, viewed or heard on the Internet. To create web pages, an HTML editor is a necessity. HTML editors apply the necessary .html tags for publishing on the Internet while providing a word processor-like interface to the designer. Popular HTML editors are Adobe PageMill™, Netscape Composer™ and Microsoft FrontPage ™. Word97 has the capability to save word documents as HTML files. Features of each HTML editors are shown in Table 8.2 below.

Office 97	Recommended for new Internet instructors. Allows authoring of html documents in Word with a "Save as HTML" option. Can also edit html document using Word. • need to do minor editing of converted html document • most of the Word features (table, font color, etc) are easily converted • include tables, images, horizontal lines and hyperlinks in your document
Netscape Composer	WYSIWYG (What-You-See-Is-What-You-Get) HTML document creation • Add, remove and modify text • Drag and Drop hyperlinks and images from the bookmark, mail, news or browse windows • apply paragraph and character styles to text as you would with your preferred word processor • include tables, images, horizontal lines and hyperlinks in your document
Microsoft FrontPage	Microsoft FrontPage 98 is a quick, effective way to create and manage professional-quality Internet or intranet sites without programming • Easy-to-use, leading edge features let you create professional Web sites without programming • Create WYSIWYG frames pages and draw HTML tables in the WYSIWYG FrontPage Editor • Drop in sophisticated, interactive functionality using FrontPage components

Table 8.2 - HTML Editor features

After creating the modularized instructional materials, the next step is to make it available to students online. The process for accomplishing this will depend on the online course software package available at the college and the role of the instructional technology support personnel at the institution.

Multimedia

Multimedia (also referred to as "hypermedia") is information presented using authoring software that integrates multiple media such as video, sound and graphics. Older forms of multiple media such as slide shows, overhead projector with transparencies and viewing movies with video cassette recorders are still widely used methods of delivering instruction but which require separate viewing with different equipment. Additionally, the original formats of these media severely limit its presentation options and ability to reach audiences not physically present in the classroom. Multimedia authoring tools such as PowerPoint™, Hyperstudio™, and Macromedia Director™ allow different forms of digitized content to be organized and presented as a unit of instruction. The software packages also include more advanced presentation options such as the Internet and CD-ROM.

Interactive CD-ROMs

Textbook publishers are distributing CD-ROMs with books to supplement traditional classroom instruction and assignments. Multimedia offers the opportunity to give students more complete and individual control over the audio/visual information presented to them, allowing students to set their own pace through the material, to stop wherever and whenever they please, and to review materials as many times as needed to understand the information. Multimedia offers a very personal, nonjudgmental learning environment on which admitting ignorance and asking for another explanation of the subject are as simple and painless as pressing a button (Lynch, 1998).

The CD-ROMs include interactive exercises and video clips and can provide remedial instruction. When available, instructors need to become familiar with the CD-ROM contents to determine the fit with existing instructional materials and assessment instruments.

Presentation Creation

Although the use of multimedia for delivering instruction is increasing, the printed word remains the most obvious and dominant medium used to transmit information whatever the context (Stewart, 1995). When creating a presentation, the instructor must first enter the textual information for the unit of instruction. As each slide is designed, multimedia content should be included that will enhance the instruction and engage the learner. To include multimedia content in the presentation, it must be digitized. Content is digitized using peripheral equipment and its corresponding specialty software or the use of industry standard packages such as Adobe PhotoShop™ for manipulating scanned images. Table 8.3 below depicts the media in its original for and the computer peripheral equipment needed to create an electronic version of the content.

The use of digital cameras and desktop video cameras allow for the easy capture of digitized content. Depending on the type of digital camera, it will store the pictures on a memory card or floppy diskette in either .jpg or .pict

Media Form	Digital Equipment Needed:
Photograph	Scanner, Digital Camera
Slides	Scanner with Transparency Adapter
X-Rays	Scanner with Transparency Adapter
Overhead Transparencies	Scanner with Transparency Adapter
Videotape	Video Editor
Still Image from Videotape	Video Editor
Graphics	Scanner

Table 8.3 — Digital Equipment needed to convert Various Media Forms

file format. The desktop video cameras capture either video clips or still images in the .bmp format for Microsoft Windows-based computers or .pict format for Macintosh computers.

Whenever possible, file formats that are viewable on both Windows-based computers and Macintosh workstations should be used. The file formats which can be used in multimedia instruction will depend on the authoring tool used to create the presentation as some authoring software only allow certain video or graphic file formats. Quicktime movies, .jpeg, .gif, .tiff and .pict graphic files are cross-platform and can be included in most authoring software presentations.

In the Office97 release, PowerPoint has an AutoContent Wizard which creates a presentation by requesting information from the presenter about the type of presentation (strategy, status), output options (presentation, Internet kiosk), presentation style (on-screen presentation, color or black and white overheads), and presentation options (title, author). Given this information, the wizard creates and editable presentation with a pre-selected background design and text which prompts the instructor for information to customize the slide show to meet their instructional goals.

Copyright and Fair Use

Be aware of the limitations on including copyrighted multimedia content in a presentation. The four basic copyright protections owned by the copyright holder are:

1. The right to make copies of the work
2. The right to sell or otherwise distribute copies of the work
3. The right to prepare new works based on the protected work
4. The right to perform the protected work (such as a stage play or painting) in public

Fair use is the most significant limitation on the copyright holder's exclusive rights. Educational multimedia projects typically incorporate an educator's original materials such as course notes or commentary with various copyrighted media formats such as video, music, text and graphic illustrations. Generally speaking, the use of copyrighted works for nonprofit or educational purposes is most likely to be considered fair use. Although there are no universal guidelines, fair use is determined by four factors:

1. Purpose and character of the use,
2. Nature of the copyrighted work,
3. Amount and substantiality of the portion used,
4. Effect of use on the potential market for the copyrighted work.

Fair use of copyrighted material in multimedia projects lasts for two years; after which time permission should be obtained before continued use of the project. Copyright permission must be requested under the following circumstances:

- Intended use of the project is for commercial or non-educational purposes
- Duplication of the project is more than the two copies allowed by the guidelines
- Plans to distribute the project are beyond the scope of the guidelines

Faculty guidelines for fair use of multimedia materials are as follows:

- Including portions of copyrighted works when producing multimedia project for teaching in support of curriculum-based instructional activities at educational institutions.
- Faculty may use their project for:
  Assignments for student self-study
  For remote instruction with a secure network designed to prevent unlawful copying
  For conferences, presentations or workshops
  For professional portfolios

Media Format	Fair Use Limitations
Video	10% or 3 minutes, whichever is less
Text Material	Up to 10% or 1000 words, whichever is less
Text Material - Poems	Entire poem of less than 250 words • But no more than 3 poems by one poet • Or five poems by different poets from a single anthology In poems of greater length • Up to 250 words • But no more than three excerpts by a single poet • Or five excerpts by different poets from a single anthology
Music, Lyrics, & Music Video	• Up to 10% • But no more than 30 seconds of music and lyrics from a single musical work • Any alterations to a musical work shall not change the basic melody or the fundamental character of the work
Illustrations & Photographs	• Photograph or illustration may be used in its entirety • Not more than 5 images by an artist or photographer • Not more than 10% or 15 images, whichever is less, from a single published collected work

Numerical Data Sets	• Up to 10% or 2500 fields or cell entries, whichever is less, from a database or data table ▶ A field entry is a specific item of information, in a record of a database file ▶ A cell entry is the intersection where a row and a column meet on a spreadsheet
Copying & Distribution Limitations	Including the original, only a limited number of copies may be made of a project. • Two use copies, one of which may be placed on reserve • An additional copy for preservation to be used or copied only to replace a use copy that has been lost, stolen, or damaged • For jointly created projects, each principal creator may retain one copy but only as permitted by use and time restraints previously outlined.
Downloading from the Internet	• Internet access does not automatically mean that works can be reproduced and reused without permission or license • Some copyrighted works may have been posted to the Internet without authorization of the copyright holder • Attribution and Acknowledgement requires: ▶ Crediting copyright ownership ▶ Identifying the source ▶ Including the copyright notice ▶ Special provisions for remote use

Table 8.4 — Stipulations on Fair Use for Various Media Formats

Presentation Integration into Instruction

To enable the students to easily view the presentation, presentation must be projected on a screen, wall or wide screen television. There are several options available for projecting instructional materials such as a mobile unit, document camera or TView®. Irrespective of the projection options available in the classroom, a copy of the presentation needs to be installed on the personal computer attached to the projection device.

As the name suggests the mobile unit is on a cart which allows instructors to share the equipment. The unit above, consisting of a computer connected to an overhead projector with a LCD panel, is fairly common because it is inexpensive and reuses existing equipment. The mobile unit at left uses a more expensive projection unit.

An economical alternative to a projection system, TView uses a television and computer to project and display presentations, games and the Internet. It supports resolutions up to 1024x768, insuring clear and sharp presentations. It includes a wireless remote control.

Conclusion

The Gartner Group reports that more than 80% of traditional U.S. colleges and universities will use distance learning technologies and techniques in one or more "traditional" academic programs by the year 2002. "Just in Time" learning and "on-demand" education will be available through the combination of fiber optics, compressed video, interactive television, and virtual learning environments (Miller, Clouse, 1993-94). Similar to all other advances in the telecommunications industry, distance education technology will continue to improve and become more affordable and accessible for both educational institutions and remote learners. In the near future, high-speed computer and Internet service will be as commonplace in the home as television and radio. In total, these events will result in a broader definition and scope of the term "instruction" to include delivery using distance education technology. Consequently, the scope of definition of "instructor-led" will need to follow suit. Distance education technology addresses the needs of the increasing population of remote, nontraditional students. For these students, distance education technology will be the preferred method of attaining a college education and their only viable option.

References

Bates, A.W. (1995). *Technology, Open Learning and Distance Education.* New York: Routledge.

Boettcher, J. V. (1999). Copyright and intellectual property. *Syllabus*, 34-36.

Bourne, J. R., McMaster, E., Rieger, J., & Campbell, J. O. (1997). Paradigm for on-line learning: A case study in the design and implementation of an ALN course. *Journal of Asynchronous Learning.*

Chou, P.H. (1994). *Guide to Managing a Telecourse/Distance Learning Program* Suisan, CA: Learning Resources.

Cook, D. L. (1995). "Community and Computer-Generated Distance Learning Environments." In Rossman, M.H. & Rossman, M.E. (eds.) *Facilitating Distance Education.* San Francisco: Jossey-Bass, pp. 33-40.

Florini, B.M. (1990). Communications technology in adult education. In M. W. Galbraith (Ed.), *Adult Learning Methods.* Malabar, FL: Kreigor.

Hanna, D. E. (1998). Higher education in an era of digital competition: Emerging organizational models. *Journal of Asynchronous Learning.*

Kearsley, G., & Moore, M. G. (1996). *Distance education: A systems view.* Belmont, CA: Wadsworth.

Kearsley, G. (1998). Distance education goes mainstream. *T.H.E. Journal*, 22-26.

Lynch,P. (1998). Stacking books: Adapting print projects to multimedia. *Syllabus*, 50-51.

Miller, C.D., and Clouse, R. W. (1993-4). Technology-based distance learning: Present and future directions in business and education. *Educational Technology Systems, 22*(3), 191-204.

Miller, G. E. (1995). "The undergraduate curriculum and distance education." In Rossman, M.H. & Rossman, M.E. (eds.) *Facilitating Distance Education.* San Francisco: Jossey-Bass, pp. 51-60.

Phipps, R. A., Wellman, J. V., & Merisotis, J. P., (1998). *Assuring quality in distance learning: A preliminary review.* Washington, DC: Council for Higher Education Accreditation.

Rao, P. V., & Rao, L. M. (1999). Strategies that support instructional technology. *Syllabus*, 22-24.

Stewart, R. D. (1995). "Distance Learning Technology." In Rossman, M.H. & Rossman, M.E. (eds.) *Facilitating Distance Education*. San Francisco: Jossey-Bass, pp. 11-18.

Trier, V. (1996). Distance Education at a Glance. *Guide #10 Distance Education: Research* [On-line] Available http://www.uidaho.edu.evo/dist10.html

Tinnie A. Banks, M.S., is currently the Instructional Design Media Coordinator at Lorain County Community College, Ohio. She is also a doctoral student at Kent State University majoring in Instructional Technology.

Management of Adjunct Faculty on Branch and Off-Campus Sites

By Jo Lynn Autry Digranes
and Swen H. Digranes

Overview

This chapter is intended to discuss issues related to adjunct faculty at branch and off-campus sites, including:

- The administrative types of branch and off-campus sites,
- The recruitment, orientation and professional development, and evaluation of adjuncts, and
- The special needs of adjunct faculty involved in distance instruction.

Introduction

Growth in the numbers of adjunct faculty brings new challenges to academic administrators. According to the *Almanac Issue of The Chronicle of Higher Education* (1999), 41% of the faculty in 1995 were part-time. That figure increased from 36% in 1985 and 30% in 1975. The numbers are typically even greater at community colleges. Palmer (1999) states, "(t)he use of part-timers at community colleges grew steadily for over 30 years—from 38%in 1962 to 40% in 1971, 50% in 1974, and 64% in fall 1995" (p.45). Increasing numbers of branch campus and off-campus sites, often staffed primarily by adjuncts, further complicates the supervision of instruction. Branch campus percentages of adjunct instructors are many times higher than even the percentages quoted for all institutions, further distancing this group of "invisible faculty" (Gappa & Leslie, 1993). Maintaining the academic integrity of the institution requires additional planning and organization when dealing with adjunct faculty at branch and off-campus sites.

The focus here is the identification of administrative structures for adjunct management on branch campuses and off-campus sites and a discussion of the resulting issues in recruitment and selection, orientation and professional development, numbers of adjunct faculty evaluation, and finally support of adjunct faculty on branch or off-campus sites. Recommendations for dealing with these issues are also provided.

Administrative Structure

The first consideration in managing adjuncts on branch or off-campus sites focuses upon the administrative structure. Ultimately the academic administrator will be responsible for management of adjuncts, but the presence of a branch campus or off-campus site adds complexity to the structure. Several organizational models are utilized with branch campuses and off-campus sites; some of the most common include:

- A completely developed administrative structure, including an academic administrator and full-time faculty assigned to the site.
- A campus administrator who directs activities on the branch or off-campus site but who may or may not have authority over academics; and

where a parent campus administrator is still the central person responsible for the academics.

- Limited or no administrative personnel with perhaps support personnel only and a parent campus administrator who is responsible for the academics.

A large branch campus or off-campus site may operate independently with a full administrative staff. The staff typically includes an administrator responsible for both full-time and adjunct faculty. The campus may even be accredited as a separate institution. Many large colleges have adopted this structure; the academic administrator reports to a central academic administrator, but operates as if on an independent campus. Comprehensive institutions, regional colleges, and community colleges are all examples of this type of organization. Many doctoral-granting universities provide branch campuses and off-campus sites; they may be two-year community college branches, graduate sites, or variations on the home institution.

Branch campuses or off-campus sites that have a fully developed administrative structure would operate very much as a home campus in the management of adjunct instructors. All aspects of recruitment and selection, orientation and professional development, evaluation, and support would emulate those on the home campus; work with adjunct faculty would not be from a distance. Connections such as Human Resources may come from the parent institution. These connections, however, appear transparent to the adjunct instructors. The major difference may lie in the focus of the campus. Branch campuses typically mirror the community or area they serve. Their academic programs may vary from those offered on the home campus, resulting in an adjunct faculty pool from different academic backgrounds with dissimilar instructional functions and diverse professional development and support needs.

On other, typically smaller, branch campuses or off-campus sites there may be a chief administrator, such as a provost or dean, who oversees all campus operations. If the administrator performs academic functions, he or she will typically report to a central academic administrator. Hiring, professional development, and evaluation may be done by the parent campus. These tasks may be conducted by the central administrator, by the academic divisions/colleges, or by some combination of these at the home institution. Support functions for adjunct faculty may be the most important provided by this type of organizational structure.

The final example is commonly found at small branches or off-campus sites. There may or may not be an administrator. There may or may not be support personnel, particularly if the site is a rented/leased instructional site, such as a public school or office building. A security guard or janitor may be the only other staff person in the building. An administrator at the parent institution is responsible for managing the adjuncts and providing all professional development, evaluation, and support functions. This model is particularly challenging for the manager of adjunct faculty, as well as for the adjunct instructor who teaches at this site model.

The last two models will be the focus here. Issues in the recruitment and selection, orientation and professional development, evaluation, and support areas are particularly important when managing at a distance. The next section addresses issues that arise with branch campuses and off-campus sites that do not operate independently.

Discussion of Issues

Whatever the structure of services at the branch campus or off-campus site, a major consideration is the degree of full-time faculty involvement. Cook (1995) emphasizes that to ensure academic quality, full-time instructors must be involved. He states:

> Important issues regarding academic quality are involved: the full-time faculty who design the curriculum establish the goals and objectives of the program; they also determine program and course requirements, texts, bibliographic and information resources, project assignments, grading procedures, and, in some instances, teaching techniques. While administrators can distribute information to part-time faculty about these matters, the nature and context of the discussions that brought them into existence can only be conveyed by the faculty (p. 5).

He recommends that full-time faculty workloads be adjusted to include work with adjunct faculty. Since full-time faculty drive the curriculum, they should be involved in recruitment and selection, orientation and professional development, evaluation, and support of adjunct instructors, whether located on the home campus, a branch campus or off-campus site.

In addition to full-time faculty there may be multiple administrators involved in the management aspects related to adjunct faculty at branch campuses and off-campus sites. Roueche, Roueche, and Milliron (1996) emphasize integrating part-time faculty into the institution through participation, communication, and socialization. These are even more important with adjuncts at a distance. Key considerations are discussed in the next sections concerning their recommendations.

Recruitment and Selection

The recruitment and selection process is key to further efforts, whether adjuncts teach on the main campus or a distant site. However, the actual process may vary greatly. Identifying adjunct faculty credentialed for teaching may be the responsibility of the main or branch/off-campus site administration, depending upon ultimate accountability for supervision of instruction.

The primary question lies in whether adjuncts should be recruited from the location of the branch/off-campus site or from the home campus location. An independently functioning branch/off-campus site would probably recruit from the site. Other administrative structures may recruit locally or from the home campus site, often depending on the distance between the branch/off-campus site and the parent institution. Recruitment and selection will also depend upon the specific program areas needs; if a branch/off-campus site offered a specialized program that catered to area business and industry, personnel from those entities may offer the credentials needed for teaching in the program. A campus's web site could publicize adjunct openings in addition to the more routine methods such as newspaper advertisements.

Related to the decision to hire main campus adjuncts for branch/off-campus sites is travel reimbursement. If adjunct faculty members are selected from the parent institution location, costs of travel to the distant site should be considered in budgeting for adjunct salaries and expenses.

Certainly full-time faculty should also be involved in the screening and hiring process because they are most familiar with curriculum content. Screening should be as rigorous as for full-time faculty, but with fewer personnel involved within a shorter time frame. One personality characteristic that should be emphasized in selection is the ability to work independently. In some cases, assignment of experienced adjuncts to branch or off-campus sites, even with travel involved, may be preferable to selection of new adjuncts. A major difference in working with branch campuses or off-campus sites is site location. If adjuncts are recruited/selected from the branch/off-campus area, the full-time faculty members may have to travel to be involved in the selection process. Again, time and travel expense considerations are aspects to be considered.

Orientation and Professional Development

Orientation for adjunct faculty at branch campuses/off-campus sites consists of two primary areas, instructional and logistics. Instructional orientation would include an introduction to teaching and classroom management. Logistics includes details on classroom location, parking, payroll, mail, and copying. These practical aspects are very important because the adjunct will not be teaching on the main campus where support services are typically more visible and easier to access.

There are several methods for providing orientation and professional development at a distance. In the instructional area, meetings/workshops typically provide orientation/instruction in teaching and classroom management. In discussing faculty orientation, the *Dean and Provost* publication (1999) suggests, "(using) orientation sessions as a bridge to other faculty development initiatives offered through the year" (p.8). With adjunct faculty at a distant site combining orientation with professional development is an efficient method. When working with branch campus and off-campus sites, offering those meetings and/or workshops at the location is a primary consideration, particularly if adjuncts live or work in the area. Inviting adjuncts to the main campus for workshops may also be a suitable method; this is particularly good for the promoting stronger relationships to the campus.

Roueche, Roueche, and Milliron (1996) suggest involving part-time faculty in coordinating and delivering staff development. This can be particularly effective if the professional development opportunities are on the distance sites; the participation can also encourage a feeling of connection for the adjunct. The adjuncts can provide insights regarding distant site teaching that a full-time faculty member may not have experienced.

Another common method is the use of an adjunct faculty handbook that includes articles focusing upon instructional techniques and instructional theories. The handbook typically provides instructional models, such as a sample syllabus format and general procedures for classroom instruction and management. Handbooks work well because they are easy to provide to adjunct instructors assigned to distant sites and can be posted on the campus web site. Library resources, such as books and references on teaching, should also be available. For the adjunct instructor on a branch or off-campus site, on-line access to these library and other instructional resources would be advantageous. Providing the adjunct with off-campus online access to collegiate services and resources would support a variety of needs, including professional development and orientation.

One of the best resources may still be a personal contact, preferably a faculty mentor. The faculty mentor should ideally be from the same discipline, but a full-timer from another area or even a "veteran" adjunct could still provide coaching on instruction and classroom management. If possible, the faculty mentor should regularly travel to the site to meet with the adjunct, particularly during the first semester of teaching. Communication and socialization can be through personal visits, telephone, and telecommunications. Setting up a chat room or listserv may be an additional resource. As Cook (1995) suggests the responsibilities associated with working with an adjunct at a distant site should be factored into the full-time faculty member's workload, particularly if the full-time faculty member has to travel to the distant site.

For imparting information on logistics, initial group or individual meetings can provide necessary information. Some of the logistical orientation will need to be covered during the screening process; a campus tour can be included during an interview or hiring meeting if held at the distant site. Balch (1999) suggests that "… sessions should be well structured with useful information, provide a warm atmosphere, and allow ample time for questions and comments" (p.14). This is particularly important for the adjuncts working at branch or off-campus sites. However, any information provided in a meeting should be also provided as either a hard copy or on-line manual or publication.

Some schools create a manual specifically designed for adjunct faculty at branch or off-campus sites. Other schools use a single adjunct faculty manual. The manual may contain information on the branch or off-campus sites, or it may be general manual supplemented by an informational manual or publications from a distant location. At Connors State College, we provide a general manual for adjunct instructors. The general manual includes some information on the branch campus, but specific information is included in a packet prepared by the branch campus for adjunct faculty members.

Recommended information specific to the distant site for these manuals or publications should include:

- Campus address, telephone, web site, and site maps
- Campus contacts (lists of administrators, etc.)
- Campus hours
- Academic calendar for the campus, with all relevant dates
- Campus regulations
- Profile of students on the branch campus or off-campus site
- Mail services
- Copying/printing services
- Library resources
- Computing and media resources
- Security services
- Employment/payroll procedures
- Inclement weather notification
- Main campus contacts

- Clerical services
- Parking

Providing copies of school catalogs and other general publications can also assist new adjuncts.

Communication is the key in the area of logistics, as it is in other areas. Employ as many methods of communication with adjuncts on branch campuses or off- campus sites as possible. Telephone calls, telecommunications, newsletters, manuals, and meetings are all important (Digranes & Digranes, 1999). Ensure that adjunct faculty members have all necessary printed documents and that they are included in campus communication channels, for both the main campus and the distance site. Also ensure that the information is updated each semester. If at all possible, provide e-mail accounts for the distance site adjunct instructors. Off-campus computer access is another service that can help to connect the—adjunct to the school. Adjunct managers should not be afraid of "overkill" when it comes to communications—the more methods the better.

In dealing with the logistics, remember to establish a primary contact for the adjunct, preferably a full-time faculty mentor. An alternative would be another adjunct faculty member who has been employed for several semesters and who has become very familiar with both the parent institution and the distance site. The faculty mentor may not be able to answer some questions, such as those dealing with employment issues, so providing additional contact information will assist the adjunct on a branch campus or off-campus site to concentrate on classroom teaching rather than on the little details.

Evaluation

Evaluation of off-campus adjunct faculty is critical, since observation may not be convenient and informal interaction is less likely to occur. Evaluation should include both student and administrative/faculty review.

Student evaluation typically consists of questionnaires/surveys. The student evaluations should reflect the same measures of academic and instructional methods that are used for full-time faculty. Variation in questions included on student evaluations may be based upon the facilities and the academic support available at the site. Adjunct managers should ensure that the evaluations are conducted, collected, and evaluated in as timely a manner as those on the home campus.

Administrative/faculty review should include observation of teaching and a structured interview. Eggers (1990) describes a program at Lincoln Land Community College that involved the training of master teachers

> … (t)o function as evaluators for part-time, off-campus instructors. During the academic year, each part-time, off-campus instructor is visited by a team evaluator with expertise in the evaluatee's discipline. The evaluator rates observed teaching behaviors with a valid and reliable instrument, and prepares a summary of the instructor's teaching strengths and weaknesses. Following the observation, the evaluator confers with the evaluatee in the spirit of helping relationship. In a dialogue between evaluator and evaluatee, a plan for teaching improvement is constructs (p.3).

Providing time and travel support for the administrator or full-time faculty evaluator to conduct the observation or interview will help to assure the success of this evaluation component.

Balch (1999) states, "Many institutions are recommending that part-time faculty develop and maintain a teaching portfolio documenting instructional activities" (p.13). This would provide an alternate, but effective method for "evaluation at a distance." Campbell et al. (1997) recommend a "working portfolio" that is "characterized by [an] ongoing systematic collection of selected work in courses and evidence of community activities" that "would form a framework for self-assessment and goal setting" as opposed to a "presentation portfolio" that is more of a reflection of the adjunct's work (p.3). Included in the working portfolio would be curricular units, teacher-made materials, assignments, and videos of teaching. Balch (1999) suggests sample tests, student evaluation results, reference letters, research, community involvement, and honors and recognition. If there are particular teaching focus areas at an institution, the portfolio should include artifacts that represent instruction designed to highlight those focus areas. The working portfolio would provide an excellent representation of the adjunct instructor's teaching activities.

Evaluation at a distance may require more artifacts, such as a working portfolio, than on-campus evaluation. It certainly requires more organization to ensure that evaluation is consistent with that conducted on the home campus.

Support Services

Support services include academic, clerical, and other support areas. Academic support involves computer and media resources, curriculum support materials, library materials, textbooks and supplemental materials, and teaching supplies. Clerical support covers word processing of documents, copying, printing, and other related services. Additional services include availability of office and student conference space, maintenance and janitorial, security, cafeteria or vending, childcare, parking, and administrative office support, such as Payroll.

Academic support may vary greatly from that on the main campus. The same services, or the availability of services, should be provided to ensure quality instruction. The library resources may have to be delivered to the branch or they may be made available on-line. A community library can provide library resources through a partnership with the parent institution's library.

Computer and media resources, though available, may be more limited than on the main campus. Technology and technological support are major issues at distant sites; offering classes at a site leased by a college does not ensure that the technology is compatible with the curriculum offered on campus. Ensuring consistency, as well as guaranteeing that the equipment works, continues to be a major concern. Technological support should be made available for adjunct instruction at distance sites, whether through the main campus or through the distance site location.

Curriculum support materials, textbooks and supplemental materials and teaching supplies might be available through a bookstore located on the branch or they may have to be ordered and delivered to the campus. On-line campus bookstores can make this job easier. The adjunct manager or faculty mentor can also help by contacting textbook publishers to obtain teacher's manuals and other text resources for the adjunct. Preplanning and organization are important since there will be a time lapse in obtaining materials. For those who work with adjuncts, either on-campus or off-campus, keeping extra teacher's manuals and supplemental materials on hand will assure all adjuncts have the necessary tools available at the start of class.

Clerical services may or may not be provided at the branch site. If services are provided at the main campus, there will again be delays in sending and receiving materials. Providing computers and printers for adjunct instructors can limit the need the clerical support. Copying can be done by the adjuncts if a copier is provided.

Office and/or conference space is also important to provide adjuncts at the branch campus or off-campus site. Facilities may not be available for individual or division-based offices and conference areas, but one central space may be available. The space should offer individual conference areas for assisting students. Providing an identified space for adjunct instructors is not only a useful service, but can also serve as another method of validating the importance of the adjunct.

Other support services will vary. It is essential that the adjunct instructor be able to access information regarding those services and be able to communicate with those areas. Where to legally park or locate a vending machine can be as major a challenge for the adjunct as locating a security guard for an escort through a dark parking lot.

Conclusion

Working with adjunct faculty at branch or off-campus sites will require more organization and structure than working with those on the main campus. It also requires an administrative commitment to involve full-time faculty with adjuncts teaching off-campus, ensuring that participation, communication, and socialization occurs (Roueche, Roueche, & Milliron, 1996). Another theme that emerges is the use of technology; technology can be a major contribution to work with adjuncts at a distance.

That commitment should emphasize socialization (Roueche, Roueche,

& Milliron, 1996) through collegiality and appreciation of the adjunct faculty members who serve on all campus sites. Social events, such as receptions or potlucks, could be planned. These could be held on the branch campuses, inviting administrators and full-time faculty and adjuncts from the home campus. Adjuncts could also be invited to events held on the main campus. Special recognition for the adjuncts, whether a certificate or a banquet recognizing their teaching contributions, is also a good idea. Authors (Balch, 1999; Roueche, Roueche, & Milliron, 1996) suggest that the part-time faculty be recognized for their years of service and/or teaching excellence. Discounts in the bookstore, tickets to campus events, fitness center memberships, and other special services can indicate the value placed on adjuncts. Tuition discounts are another suggestion from Balch (1999) who states,

> The personal factor, one-on-one conversations; invitations to special events by telephone rather than through mailboxes; and opportunities to learn about the students, the state of the campus, and the goals for the future will be the key ingredients toward a systematic and successful integration of our part-time faculty (p. 17).

Higher education today is a blend of synchronous and asynchronous learning, traditional and nontraditional students, full-time and adjunct faculty, and single campus, multi-campus institutions, branch campuses/off-campus sites, and virtual institutions. We must adapt to this continually changing blend, ensuring that we offer quality instruction to meet the needs of the students we serve.

References

Almanac Issue. (1999). *The Chronicle of Higher Education. XLVI*(1), 38.

Balch, P. (1999). Part-time faculty are here to stay. *Planning for Higher Education, 27*(3), 32-40.

Campbell, D. M., Cignetti, P. B., Melenyzer, B. J., Nettles, D. H., & Wyman, R. M. Jr. (1997). *How to develop a professional portfolio: A manual for teachers*. Needham Heights, MA: Allyn &Bacon.

Connors State College. (1999). *Adjunct faculty handbook* (rev. ed.). Warner and Muskogee, OK: Author.

Cook, W. A. (1995, January). *Empowering faculty to manage off-campus degree program: Redefining faculty workloads and service*. Paper presented at the American Association of Higher Education Conference on Faculty Roles and Rewards, Phoenix, Arizona.

Digranes, J. L., & Digranes, S. H. (1999). Communication with adjunct faculty - Working with a branch campus. *Adjunct Info: A Journal for Managers of Adjunct and Part-time Faculty, 7*(4), 1.

Eggers, P. (1990, April). *Part-time, off-campus instructors: A support program for improving teaching effectiveness*. Paper presented at the Annual Convention of the American Association of Community and Junior Colleges, Seattle, Washington.

Gappa, J. M., & Leslie, D. W. (1993). *The invisible faculty: Improving the status of part- timers in higher education*. San Francisco, CA: Jossey-Bass.

Orientation programs help new faculty feel connected to campus. (1999). *Dean & Provost, 1*(1), pp. 1, 8.

Palmer, J. C. (1999). Part-time faculty at community colleges: A national profile. *The NEA 1999 Almanac of Higher Education*. Washington, DC: National Education Association.

Roueche, J. E., Roueche, S. D., & Milliron, M. D. (1996). Identifying the strangers: Exploring part-time faculty integration in American community colleges. *Community College Review, 23*(4), 33-48.

Jo Lynn Autry Digranes, Ph.D., is Vice President for Academic Services and Technology, Connors State College, Warner and Muskogee, Oklahoma.

Swen H. Digranes, Ph. D., is a Professor, College of Education, Northeastern State University, Tahlequah, Oklahoma.

Evaluation of Adjunct Faculty in a Process for Effectiveness

By Sharon L. Stoops

Overview

This chapter addresses the issues associated with evaluating adjunct and part-time faculty, including:

- Evaluation practices,
- Historical background of faculty evaluation,
- Student evaluation practices and procedures as well as student biases,
- Other tools for use in faculty evaluation, and
- The process for developing faculty development instruments.

Introduction

When one walks into just about any academic departmental office during the last week of a semester, an all too familiar chaos will greet the visitor. Students are standing in line at the secretary's desk, most wanting to contact an instructor—usually an adjunct instructor who has no other point of contact on campus. There will be a pile of phone messages on the secretary's desk—messages for adjuncts she hasn't found time to deliver yet—and the phone continues to ring. She is also trying to collect end-of-term grade reports and other required paperwork from instructors as well as receiving from passing instructors documents for the next term—copies of syllabi, requests for materials, etc. On the adjunct manager's desk there are two new piles of materials: one almost two feet tall that consisted of student evaluations of adjunct instructors for the ending semester and a second pile of almost 100 contracts for adjunct faculty for the upcoming semester, awaiting the manager's approval. If one listens closely, the observer may overhear a phone message that an adjunct instructor has suffered a heart attack and been hospitalized; his wife will try to get grades to the department later in the week. Then there are those calls from the registration office or branch campuses, reporting all sections of a class are full and asking that another one be added. And it's barely 8:00 a.m. But this is just another all too frequent moment in one departmental office of any college that relies heavily upon adjunct faculty.

Unfortunately, this moment is probably not an anomaly since records from the National Center for Education Statistics show that use of adjunct faculty (part-time or contract faculty) occurs in all types of post-secondary education institutions in the United States. It is safe to say that almost all faculty supervisors, from reassigned faculty coordinators to department chairs to academic deans, will at one time or another have to deal with adjunct faculty and the ensuing opportunities and problems.

This chapter is meant to summarize what academic writers and researchers have said about the evaluation of adjunct faculty in institutions of higher education: There have been no hints or predictions that the use of adjunct faculty is likely to end or even decrease anytime in the near future.

In fact, the predictions are that with the tightening of institutional budgets, the hiring of part-time personnel at all levels will increase. Even the trend toward increased course offerings via distance education and alternative delivery systems is likely to increase the reliance upon contract instruction, especially as institutions find they can "hire" experts from anywhere in the country or even in the world.

Are there problems associated with the use of adjunct faculty? If so, what might these be? Almost all post-secondary institutions use adjunct faculty to some extent. Community colleges and other two-year institutions rely heavily upon such faculty. National statistics tell us that the use of adjunct faculty by U.S. higher education institutions is as high as 38 - 57 %, based on whether the measure refers to headcount or percent of courses taught. In community colleges, adjuncts account for as much as 67 % of all faculty; women and minorities make up the majority of adjunct numbers (Grusin & Reed, 1994).

Why do colleges use adjunct faculty? Often college administration will tell us that use of adjuncts provides valuable, up-to-date expertise from practitioners in the field for specialized courses. This reasoning is legitimate in a few cases. There are a few such experts who teach "just for the fun of it" while they devote most of their time to a "real" job, but many adjuncts in these positions command high stipends for presenting their expertise and teach only upper classmen in very specialized courses. The reality of staffing in most post-secondary institutions is that such practice is an exception rather than the general rule.

Much more often, the reliance upon adjunct faculty is more prosaic. Due to unexpected increases in enrollment, schools may find they have an extra demand for course sections that cannot be absorbed by full-time faculty. The reality of life in community colleges, especially, is that students are not turned away because scheduled course sections are full. Administration usually urges chairs to create new sections and "find" someone to teach them. Of course, if such courses would happen to be off-site, it makes sense to use a qualified local instructor rather than send someone from the home campus. One problem not easily overcome is the available hours some of the best potential adjunct have to teach. Many of the best adjuncts are available only for evening and weekend classes because they hold jobs with regular daytime hours. This is especially true of secondary school teachers who are an excellent source for many of basic classes. For some subject, especially mathematics and science, there is a dearth of qualified adjuncts for daytime classes. The search for qualified adjunct faculty can be an almost endless occupation for some chairs.

Another significant, and unfortunately far from occasional, reason for the reliance upon adjunct faculty for delivery of instruction is that it is less expensive to support adjunct than full-time faculty. In many instances, the part-time pool is so large, colleges have a buyer's market in which to find qualified people willing to teach for low wages. In any case, not having to pay for such benefits as retirement and insurance provides an institution with a means to cut personnel costs. (In some states, adjunct faculty can legally organize and can command such benefits. Some institutions provide benefits such as health insurance for adjuncts as a matter of course. These instances, however, are still not the majority.)

It is little wonder that "institution-hopping" takes place among the ranks of adjuncts. They go where the higher pay and the larger contract is offered. Last minute changes are frequent occurrences. Getting a well qualified, experienced adjunct instructor is often more luck than anything else, institutions often get what we pay for—and not necessarily because the adjunct means to shortchange. It is a fact of life that one has to survive fiscally, and an adjunct often does so by hiring out to multiple institutions or accepting contracts for the least desirable situations simply to make ends meet. Time and energy (traveling takes both) demands take their toll. Few institutions do much to ensure adjunct faculty have everything, including information, to perform their jobs adequately, let alone, easily. What an institution gets is an adjunct staff who often deal with the most vulnerable students (those at the lowest levels, in basic courses) while the adjuncts have only tangential connections with the institution themselves. Problems are compounded because these are also the instructors who teach night and weekend courses where they have the least direct supervision and when students have the least access to other support. What we have is a recipe for problems and headaches for supervisors.

Styne (1997) aptly calls adjuncts "the slave laborers of the '90s." Personal experience and other anecdotal evidence suggest that those who manage adjunct faculty, other than having full-time status, are not in a situation much better. Styne's experience agrees:

> A full-time faculty member serves as coordinator of adjunct faculty. The coordinator is released from teaching one class to do the job, and so far, each has chosen to serve for just one academic year. These coordinators have played important roles in developing procedures, preparing forms, and providing day-to-day supervision and evaluation of part-time faculty. The regular change of coordinators reflects the difficult and time-consuming nature of the job (p. 51).

Gappa and Leslie (1993) pointed out that there are false economies achieved by the hiring of part-time faculty, citing that increased numbers of part-timers mean fewer full-time faculty to handle advising, curriculum development, program coordination, committee work and other departmental responsibilities. If a department relies upon full-time faculty to serve as mentors and trainers of adjuncts, ratios can quickly become unmanageable.

Now add to this mix, the constantly developing cry for accountability by a public that sees large sums of tax dollars going to support higher education at the same time tuition spirals upward faster than inflation. Many of these taxpayers want better futures for their offspring, but many, themselves, have not received a college education. They do not understand the economics of educational institutions but understand the demands on their tax dollars. This means pressure is being brought to bear on institutions to prove those students are being taught effectively and efficiently. Outcomes assessment has become a buzzword and goad for higher education.

Evaluation Practices

It usually falls to the department chair to find, hire, train, and otherwise shepherd the adjuncts used by the department. It also means that the chair is charged with the evaluation of such personnel—especially during the crucial first semester of work. How well a chair performs such tasks affects the quality of instruction provided. The evaluation process is one way a chair has to control some of the variables; chairs themselves are scrutinized as to how well they do the job. Chairs are being held accountable for student success and teaching effectiveness. An institution's reputation can be affected by how well its faculty and administration perform; how effective they are. Demonstrated effectiveness affects an institution's marketability—which brings us once more to financial concerns. Institutions have to get FTE, retain FTE, and graduate FTE; and faculty and their performance play the pivotal role. The bottom line for supervisors is that program integrity must be upheld, student complaints held to a minimum, goals met, and cost contained. Chairs need to efficiently weed out any poor hires and determine where, if any, development of faculty will be effective. Hence the need to develop a strong evaluation practice—hopefully one which does not demand time which is not available.

Styne (1997) describes the evaluation procedure at Wilbur Wright College. Her experience seems to mirror or echo the descriptions heard from many managers of adjunct faculty:

> We are required to evaluate new part-time faculty in their first and second semesters, using a one-page evaluation form provided by the dean of instruction. A coordinator of adjunct faculty, the department chair, or occasionally another senior teacher we designate, visits a class session selected from among those listed by the teacher as the best ones to visit. Copies of the evaluation forms go to the dean of instruction and to the part-timer being evaluated, and the evaluator discusses the findings with the teacher. We try to make positive suggestions, especially in cases where the visit seems to show a need for improved teaching techniques. Should these visits reveal any serious problems, or if there are serious student complaints about the teacher, the dean of instruction also visits a class (p. 54).

Styne's evaluation process seems typical for two-year colleges. She expresses frustration and doubts about her college's system just as many other adjunct managers do. But like Styne, most concede the necessity of some kind of evaluation for adjunct faculty. The doubts seem to appear when deciding how to evaluate, what form the evaluation should take, and what should be done with the results.

By having some understanding of how and why evaluation practices are used, it will be possible to see how evaluation practices might be adapted for use with adjunct faculty. First of all, very little research seems to have been done regarding the role and use of part-time faculty and the quality of instruction, but the number of anecdotal writings regarding the subject are increasing. One research report of note, Grusin and Reed (1994), focuses upon the role of adjunct faculty in instruction of journalism. The study found that adjuncts teach an average of 20% of all journalism classes each term in the schools reporting (well below the reported national average), but the range was between 2% and 90%. These numbers represented increases during the past several years with highest increase in the use of adjuncts attributed to enrollment growth and leaner budgets (p. 19).

Grusin and Reed (1994) reported that in many cases, "schools have no formal, written selection policy" (p.19) for the hiring of adjunct faculty and criteria for credentialing vary widely; pay and benefits also vary with average pay per course being just under $2000 (p. 20). Anecdotal accounts and personal experience support these findings as applying to other instructional areas as well.

Other issues identified by the Grusin and Reed (1994) study included reports of little orientation and guidance for new adjuncts; a little over half (58%) are required to have office hours; few participate in social events and faculty meetings at the school—in short, adjuncts seem to receive little supervision. Of administrators polled, "78.9% said they have no written supervision policies for adjuncts" and "45% never monitor (observe) adjuncts' teaching." Of those who did not monitor teaching, "74% said they always have students evaluate the part-time faculty" (p.21).

Some Background on Faculty Evaluation

From the historical aspect, we know that formal faculty evaluations used in U.S. higher education and research regarding them date as early as the 1920s with earliest research being dominated by Remmer and Purdue University (Marsh, 1987). The formal assessment of faculty arose with the concept of tenure; those granting tenure looked for a way to document the "merit" upon which they decided the award. Unfortunately, especially in early days, the process was often subjective and not openly discussed, a situation that led to some misunderstanding of the process. With the adoption in 1940 of the AAUP Statement of Principles on Academic Freedom and Tenure, the awarding of tenure became the domain of the faculty and the criteria for the award become more standardized. Post-World War II growth in higher education allowed for increases in faculty ranks, but public support and funding weakened following the campus unrest and high inflation of the late 1960s and early 1970s. Administrations had to refocus their practices for hiring faculty and look for ways to decrease salary expenditures or, at least, demonstrate some soundness in their personnel decisions. By the mid- to late-1980s, public voices were questioning the "teaching role" of post-secondary institutions and demanding more quality. Institutions began looking critically at the function of the faculty; accountability became the focus (Brascamp & Ory, 1994).

Administrations began to evaluate classroom instruction as well as faculty research, publication, and service to the institution and community. Haste to include all of this in response to the increasing pressures of budget and public opinion, however, led to some inaccurate data-gathering methods, which in turn led to some flawed decisions. In consequence, faculty who were already uneasy about others judging their competency have become more skeptical, defensive, and resistive to evaluation, often citing "invasion of professional privacy," subjectiveness in interpretation of gathered data, and lack of knowledge of what constitutes effective teaching, not to mention problems in validity, objectivity, and reliability of the system (Seldin, 1980, p.7).

Changes in law, such as the 1972 amendment to the Civil Rights Act that extended prohibition against discrimination in employment to colleges and universities, have changed and opened up hiring and evaluation processes. Post-secondary institutions have found that they need to establish objective non-biased goals and standards, then apply those equally and fairly to all faculty. Most institutions have, indeed, put in place objectives and standards for all full-time personnel.

The evaluation process referred to above, is a summative process—one which is used to make personnel decisions such as promotion, awarding of merit pay, or awarding of tenure. This still remains a primary and necessary aspect of evaluation despite all objections of faculty to the contrary.

The role of formative evaluation has taken nearly equal significance and is still expanding. As assessment of instructional ability became a significant component of the summative evaluation process, it became apparent that many faculty chosen for their brilliance in research fields or for their subject matter knowledge were often not trained to teach and train others—undergraduate students, especially. New or beginning instructors, including a large proportion of adjunct faculty, often need development as instructors, whether on tenure track or not. It was quickly discovered that the mere gathering of data about teaching effectiveness, even when shared with the instructor concerned, did not necessarily lead to better teaching habits and instructional effectiveness. Thus, during the past two decades, colleges and universities have worked to develop formative evaluation processes linked with professional development programs—at least for full-time faculty.

Formative evaluations include any instrument or method used to gather information that can be used by an instructor—perhaps with the help of a department chair, mentor, colleague, or development specialist—to change and improve his or her instruction. Evidence indicates that tools used in formative evaluation work best if they are not part of a summative process. Centra (1993) states that "the reason has more to do with teachers than with the evaluators: teachers will not be as open to discussing weaknesses or seeking advice from people who will also judge them" (p.5). Perhaps from the evaluator's point of view, it is just as difficult to objectively judge someone whom one has spent time and effort helping to develop.

A number of researchers and writers about evaluation have noted another foible of the process. Faculty who are among the ranks of those who insist that formative and summative elements be kept separate often themselves move the formative to the summative when it is to their benefit, for example, by including results of a formative evaluation in a portfolio submitted for merit pay consideration. Student evaluation of instruction, an instrument type originally designed as formative has proven to be so valid and reliable an indicator that it is now widely accepted as a summative instrument. Argument still abounds about this matter and faculty are still raising concerns about the use of such an instrument. These caveats and suspected biases will be visited later.

Despite the apparent necessity to keep the formative separate from the summative elements of evaluation, recent studies seem to demonstrate a necessary co-dependency. Arreola (1995) agrees:

> Faculty evaluation systems, no matter how well designed, which are implemented without reference to faculty development programs are inevitably viewed by the faculty as being primarily punitive in intent … On the other hand, faculty development programs which are implemented without clear reference to information generated by faculty (summative) evaluation systems tend to be disappointing in their effect, no matter how well designed or funded. The reason for this is simple … Without reference to a faculty evaluation system, faculty development programs tend to attract primarily those faculty who are already motivated to seek out resources and opportunity to improve their performance (p. 3).

Most current researchers and writers in the field agree that to build a successful evaluation program, an institution must have an interconnected formative and summative process that

- visibly supports the values of the institution,
- is supported by the administration and accepted by the faculty,
- evaluates those aspects of the faculty role that are considered important and are rewarded.

The particular set of instruments used for gathering data and how summative data is reported seem to be of much less importance than that criteria be well thought out and communicated, that standards are just and used fairly, and that all involved understand the process and its consequences and rewards.

"Evaluation of faculty ... should be viewed in the larger perspective of the evaluation of the purposes of institutions of higher learning" (Seldin, 1984, p.107). Faculty on most campuses are expected to be much more than classroom presenters. Evaluation needs to be based on those elements of the faculty role and should reflect the value given to each element. These elements might include research and publication, advising of students, and service besides instruction. For most faculty, especially those in non-research institutions and community or two-year colleges, the greater weight or value would be given to instruction. Adjunct faculty would be evaluated almost exclusively for instruction with that aspect defined and its important components identified.

Can any type of effective and interconnected process be established for adjunct faculty? Lack of resources will probably lead most institutions to continue much as they are now, having managers of adjuncts struggle through the best they can. However, some concentrated thought and consideration can lead to improvement if evaluation of adjunct faculty is considered as one necessary component of an important personnel process which includes hiring, orientation, evaluation, development, and promotion/termination. Substantial thought must be given to the selection of evaluation instruments and the uses to which the results are put.

Institutions have some very basic requirements or responsibilities for which all faculty must be held responsible and as such should be considered in any evaluation. These include such things as instructing a minimum of class sections, attending class meeting times, preparing suitable course syllabi and materials, and completing paperwork (such as grade reports) in a timely fashion. Most researchers feel that evaluation instruments should closely reflect the duties and responsibilities valued. Arreola (1995) goes so far as to devote almost an entire chapter defining of such things as learning ("Persistent, measurable, specified change in the behavior of the student resulting from an experience designed by the teacher") and instruction ("A set of experiences which induces student learning"). Arreola also defines other key component including content expertise, instruction delivery skills, instructional design skills, and course management skills—areas he feels are ones important to measure when focusing on instruction during the evaluation process. It can be deemed that students might not be the best judges of some of these criteria.

Almost all recent writing devoted to faculty evaluation agree that data gathered, whether for formative or summative purposes, should come from a variety of sources. These sources can and should include students, instructors doing self-evaluations, colleagues who do classroom observations, and supervisors. In some cases, information from alumni and persons outside the institution, such as employers of graduates or members of the community that have been served by the faculty member in a service role might be valid. Arreola (1995) recommends that sources of information and weights to be given those evaluations should be negotiated by the instructor and the supervisor prior to the evaluation period. While such negotiation is not practical when dealing with most adjunct faculty, these faculty, nonetheless, should be informed "up front" what the evaluation process will be, what the criteria are, and who will be the evaluator(s).

Student Evaluation of Instruction

It must be conceded that a major component of faculty evaluation will continue to be the student evaluation of teaching effectiveness in some form. Since student evaluation of instruction has been researched for over 70 years, it makes sense to look at the research findings although, as Wachtel (1998) points out in his review of research, the range of findings is broad and often conflicting.

Despite some argument to the contrary, it seems that most people, including students, can indeed identify characteristics of good teaching and several studies have shown that a high level of agreement can be found when lists of characteristics of good teaching are developed and ranked. According to Seldin (1980), the most important identified characteristics of a good instructor focus on instructor knowledge, method of instruction, instructor-student rapport, teaching behaviors, enthusiasm in teaching, concern for one's teaching, and overall enhancement of the learning process (p.72-73).

Seldin's findings are supported by research involving an evaluation called the Snell Educator Effectiveness Index which has been used in theoretical research for education. The index is composed of five teacher characteristics or traits that were identified and validated through a number of studies. The five traits identified by a wide variety of students as being most desirable in an instructor include "the ability of a teacher to be INTERESTING, KNOWLEDGEABLE, ORGANIZED, FAIR, and FRIENDLY" (Snell and Mekies, 1992, p. 286). Through a number of trials and groups controlled for various demographics, INTERESTING was found to be most important to students, followed very closely by KNOWLEDGEABLE (p.287).

Snell and Mekies prepared the Index with an essay portion to produce what they feel is a practical tool for faculty evaluation. But they emphasize that the essay portion should only be used in a double blind situation where a second party hands out evaluations, collects them, and delivers them to the instructor's supervisor. The remarks should be given the instructor in their entirety after grades are posted (p.287), but the researchers are very careful to indicate that instructors and their supervisors should be the ones to decide whether the instrument is used for formative or summative evaluation.

Student Evaluation Biases

A number of possible biases could cause problems with instruments used to evaluate instructors. However, almost any possible bias that could appear in such ratings has received scrutiny and been subjected to research for several decades, especially to determine what biases are common in certain types of instruments and to what extent. It might seem obvious that the instrument type receiving the greatest attention would be the student evaluation of instruction. Feldman (1992 and 1993) especially has published some very thorough studies used to determine what impact elements such as gender of instructors might have on overall student ratings of instruction. Feldman's major finding was that students' gender is an important element in that females tend to rate female instructors slightly higher; males tend to rate male instructors slightly higher. The differences found, while statistically noticeable, were not consistent among studies. Some influencing factors might include the instructional field and what the historical gender dominance of the field might be. Feldman (1993) summarizes his findings:

> In a sense, college students favored men when globally perceiving and evaluating the college "teachers" they were asked to rate in experimental research in the social laboratory. Although the majority of laboratory studies found no differences in overall evaluation as professionals between male and female "teachers," in those studies where differences were found, male "teachers" received more favorable ratings than did their female counterparts. No laboratory study found that women on average received higher overall ratings than men across experimental conditions. In the present analysis of college students' evaluations of their actual college teachers, results were somewhat different. Again, the majority of the studies did not show a statistically significant difference between the two genders. Here, however, when statistically significant differences were found, more of them favored women than favored men (176).

Feldman's studies also include scrutiny of such elements as class level of the course, difficulty of the course (or instructor), personality characteristics of the instructor, as well as perceived professionalism, competence, confidence, etc. Feldman listed a number of considerations that could have been influential in the findings of his studies. These may be factors that institutions may wish to consider when choosing or using specific instruments; there is no likelihood, however, that any instrument will be without some bias:

- **The course grade expected by the student**—Braskamp and Ory (1994), Centra (1979), Marsh (1987) and others have found a moderate correlation between the grade expected by students and the rating given the instructor; students expecting higher grades tend to give higher ratings to the instructor. A concern for administrators here might be whether faculty wanting better ratings will tend to inflate grades or be more lenient. This could be a strong factor in the adjunct situation. Goldberg and Callahan (1991) found a positive correlation between the fact that adjunct faculty gave higher grades than full-time faculty and that students rated adjunct faculty higher than full-time faculty, even when the students were unaware of the faculty members' status.

- **Popularity of instructor**—Atamian and Ganguli (1993) found that "students in general, and male students in particular, do not use similar criteria for judging effectiveness and popularity of instructors ... Female students, on the other hand, appear to judge their least favorite instructor to also be least effective ..." Other reports linked popularity of instructor with class size and other variables which need further study.

- **The reasons for taking a course (elective or required)**—Feldman (1978) found that students who elected to take a course tended to rate the instructor of that course higher than they rated an instructor of a course they were required to take.

- **The workload of the course (difficulty of the course)**—Wachtel (1998) finds this to be an area needing further study. The fear is that faculty will reduce homework and make exams easier, but there is some indication from research that some increase in the workload of a course leads to higher ratings. Wachtel cautions that the instructor's perception of difficulty and pace seems to vary from the perception of the students, and math and science courses may prove exceptions to any findings based on other courses (p. 198).

- **Class size**–most researchers investigating the effects of class size on instructors' ratings have reported that smaller classes tend to produce the highest ratings; on the other hand, Feldman (1978) suggests that there is a curvilinear relationship with the largest classes also bringing higher ratings.

- **Level of course (might also relate to maturity of student)**—Marsh (1987) and Feldman (1978) each found that higher level courses tended to produce higher ratings for instructors. It appears that no other particular factor which might explain the phenomenon—such as age of student, rank of instructor, class size, etc.—has been studied in this context.

- **Instructor's rank**—research involving the effect of an instructor's rank upon student ratings appears to find no significant relationships. Wachtel (1998) reported that a minority of studies which reported significant relationships also found that the relationship tended to be inverse when concentrating on age and experience of the faculty member (not rank).

- **Academic subject**—Subject matter does, indeed, seem to have an effect on ratings with mathematics and sciences consistently ranking lowest. The reason for the low rankings for these types of classes have not been definitely identified, but even supporters of student evaluations of instruction caution against comparing ratings of teachers of math and science with ratings of teachers from other departments.

- **Minority status or physical appearance of the instructor**—There seem to be no thorough studies dealing with either issue. Wachtel (1998) reported that Buck and Tiene, in an 1989 study, "found significant inter-action between gender, attractiveness, and authoritarianism ..."(p.201), but this study appears to stand alone currently. With the emphasis on developing multicultural diversity in faculty and staff and the knowl-edge that minorities and women make up a large percentage of adjunct faculty, this could be a crucial area needing research.

- **Evaluation administration conditions**—Researchers appear to be in accord that blind administration of the instrument is most effective (the students should not feel that instructors handle the material in any way) and students should remain anonymous. Also, as much as possible, a course evaluation should not coincide with the timing of a major exam-ination in the course. Braskamp and Ory (1994) insist that students need to be informed how the results of the evaluation will be used.

Those in judgmental roles will need to be sensitive to these possible biases and act accordingly. A variety of sources of data should help minimize the overall effect of a biased instrument.

According to Wachtel (1998):

> ... after nearly seven decades of research on the use of student eval-uations of teaching effectiveness, it can safely be stated that the majority of researchers believe that student ratings are a valid, reli-able, and worthwhile means of evaluating teaching ... In fact, Marsh (1987) contends that student evaluations are the only indicator of teaching effectiveness whose validity has been thoroughly and rig-orously established (p.192).

Wachtel (1998), in his review of research, neatly lists most of the common arguments against the use of student evaluation of instruction and counterpoints them with research done disproving the stated apprehension. A summary of his conclusions from his review of research include the following points:

- "Feedback from student ratings can help to improve instruction ... They alone will not automatically improve teaching and sustain that improvement without other types of feedback.
- "The use of student ratings increase the likelihood that excellence in teaching will be recognized and rewarded.
- "Student ratings have been shown to be positively correlated with student learning and achievement, i.e. students rate most highly those instructors from whom they have learned the most ... (t)hese correlations are only moderate.
- "Student ratings are positively correlated with ratings by alumni.
- "There is abundant anecdotal evidence of faculty hostility and cynicism toward the use of student ratings" (pp.192-194).

While Cashin and Downey (1992) find that student evaluation of faculty is of consistent enough quality to search for global rating items which would enable the construction of very brief, summative tools, Tagomori and Bishop (1995) agonize that such evaluations are often adopted by institutions based on what other institutions are using rather than on validated studies. They feel many such evaluations are filled with vague, subjective, and poorly correlated items which render any scores to be useless. Weissberg (1993) compares use of standardized teaching evaluations by colleges and universities to be "reminiscent of the heyday of American automobiles when poorly made, unsafe cars were justified by the industry because 'the public likes them, why else would they buy them?' " (p.7). Weissberg feels that more enlightening tools for evaluating teachers' and institutions' effectiveness can be found than student satisfaction with classes—such as comprehensive exams to see what students have really learned.

It should be apparent that the final verdict pertaining to the reliability and effectiveness of student evaluations is still out. But in lieu of better tools, supervisors who select such forms need to use some directed research to find the instrument best suited to their particular needs and circumstances.

Other Tools

What besides a student evaluation of instruction could be considered for evaluation of an instructor's effectiveness? Keig and Waggoner (1995) list the following: "direct classroom observation, videotaping of classes, evaluation of course materials, an assessment of instructor evaluation of the academic work of students, and analysis of teaching portfolios" (p.1). Keig and Waggoner weight their recommendations towards a formative peer evaluation process and cited six instructional events identified by Hart (1987) as elements of instructional delivery that can and should be critiqued by "knowledgeable colleagues" in the process. These elements included such things as the physical setting for a class, the instructor's procedures, the instructor's and the students' use of language when interacting, roles played by class participant, the relationship of a course to other courses, and outcomes (student learning) (p.1-2). Keig and Waggoner see the use of videotaping as one way to evaluate the elements listed above as well as validate other feedback. Appendix 10.1 shows Ivy Tech's observer evaluation.

DeFina (1996) finds that student and peer evaluations can be capricious and that self-evaluations seldom have specific guidelines. She feels portfolios are a more credible means of assessment and recommends that a portfolio include a narrative section (describing the instructor's teaching philosophy, responsibilities, and methods), course projects, assignments and activities; motivational instructional techniques, professional development activities, methods of staying current, and goals and activities for self-improvement. Evidence which should be provided might include samples of student work (graded), student performance indicators, representative course syllabi, student evaluation reports, outlines of presentations given, and achievements and awards. DeFina emphasizes that evaluators should expect succinctness and hard evidence in a portfolio. Centra (1993) found that even portfolios that were not ideally designed correlated reasonably well with student evaluations and other evaluation forms. Both DeFina and Centra seem comfortable with use of portfolios as summative evaluation tools.

Formative evaluation tools can include most of the items discussed above. The difference still remains with the use to which the results are put. Formative evaluations are used to determine the strengths and weaknesses of an instructor's presentation and preparation in order for development and improvement to take place.

With adjunct faculty, formative types of evaluation may be considered wastes of time if the institution cannot find a way to provide for and encourage participation in developmental activities. Millis (1994) suggests that:

> Teaching improvement activities can include skill-building workshops, seminars, conferences, or retreats, lasting from one hour to several days. Topic-oriented luncheon (often "brown bag" affairs) and special interest groups addressing teaching interests such as critical thinking or cooperative learning provide networking opportunities. Some campuses encourage faculty to visit the classes of colleagues or to have a peer visitor share observations. Many campuses offer targeted teaching development opportunities with themes related to multiculturalism, classroom research, cooperative learning, teaching portfolio preparation, writing across the curriculum, or teaching and technology (p.461).

Since many of these activities are planned for full-time faculty, anyway, it would take little extra expense or time to include adjunct faculty. Incentives to encourage adjunct participation, however, would need to be considered. Institutions should not overlook the effectiveness of newsletters and mentoring programs and, especially, the sharing of news recognizing achievements and awards of adjunct faculty. A library that can provide readily available resources and periodicals for teaching is also essential. When such activities and resources are provided, formative evaluations can then be used to direct affected faculty to those sources and activities most likely to assist improvement.

Cautions for Managers

Two other items need to be considered for consideration by a manager of adjunct faculty (in fact, of any faculty). The first has to do with the quickly escalating use of alternative delivery of instruction. Evaluation forms that may have worked in the traditional classroom setting may be entirely inappropriate for a course delivered via the Internet or by video-conferencing. New studies are just beginning to appear in the literature, which seek to determine effective evaluation methods. Such developments will need to be monitored, and as tools are made available, adapted for use in individual institutions. This will be especially important for courses delivered by adjunct faculty who seldom have the opportunity to meet face-to-face with their supervisor.

A second item is a caution concerning personnel policy. Most human resources personnel will tell supervisors that all personnel decisions must be documented. Any evaluation tool should provide the evaluated individual with a chance to respond to any findings and conclusions as well as provide for signatures of all that review and accept the material as accurate. This is very important in situations, where, for example, after hiring a minimally adequate adjunct to teach a course for a number of terms, a fully qualified instructor is found to replace the first. In today's litigation-happy environment, an adjunct manager may have to prove that there is sufficient reason to not rehire even a temporary part-time instructor. There are many other personnel situations that can trip up even the most well-meaning supervisor if the documentation to support decisions is not available.

Evaluation Instrument Development Process

Preparation for selection of an instrument seems the most critical part of the evaluation process—what is used to measure effectiveness needs to measure the correct elements. Faculty and administration need to work together to develop the process. One example of how such a process might work is the recent workings of a statewide committee for Ivy Tech State College in Indiana. That committee made up of representatives of both faculty and administration deliberated nearly 18 months before any instrument was designed or chosen. The first step taken was to establish and state the purpose for evaluation of instructors. Step two consisted of the identifying of the general role and responsibilities of an instructor in the college, then the identification of "quality indicators" which could be used to judge effectiveness. The committee actually composed a generic job description for instructors which lists the areas of responsibility and the roles expected of any instructor plus an addendum for those faculty serving as program chairs. These elements were circulated to all 22 campuses of the college, soliciting comments and criticisms. Once these elements were agreed upon, the committee designed an instrument for use by supervisors for classroom monitoring (or observation). In the interest of time and economy, the committee decided that an instrument for student evaluation of instruction currently used statewide would be kept through an entire evaluation cycle at which time the process and elements would be further scrutinized. An entire process for the evaluation of faculty was written and put forward to all elements of the college—upper administration, campus administration, faculty, legal service, and human resources—for adoption. The process is in its first-year trial period, so its effectiveness cannot be measured. The process used by other colleges, of course, would need to be different due to different circumstances and values but all those who must use the evaluation instrument need to be included in its creation.

Conclusion

Many institutions have posted their personnel policies and even examples of evaluation tools on the Internet. Administrators looking for ideas to adapt for their own situation can easily and quickly access a multitude of examples. A sobering caveat is offered, however, by Grusin and Reed (1994) who remind us that there are few incentives for managers to improve current practices, especially because the use of adjuncts costs less than the use of full-time faculty and because accrediting bodies do not demand or enforce higher standards. Even though managers know they should do better, they face many uphill challenges. Program improvements needed on most campuses include the incorporation of a manual of standards and practices to guide the hiring, supervision and evaluation of adjunct faculty, a formal mentoring system, incentives to participate in development activities, and rewards for outstanding teaching among adjunct faculty.

Say Grusin and Reed (1994),

> To fail to treat adjuncts like real faculty is to devalue both the part-timer and the teaching profession by sending a message that "anyone can teach." Most of all, schools that do not acknowledge and mentor adjunct faculty fail in their responsibility to students who sign up in good faith for courses taught only by "staff" (p.25).

If we supervisors of adjunct faculty at our institutions were to be evaluated for effectiveness in the management of adjunct faculty, how would we fare?

References

Arreola, R. A. (1995). *Developing a comprehensive faculty evaluation system: A handbook for college faculty and administrators designing and operating a comprehensive faculty evaluation.* Boston: Ankar.

Atamian, R., & Ganguli, G. (1993). Teacher popularity and teaching effectiveness: Viewpoint of accounting students. *Journal of Education for Business, 68,* 163-169.

Braskamp, L. A., & Ory, J. C. (1994). *Assessing faculty work: Enhancing individual and institutional performance.* San Francisco: Jossey-Bass.

Cashin, W. E., & Downey, R. G. (1992, January). Using global student rating items for summative evaluation. *Journal of Educational Psychology, 84,* 563-572.

Centra, J. A. (1979). *Determining faculty effectiveness.* San Francisco: Jossey-Bass.

Centra, J. A. (1993). *Reflective faculty evaluation: Enhancing teaching and determining faculty effectiveness.* San Francisco: Jossey-Bass.

Feldman, K. A. (1978). Course characteristics and college students' ratings of their teachers: What we know and what we don't. *Research in Higher Education, 9* (2), 199-242.

Feldman, K. A. (1988). Effective college teaching from the students' and faculty's view: matched or mismatched priorities. *Research in Higher Education, 28*(3), 291-344.

Feldman, K. A. (1992). College students' views of male and female college teachers: Part I—Evidence from the social laboratory and experiments. *Research in Higher Education, 33*(3), 317-375.

Feldman, K. A. (1993). College students' views of male and female college teachers: Part II—Evidence from students' evaluations of their classroom teachers. *Research in Higher Education, 34*(2), 151-211.

Gappa, J. M. , & Leslie, D.W. (1993). *The invisible faculty: Improving the status of part-timers in higher education*. San Francisco: Jossey-Bass.

Goldberg, G.,& Callahan, J. (1991). Objectivity of student evaluation of instructors. *Journal of Education for Business, 66*, 377-378.

Grusin, E. K., & Reed, B. S. (1994). The role of part-time faculty in the quality of instruction. *Journalism & Mass Communication Educator, 48*(4), 15-22.

Keig, L., & Waggoner, M. D. (1995). *Collaborative peer review. The role of faculty in improving college teaching*. Washington, DC: ERIC Clearinghouse on Higher Education. (ERIC Document Reproduction Service No. ED 378 924).

Marsh, H. W. (1987). Students' evaluation of university teaching: Research findings, methodological issues, and directions for future research. *International Journal of Educational Research, 11*, 253-388.

Millis, B. J. (1994). Faculty development in the 1990s: What it is and why we can't wait. *Journal of Counseling and Development, 72*, (5), 454-469.

Seldin, P. (1980). *Successful faculty evaluation programs: A practical guide to improve faculty performance and promotion/tenure decisions*. Pleasantville, NY: Coventry Press.

Seldin, P. (1984). *Changing practices in faculty evaluation*. San Francisco: Jossey-Bass.

Snell, J. C., & Mekies, S. (1992). Snell Educator Effectiveness Index: An instrument for faculty evaluation by students. *Journal of Instructional Psychology, 19* (4), 286-290.

Styne, M. M. (1997, February). Those unfamiliar names and faces: The hiring, management and evaluation of part-time faculty. *Teaching English in the Two Year College, 24* (1), 50-54.

Tagomori, H. T., & Bishop, L. A. (1995). Student evaluation of teaching: Flaws in the instruments. *Thought and Action, 11*, 63-78.

University of Minnesota (1999). Protocols for student evaluation and peer review of faculty teaching contributions and policy on evaluation of teaching contributions.
<http:www1.umn.edu/usenate/policies/stueval.html> available July 7, 1999.

Wachtel, H. K. (1998, June). Student evaluation of college teaching effectiveness. *Assessment and Evaluation in Higher Education, 23*(2), 191-211.

Weissberg, R. (1993). Standardized teaching evaluations. *Perspectives on Political Science, 22* (1), 5-8.

Sharon L. Stoops is currently the Chair of the General Education and Support Services Division of Ivy Tech State College, Indiana. Sharon is also ABD and participating in the dissertation exercise toward a Ph.D. in Education Leadership, Administration, and Foundations from Indiana State University.

Chapter 10 Appendices

Appendix 10.1 — Ivy Tech Classroom Observer Evaluation Form

Ivy Tech State College
Course Evaluation

INSTRUCTOR: _____	COURSE: _____
OBSERVER: _____	DATE: _____
TIME OBSERVED (to)	

Please rate each of the following from 1 to 5 with 1 being strongly disagree and 5 being strongly agree; or 'Yes" or 'No' as applicable. If the measure was not observed mark N/O. Please include comments concerning the measure.

CURRICULUM REVIEW

	No			Yes	N/O	COMMENTS
1) The syllabus course description agrees with the state description	1			5		
2) The syllabus course objectives agrees with those in the state description	1			5		
3) The syllabus contains a weekly outline	1			5		
4) Topics are presented in a logical sequence	1	2	3	4	5	
5) The syllabus provides for each of the course objectives	1	2	3	4	5	
6) The syllabus contains information necessary to determine grades	1			5		
7) The syllabus contains necessary classroom policies	1			5		
8) The syllabus references required texts, resources and how they will be used	1			5		
9) The instructors office hours included	1			5		

ASSESSMENT REVIEW

1) Tests relate to course learning objectives	1	2	3	4	5	
2) Projects are appropriate to course objectives	1	2	3	4	5	
3) Appropriate records are maintained to determine student achievement	1	2	3	4	5	
4) The instructor prepares appropriate evaluation activities and instruments (usage of tests, lab work, other exercises)	1	2	3	4	5	

CLASSROOM REVIEW

1) The instructor presents material as it relates to the syllabus	1	2	3	4	5	
2) The instructor presented an overview of the lesson	1	2	3	4	5	
4) The instructor communicated effectively (grammar, spelling, voice volume)	1	2	3	4	5	
5) The instructor defined terms, concepts, and principles	1	2	3	4	5	COMMENTS:

Appendix 10.1

Ivy Tech State College
Course Evaluation

		1	2	3	4	5		
6)	The instructor presented examples to clarify points	1	2	3	4	5		
7)	The instructor related new ideas to familiar concepts	1	2	3	4	5		
8)	The instructor encouraged students' participation in class	1	2	3	4	5		
9)	The instructor explained material in response to students/questions	1	2	3	4	5		
10	The instructor provided assistance to students when needed.	1	2	3	4	5		
11	The instructor engaged students in participatory and productive learning activities	1	2	3	4	5		
12	The instructor used various teaching aids (media, AV)	1	2	3	4	5		
13	The instructor demonstrated knowledge of subject matter.	1	2	3	4	5		
14	The instructor established and maintained an atmosphere which facilitated learning	1	2	3	4	5		
15	The instructor was prepared (class began on time, materials ready, used classtime productively)	1	2	3	4	5		
16	The instructor adapted teaching methods to students enrolled	1	2	3	4	5		
17	The instructor treated students with respect and equality	1	2	3	4	5		
18	The instructor maintains safe environment in classroom/lab.	1	2	3	4	5		

What were the major strengths observed?

What suggestions for improvement can be made?

Date reviewed and discussed: _____

Observer: _____

Faculty member observed: _____

Reviewed by (Chair/DofI): _____

11

Maintaining Quality in Higher Education

By Albert B. Smith, Bonita Butner, Brent Cejda, and John Murray

Overview

This chapter consists of four major sections related to maintaining and improving quality in institutions of higher learning:

- quality management and part-time faculty,
- hiring and developing quality part-time faculty,
- instructional quality and part-time faculty, and
- program evaluation for enhancing quality.

Each section offers some specific recommendations for academic managers who are looking for new ways to enhance the quality of their programs and their work with part-time instructors.

Introduction

In a recent article in the *Chronicle of Higher Education*, Leatherman (2000) noted that colleges are continuing to hire more part-time faculty members. He reports on a study conducted by the U.S. Department of Education. This study, based on a survey by the department's National Center for Educational Statistics, showed that two-year and four-year colleges and universities were hiring more faculty members than they did in 1995. Here are some of the figures from this report:

In 1997, 682,650 faculty members worked at four-year institutions—35,591 more than in 1995. But of those new hires, 11,083 were full-timers and 24,508 were part-timers.

During that same period, the number of faculty members at two-year colleges increased to 307,163, from 248,415. Of the 22,748 new hires, 31% filled full-time posts, while 69% took part-time positions.

Overall at four-year institutions in 1997, 67.4% of faculty members worked full time and 32.6% worked part time. In 1995, the comparable proportions were 69% and 31%. At two-year colleges, 35.4% worked full time and 64.6% worked part time, compared with the 36% who were full-timers and 64% who were part-timers in 1995 (pp. 1-2).

From this data, one can clearly see that part-time faculty need to be considered in any discussions of maintaining quality in higher education.

Quality Management and Part-time Faculty

In the early 1980s, it became apparent that companies in the United States needed to change their ways of doing business if they were to survive. Products made in other countries were less costly to manufacture, were produced faster, were of higher quality, and were sold at lower prices than American products (Freed & Klugman, 1997). The philosophies of three quality improvement specialists, Deming, Juran, and Crosby, contributed significantly to the development of the quality movement which has been given a variety of labels, among them "Total Quality Management" (TQM) and "Continuous Quality Improvement" (CQI) (Cornesky et al., 1992). According to Seymour (1993), higher education has adopted quality initiatives to address the four following challenges:

1. increased competition for students,
2. consumer-driven markets searching for value,
3. the accountability and assessment movements, and
4. a new service orientation that is focused on meeting student needs.

American higher education has commonly used the term quality. Every admissions office seeks quality students. Every search committee seeks quality applicants for faculty positions. Every institutional performance report documents the quality of graduates.

The wide usage of the term has led to a number of myths concerning quality and higher education, such as only highly selective colleges have quality or quality in higher education is directly related to high-cost tuition. Yet these statements and corresponding myths do not provide a clear definition of quality or provide guidance concerning how quality is achieved and maintained.

Four criteria have been used to identify quality in higher education institutions. According to Bergquist (1995), two of the oldest and most common measurements of quality in higher education are what he terms the *input and outputs* of resources. Input measurements include such things as the grade point averages or standardized test scores of entering freshmen, the percentage of faculty with terminal degrees, the number of library holdings, or the amount of institutional endowment. Outputs include measurements such as the overall graduation rate; the number of faculty publications; or the passing rate of graduates on professional exams for licensure in accounting, law, medicine and teaching.

A third measurement of quality in higher education is based on institutional mission. Bogue and Saunders (1992) stressed that, "Quality is conformance to mission specification and goal achievement—within publicly accepted standards of accountability and integrity" (p. 20). In a similar fashion, Green (1994) asserted that "a high quality institution is one that clearly states its mission (or purpose) and is efficient in meeting the goals that it has set for itself" (p. 15). The fourth measurement of quality takes a before and after approach, most often referred to as "value-added". Astin (1985) describes this approach as institutions "that have the greatest impact—add the most values as the economists would say—on the student's knowledge and personal development and on the faculty member's scholarly and pedagogical ability and productivity" (p. 61).

While consensus has not been reached concerning an exact definition of quality in higher education, some common aspects have emerged which provide a better understanding of how quality is achieved and maintained.

A review of the literature reveals nine attributes, practices and principles that are generally accepted as indicators of quality in an organization and are commonly mentioned by authorities (Chaffee & Sherr, 1992; Cornesky et al., 1992; Freed & Klugman, 1997). These indicators have been labeled as "quality principles" (Freed & Klugman, 1997). The principles and their relationship to managing a department are outlined below:

1. **Leadership must support a quality culture** and

2. **Leaders create a culture of quality.** Institutional leaders need to support the implementation and maintenance of a quality culture by ensuring that the necessary resources are available to support quality initiatives. Even the most talented part-time faculty member will have difficulty in providing quality instruction without at least a minimum of instructional support. In addition, both top-down and bottom-up leadership is needed for participative decision making that will improve the quality of higher education. Departmental leaders must be effective communicators who can bridge the often disparate interests of the respective constituencies of administration, faculty, students, and alumni. Of keen importance is effective communication and representation between and among the full- and part-time faculty in a department.

3. **The institution must be vision, mission, and outcomes driven.** Educational institutions exist for a purpose and this purpose is defined by the expectations of all stakeholders. For colleges and universities, these stakeholders include administrators, faculty, students, parents, trustees or directors, alumni, employers, accrediting organizations and bodies, funding entities and society as a whole. Departmental leaders are

responsible for ensuring that the vision and mission of the institution is represented in the programs and activities of the department. Moreover, measurable outcomes will greatly influence the stakeholder's perceptions of department and institutional quality. Both full- and part-time faculty must be aware of desired departmental outcomes and how these outcomes relate to the overall vision and mission of the institution.

4. **The institution must be systems dependent.** Institutional quality is a result of the interaction of interdependent parts of a system. In other words, a change in one part of the institution will affect other parts of the institution. For example, increasing the use of part-time faculty to address budgetary concerns could place additional responsibilities on full-time faculty in areas such as advising and committee service. In terms of staffing, the departmental leader must ascertain and address potential systems problems.

5. **The institution should support systematic individual development**. Continuously updating and improving knowledge and skills is a necessity to quality higher education. The departmental leader needs to work with each individual faculty member, both full- and part-time, to determine appropriate areas for continued development and must also be supportive of development efforts.

6. **The institution must make decisions based on fact.** Before a problem can be fully understood it is important to consider data that measures both the desired outcome and the process designed to achieve the outcome. Many times, there will also be relevant data necessary to develop a contextual understanding of the issue. The departmental leader will play a central role in working with full- and part-time faculty in developing the mechanisms to gather as well as present such data.

7. **The institution should delegate decision making.** If individuals are to be responsible for achieving quality, they must be able to make necessary changes. The faculty in a department is best suited to identify ideal ratios of full- and part-time faculty, specific areas of expertise desired in part-time faculty or other possible solutions to filling instructional needs. They should work with the administration in determining the

number and use of part-time faculty.

8. **The institution should encourage collaboration.** Collaboration and teamwork allows for the division of labor based on individual strengths to achieve a common goal. The departmental leader is key in developing and maintaining good relationships between full- and part-time faculty as well as identifying both opportunities for collaboration and teamwork as well as the appropriate individuals for such efforts.

9. **The institution should plan for change.** Vision, mission, and outcomes are based on the expectations of stakeholders and these expectations will change. The departmental leader will need to anticipate change and, when appropriate, bring the necessity for change to the attention of departmental members and top-level administrators.

Part-time faculty are a reality in contemporary higher education. Colleges and universities must attempt to control any negative outcomes related to quality that result from this reality. A systematic process for the hiring and continued employment of part-time faculty is a first step to maintain quality. This process should address aspects of quality, ranging from the vision and mission of the institution to the role of the faculty member in quality improvement efforts and outline requirements for continued employment, including individual development expectations. Most importantly, the importance of quality should be clearly articulated to part-time faculty prior to initial employment.

It is also essential that departmental leaders ensure support for a quality learning experience by integrating part-time faculty with the full-time faculty. This integration includes aspects such as orientation and providing instructional support and continuing development opportunities. Successful integration will help minimize any short-term negative outcomes as well as foster a culture of continued quality improvement.

Hiring and Developing Quality Part-time Faculty

"There is considerable evidence to support the idea that how part-time faculty are hired and used by the college is a key factor in the quality of part-time faculty instruction" (Roueche, 1999). Roueche, Roueche, and Milliron (1996) found that colleges that effectively used adjuncts took a proactive approach to the recruitment, selection, and socialization of adjuncts. These colleges do not wait until a need arises but actively develop databases of potential adjuncts in order to be more selective in hiring. There are many sources to use when developing a database of qualified adjuncts:

- Local newspapers ads announcing potential openings
- Spouses of colleagues who also have advanced degrees
- Local industry and business professionals
- Advisory committees
- Professional societies (e.g. Society for Professional Engineers, Professional Accountants Association, The American Chemical Association, and etc.) for referrals
- Department chairs at four-year institutions who may know of recent Master's graduates who might be still in the area
- Doctoral candidates who might be interested in gaining some college teaching experience while completing a dissertation
- Recent retirees both from your institution and other colleges in the area
- Other colleges within commuting distance who may have lists of potential adjuncts

Proactive colleges and universities "consider both the type of person the college wants as an instructor and whether or not the individual will be satisfied with part-time employment" (Roueche, Roueche, & Milliron, 1996, p. 43). The first step is to identify the characteristics you would like in adjuncts. Identifying the characteristics starts with an examination of two types of requirements—those that are essential and those that are critical. Essential requirements are the basic skills, credentials, etc. that are needed to be minimally qualified for the position. Often essential requirements are the minimum criteria needed to be considered for the position and are rather easy to assess. For example, a minimum requirement is graduate level training in the discipline to be taught.

After identifying the essential requirements, it is necessary to identify the critical requirements. Critical requirements are those that are necessary to be successful in the particular position you are filling. Critical requirements need to account for not only the duties of the position, but also the culture of your institution and department. Haefele (1981) points out that to determine the critical requirements the chair needs to ask "Can a person lacking quality A or B be effective in this teaching situation" (p. 42)? Identifying the critical elements not only enhances the chance that the person hired will "fit" into your institution, it also can be a way of communicating a more realistic picture of what the job entails.

The second step in interviewing is to develop a set of questions that assess the candidates on the critical requirements. Although researchers have demonstrated that interviews are often not a reliable means of selecting the best candidate, there are several steps a chair can take to increase reliability. The first step is to take the time to work with the hiring committee to develop and refine a set of questions that will probe specific behaviors. These questions are likely to be the same or extensions of the items used to inquire about the critical requirements of the job. The key is to develop questions that will elicit responses that indicate how the candidate will *act* in certain situations. Knowing what a candidate thinks are her or his three best qualities will not tell you much, if anything, about her or his behavior. Committees should ask questions like:

- Do you give students an opportunity to revise papers for a higher grade?
- What type of exams do you give?
- How do you deal with poor attendance?
- What about a missed exam?

The second step is to assign each agreed-upon question to a specific committee member to ask of every finalist. The third step is for the committee to discuss what would be acceptable answers. If the committee agrees ahead of time on what is unacceptable, acceptable, and exceptional, they can use a three point rating scale with 1= unacceptable, 2 = acceptable, and 3 = exceptional. The key to achieving interrater reliability is for the committee to spend sufficient time discussing the qualities of an unacceptable, acceptable, and exceptional answer *before* conducting any interviews. For more detail on how to increase the reliability of behaviorally oriented interviews see Murray (1998; 1999a; 1999b).

Hiring is less than half the job when it comes to hiring adjuncts. "The biggest problem appears to be institutional neglect of part-time faculty, who are routinely treated as second class citizens—the 'neglected majority.'" In large part, part-time faculty have been excluded from the *collegium*. They are not so much a neglected majority, as the "excluded majority" (McGuire, 1993, p. 1). Effectively integrating adjuncts into the culture of the college requires an effective adjunct faculty development program. Faculty development for adjuncts may need to address the following issues:

1. **Adjuncts may lack an understanding of the institutional mission, the purpose of the course in the overall curriculum, and the characteristics of the students.** Colleges that make effective use of adjuncts "give the part-timer the opportunity to learn about the culture of the organization, the mission of the community college, and the nature of the students—linking staff development and evaluation to rank advancement. Small increments in pay or a change in title can go a long way toward making individuals feel more a part of the organization" (Roueche, Roueche, & Milliron, 1996, p. 43).

2. **Adjuncts may lack an understanding of the institutional policies and procedures.** While a faculty handbook with current policies and procedures can help, handbooks are often out-of-date and often go unread (Osborn, 1990). One solution is a required orientation for adjuncts. However, adjuncts often resent these, and it can be difficult to get them to attend (Osborn, 1990). Colleges can ameliorate these concerns by paying adjuncts for their professional time and videotaping the session for those unable to attend. If you conduct an orientation session, consider carefully the agenda and include only "must know" information and try to include something about teaching and learning. If you make the orientation session worthwhile either by compensating the professionals for their time or providing useful instruction, "they will come."

3. **Adjuncts may feel they lack a connection with full-time faculty and**

administrators and thus are marginalized and unappreciated (Lyons, 1999). Colleges and universities can reduce this sense of alienation by including adjuncts in reward systems "in work projects, in curriculum discussions, in celebration of successful programs and initiatives and other rituals that define and describe the culture ..." (Roueche, 1999, p. 4). Colleges and universities need to aggressively develop strategies that connect full-time faculty with adjuncts. Such strategies can include mentoring programs, involving adjuncts' in faculty meetings, social get-togethers, or having full-time faculty sit in on adjuncts' classes to offer helpful advice on teaching. The exact strategies are less important than simply forging the connections. Also to increase adjuncts' sense of belonging and connection with full-time faculty consider providing office space, telephones, computers, and secretarial assistance. Not only will these make adjuncts feel valued, but they will also help them increase their classroom effectiveness.

4. **Adjuncts may lack knowledge of pedagogy, especially new techniques.** "While well grounded in their disciplines, adjunct instructors often initially are ill prepared to effectively satisfy the full range of needs of today's students" (Lyons, 1999, p. 4). Since adjuncts are often marginalized within an institution, they often do not participate in faculty development opportunities. Therefore, institutions need to find ways to encourage greater participation in faculty development activities. One means of involving the adjuncts is to allow them to participate in the planning of faculty development activities.

"We make attempts to orientate[sic], integrate, and develop part-time faculty without really knowing if our efforts are valuable or if they increase teaching effectiveness. We are then puzzled when the activities we design for part-timers fail to attract many participants. In short, when dealing with part-time faculty, we tend to operate more on assumption than on fact" (Osborn, 1990, p. 17).

Adjunct faculty who can better identify their developmental needs are more likely to attend if the activities meet their needs. After the adjuncts' needs have been determined, consider a series of workshops just for adjuncts. Some adjunct and full-time faculty members may be able to conduct some of the workshops. The presenters should be compensated. The workshops should be scheduled at times convenient to the adjuncts and the attendees should be given a modest stipend for attending.

Once hired, oriented, and involved in development activities, part-time faculty will represent a valuable resource in any department.

Instructional Quality and Part-time Faculty

The number of part-time and adjunct faculty in higher education continues to grow. Over the past 20 to 30 years, various reports and studies have documented a steady increase in the use of part-time faculty at both two-year and four-year institutions (Roueche, Roueche & Milliron, 1995; Committee on the Use of Part-Time Faculty, 1990). In fact, a study by Roueche, Roueche and Milliron (1995), indicates that 58% of the faculty are part-timers at AACC member colleges of 8,000 or more students. When district- and nondistrict-related colleges are examined the figure rises to 63-68%, respectively. This increase has been attributed to a number of factors. Principle among these factors is flexibility, special expertise, real-life experience, and institutional budgetary constraints.

First, adjunct and part-time faculty offer an institution increased flexibility not only in the types of courses offered but also in the scheduling of courses. Employment of part-time faculty is usually done on an academic term-by-term basis which allows the institution to react quickly to unexpected demands of increased student enrollments and requirements for specialized courses (Committee on the Use of Part-Time Faculty, 1990; Hoffman, 1980). In addition, many part-time faculty are available to teach evening courses.

Second, professional schools have long used experts from the field to lecture in their expertise area (Tuckman & Pickerill, 1988). It is suggested that these individuals bring a "unique blend" of practical experience and scholarly perspective to the classroom environment. Today, areas such as management, journalism, and technology utilize part-time faculty for the same reason. By bringing practical experience into the classroom, part-time faculty can demonstrate the link between school and work.

Finally, institutions realize an economic benefit when hiring part-time faculty. Part-time faculty are usually paid at a rate that is less than the full-time faculty rate. In Texas, a survey found that, on average, part-time faculty receive approximately 40% of the amount paid to full-time faculty (Committee on the Use of Part-Time Faculty, 1990). Roueche, Roueche, and Milliron (1995) report that salaries vary by type and geographic location of the institution. They report a national average of per-course compensation for part-time faculty of $1,000-$1,200. Institutions defend this salary schedule because of the limited participation of part-time faculty in such areas as research, committee work, and extended office hours (Hoffman, 1980; Roueche, Roueche, & Milliron, 1995).

Even with the aforementioned benefits that institutions derive from the employment of part-time faculty, concerns continue to be expressed regarding the disadvantages of hiring large numbers of part-time and adjunct faculty. Chief among these concerns are instructional quality and the ability of the institution to provide support services to part-time faculty (Hoffman, 1980; Roueche, Roueche & Milliron, 1995; Texas Higher Education Coordinating Board, 1990). As the number of part-time faculty increases, concerns that part-time faculty are less effective, are not as competent, and do not have the same commitment as full-time faculty continue to be raised. Hoffman (1980) states that "as a rule, fewer part-time instructors have advanced degrees than their full-time colleagues ... [and] also have less teaching experience" (p. 12). Similarly, Friedlander, as quoted in Roueche, Roueche, and Milliron (1995) found that:

> Part-time instructors were found to have less teaching experience, to have taught fewer years at their current institution, and hold lower academic credentials. The adjunct instructor also differed from full-timers in that he had less choice in the selection of materials to be used in his course, assigned fewer pages to read, used less instructional media, recommended or required students to attend fewer out-of-class activities, and placed less emphasis on written assignments (p. 9).

Given this information, the question becomes, is instructional quality jeopardized when part-time faculty are used? Are students the ultimate "victim" as institutions struggle to find ways to meet new demands?

Roueche, Roueche, and Milliron (1995) provide perspectives from both the institution and part-time faculty on the issue of instructional quality. When asked to provide an opinion on part-time faculty and the quality of instruction, department chairs, deans, and provosts suggested that they were either not as effective or at least as effective as full-time faculty. They also felt the range of quality was probably broader among part-time faculty than full-time faculty. However, research provides a different picture. "Empirical studies to date have found no significant differences in student rating, class retention, or student achievement in subsequent classes between students taught by part-time faculty and those taught by full-time faculty" (Roueche, Roueche, and Milliron, 1995). Part-time faculty appear to be just as competent and provide the same academic quality as full-time faculty. When examining quality from the part-time faculty perspective, several issues can be addressed. Gappa and Leslie (1993) found that 52.5% of the part-time faculty in public two-year institution had fewer than four years in their current institution, while 35% had over four years. Similarly, in a study at Johnson County Community College (KS) by Bethke and Nelson (1994), found that 30% of part-time faculty were in their first year of teaching and 56% were within their first three years of teaching. Roueche et al. (1995) suggests that concerns about length of experience may be unwarranted. They provide a counter-argument of the possibility that part-time faculty are likely to have more recent graduate training, and will therefore have more current information in their specialty area. A review of the literature, then, does not support the contention or concerns expressed by administrators and full-time faculty regarding quality instruction and part-time faculty. It would appear that part-time faculty, when selected, supervised, and used appropriately, are as effective as full-time faculty.

Another area of instructional quality concern is support services. Part-time faculty often find them either nonexistent or sorely lacking (Committee on the Use of Part-Time Faculty, 1990). Part-time faculty report that access to such services as adequate clerical help, a telephone, library privileges, and copy machines continue to be an issue in the delivery of their courses. However, most often cited is the lack of available office space (Committee on the Use of Part-Time Faculty, 1990). Lack of these support services can impact instructional quality. If part-time faculty do not have access to a telephone, they cannot make or receive calls from their students. Also, lack of office space can have a negative impact on class preparation, meeting with students, grading papers, etc. Support services are important when discussing the quality of instruction. While having services such as office space, telephones, etc. do not guarantee quality instruction, the lack of these services can adversely impact the delivery and quality of instruction. A study in Texas recommended the following as it relates to support services:

- Each college should provide an appropriate work area—preferably an office—where part-time faculty can advise, counsel, work, and visit with students; store materials; grade papers; prepare classes; and communicate by telephone with students.
- Part-time faculty should be provided with adequate secretarial help and equipment to meet their typing and copying needs (Committee on the Use of Part-Time Faculty, 1990).

The use of part-time faculty in higher education shows no signs of abating. In fact, trends in fiscal constraints, faculty labor markets, and shifting academic demands suggest that the numbers will continue to increase (Roueche, Roueche, and Milliron, 1995). However, concerns continue to be expressed about how part-time faculty are hired, how they are integrated into the academic community, and most importantly how they impact the quality of instruction (Roueche, Roueche, and Milliron, 1995). Whereas appropriate ratios for part-time to full-time faculty do not exist, institutions should demonstrate caution when hiring part-time faculty. Large numbers of part-time faculty may limit the ability of departments to engage in governance and public service activities, advising, and may not provide necessary program stability. These issues in turn may impact quality. Institutions should continually monitor their part-time faculty just as they do their full-time faculty. However, when institutions take care in the selection, orientation, development, assignment of teaching responsibilities, and support they provide to part-time faculty, research indicates that the use of part-time faculty does not have an adverse impact on instructional quality.

Program Evaluation for Enhancing Quality

While most strategies for change in higher education in the past have focused on the institution as a whole, the trend is to focus more on the departmental unit if real change in student and faculty behavior is to be achieve (Nichols, 1995). Academic and vocational departments are the physical and intellectual homes of both full- and part-time faculty. The premise underlying the recommendations for improving program evaluation here is that an "evaluation culture" must be established at the department and institutional level at both two-year and four-year colleges for program evaluation to be effective. Too often in the past top-down evaluation strategies have not been very successful. Often the top-down approach to program evaluation results in the faculty seeing the process as an exercise of little value to them or the institution. They tend to view program evaluation as something some external agency such as a regional or professional accrediting agency requires of them every 5-10 years with limited benefits. In other words, there is a lack of commitment to the process of program evaluation at the department level.

One of the best ways for leaders of colleges and departments to develop an "evaluation culture" is to first study colleges that have been successful in this area. Wergin and Swinger (1999) recently completed a national study of program evaluation that included a mailing to all campus provosts. Their efforts uncovered information on program evaluation at about 130 institutions across the Carnegie Classification Categories, primarily four-year institutions. They then selected 20 of these institutions for further study through one-and-a-half-day visits. These visits included interviews with key administrators and faculty leaders on their program evaluation practices. The results of this study are summarized here since the findings apply to both two-year and four-year college administrators and faculty. The findings are particularly relevant for department chairs who are seeking ways to improve program evaluation in their units with the involvement of both their part-time and full-time faculty. The results presented here include a discussion of:

1. Current program review practices;
2. Components of effective valuation at the department level;
3. Evaluation policies and practices;
4. Evaluation standards, criteria, and measures; and
5. Recommendations for program evaluation practice.

Five Ways to Conduct Program Evaluation

Wergin and Swinger (1999) found five different ways that campuses were evaluating their academic departments. In some cases, the campuses studied employed all five approaches. The approaches were: 1) program review, 2) outcomes assessment, 3) specialized accreditation; 4) financial accounting initiatives, and 5) internal quality assurance.

1. **Program review.** Models for internal "program review" have been around for at least 15 years (Conrad & Wilson, 1985). The reviews are usually cyclical with departments being evaluated every five to seven years. For these reviews to be successful, it is recommended here that both the full-time and part-time faculty take part in the review of department strengths and weaknesses and in the preparation of the plan for improvement. Also, for success, this form of program review needs to be summative in nature and well integrated into the life of the institution and its departments.

2. **Outcomes assessment.** This form of assessment dates back to the late 1980s (Banta et al., 1993) and is becoming a more common practice in many two-year and four-year colleges. External agencies, such as accrediting bodies and state legislatures, have been the principal backers of this approach to program review (Commission on Colleges of the Southern Association of Colleges and Schools, 1998; Nichols, 1995). The emphasis of this model for evaluation has shifted from an assessment of "inputs" to the documentation of "student learning". In using this form of program evaluation, the department chair should make sure that part-time and full-time faculty see the collection and use of this data as a necessary step

to improving the teaching and evaluation of their department.

3. **Specialized accreditation.** There are now over 100 specialized accrediting bodies that attempt to hold colleges and/or departments to standards of quality for program input and outcomes (Dill, 1998). This form of program review, while not applicable to all departments, can be another very valuable approach to program review. To be successful however, department chairs and their faculties need to focus on how well their programs meet their goals in ways that are consistent with their college or university mission, rather than with someone else's rigid or unrelated standards.

4. **Financial accounting initiatives.** Only a few higher education institutions have developed an accounting procedure called "activity-based costing" (Moore, 1998). The idea behind this form of evaluation is that departments as income and cost centers will begin to pay more attention to whether or not they are profit centers. The problem with this form of evaluation is that it may make departments more fiscally responsible but it may not give enough attention to other indicators of program quality such as student graduation rates, student job placement, etc. The ratio of part-time to full-time faculty would certainly be one consideration in this model.

5. **Internal quality assurance.** Each of the above forms of program or department evaluation tend to be essentially "top-down" or "outside-in" with the emphasis on accountability to external constituencies or stakeholders (Wergin & Swinger, 1999). Over time these externally driven forms of evaluation are not likely to succeed without some form of "internal motivation" on the part of the chair and faculty members. It will be up to the department chair to promote "continuous quality improvement" as a way of life for both full- and part-time faculty. The chair can best achieve this viewpoint by promoting collaboration and a focus on standards that will produce quality at the unit level.

The key to effective program evaluation appears to be effective unit leadership at both the college/university and department levels (Wergin &

Swinger, 1999). Outlined below are the components needed for effective program evaluation at the department level.

> Our data suggest that ... effective departmental assessment depends on three key factors; the degree to which the *organizational and cultural setting* promotes a conducive atmosphere for evaluation; the credibility and fairness of *evaluation policies and practices*; and the validity and reliability of *evaluation standards, criteria, and measures.* (Wergin & Swinger, 1999, p. 8)

Components of Effective Evaluation at the Department Level

The department chair needs to examine his or her organizational and cultural setting in order to build a department climate that is supportive of quality improvement. Listed below are six elements that Wergin and Swinger (1999) believe administrators, particularly chairs, should strive to achieve in order to have a "quality" institutional climate.

1. **A leadership of engagement.** Chairs must be able to make a clear and compelling case for the necessity of program evaluation to both the full- and part-time faculty.
2. **Engaged departments.** The department faculty need to have a continuous conversation about the quality of the various components of their program.
3. **A culture of evidence.** The chair should support a tradition of program evaluation where student outcomes assessment strongly influences teaching and curriculum decisions.
4. **A culture of peer collaboration and peer review.** Part- and full-time faculty will need to meet regularly if this goal is to be achieved.
5. **A respect for difference.** Differential faculty roles should be encouraged to achieve the highest level of department productivity.
6. **Evaluation with consequence.** Most program reviews do not go far enough. For program review to work there must be a visible impact on resource allocation at all levels of the organization, but particularly at the department level. (pp. 8-10)

In order to achieve "evaluation with consequence," the appropriate evaluation policies and practices will need to be in place at both the department and institutional levels.

Evaluation Policies and Practices

The most successful evaluation programs of the future will be ones in which departments are given a greater voice in the establishment of their programs and a chance to focus more on a process that contributes to continuous improvement over each five- to seven-year evaluation period. Effective policies and practices suggested by the institutions that Wergin and Swinger (1999) studied included the following three important elements for departments:

- **A clear purpose which fits the culture and mission of the institution** ...
- **Encouragement of a "spirit of inquiry" by the unit** ... (Preskill and Torres, forthcoming).
- **Tangible administrative follow-through** ... (p. 11-12)

One element missing in the above list would be the need for a comprehensive faculty evaluation and development system for both full- and part-time faculty. For more information on these two topics, the reader is encouraged to read Chapters Five and Six in the book *Strangers in Their Own Land: Part-time Faculty in American Community Colleges* (Roueche, Roueche, and Milliron, 1995) and the book *Evaluating Faculty for Promotion and Tenure* (Miller, 1987).

Evaluation Standards, Criteria, and Measures

Once a college and its departments have evaluation policies and practices in place, the department chair and faculty will need to establish "criteria," "standards," and "measures" for their program review system. In this case, "criteria refer to the kinds of evidence collected as markers of quality; standards are the benchmarks against which the evidence is compared; and measures are the methods used to collect the evidence" (Wergin & Swinger, 1999, p. 12). An example of these three elements is given below:

Other criteria categories that are currently being used for program evaluation include:

Criteria Category	Criteria	Measures/sources of data	Standards
Faculty Qualifications	Academic Credentials	Faculty Vitae	Appropriate Degree from Top Ten University

1. Faculty productivity,
2. Efficiency,
3. Curriculum quality,
4. Pedagogical quality,
5. Student quality,
6. Student productivity,
7. Learning outcomes,
8. Adequacy of resources and
9. Department contribution to institutional mission/priorities.

Wergin and Swinger (1999) found these nine categories represented in their research of the 20 best examples of college and department program evaluation in the US. They were also able to identify 93 criteria used by colleges in these nine criteria categories. While no two programs were found to be exactly alike in their review, their report is a valuable resource and starting point for department chairs who are seeking to improve the evaluation and quality of their programs.

Recommendations for Evaluation Practice

Wergin and Swinger (1999) offered four specific recommendations for creating more "self-regulating" institutions and for more widely accepted methods for evaluating departments. These four recommendations are listed here.

1. Be proactive in discussions of "quality"
2. Decentralize evaluation to the maximum possible extent
3. Recognize that evaluation is not for amateurs; address the development needs of deans, chairs, and faculty
4. Focus not just on enhancing collaboration and teamwork, but on "organization motivation" (pp. 18-21)

One additional recommendation that could be added to this list would be for college administrators to create a system for rewarding departments that establish effective program evaluation practices and evaluation cultures. Such rewards will be needed to institutionalize effective program evaluation at the department level.

Conclusion

If higher education institutions are to survive and prosper in the first 100 years of this new millennium, they will need to pay more attention to the quality of their management systems, hiring and development practices, instructional delivery systems, and program evaluation practices than they have in the past. In paying more attention to these four areas, institutional administrators, particularly at the department/division level, will need to work closely with their faculties, particularly their part-time faculty, who are becoming an increasingly valuable resource in times of limited resources.

References

Astin, A. (1985). *Achieving excellence: A critical assessment of priorities and practices in higher education*. San Francisco: Jossey-Bass.

Banta, T.W., et al. (1993). *Making a difference: Outcomes of a decade of assessment in higher education*. San Francisco: Jossey-Bass.

Bergquist, W.H. (1995). *Quality through access, access with quality*. San Francisco: Jossey-Bass.

Bethke, R., & Nelson, V. (1994, May). *Collaborative efforts to improve conditions for adjunct faculty*. Paper presented at the Annual International Conference of the National Institute for Staff and Organizational Development on Teaching Excellence and Conference Administrators. Austin, Texas. (ERIC Document Reproduction Service No. ED 373 822.)

Bogue, E.G., & Saunders, R.L. (1992). *The evidence of quality*. San Francisco: Jossey-Bass.

Chaffee, E.E., & Sherr, L.A. (1992). *Quality: Transforming postsecondary education*. ASHE-ERIC Higher Education Report (No. 3). Washington, DC: George Washington University, School of Education and Human Development.

Commission on Colleges – Southern Association of Colleges and Schools (1998). *Criteria for Accreditation*. Decatur, GA: Southern Association of Colleges and Schools.

Committee on the Use of Part-Time Faculty. (1990). *Study on the use of part-time faculty*. Austin, TX: Texas Higher Education Coordinating Board.

Conrad, C.F., & Wilson, R.F. (1995). *Academic program reviews: Institutional approaches, expectations, and controversies*. Washington, DC: ASHE-ERIC Higher Education Report No. 5.

Cornesky, R., McCool, S., Byrnes, L., & Weber, R. (1992). *Implementing total quality management in higher education*. Madison, WI: Magna Publications.

Dill, W. R. (1998). Special accreditation: An idea whose time has come? Or gone? *Change, 30*, 18-25.

Freed, J. E., & Klugman, M. R. (1997). *Quality principles and practices in higher education*. Phoenix, AZ: The Oryx Press.

Gappa, J. M., & Leslie, D. W. (1993). *The invisible faculty: Improving the status of part-timers in higher education*. San Francisco: Jossey-Bass.

Green, D. (1994). *What is quality in higher education?* London: The Society for Research into Higher Education/Open University Press.

Haefele, D. L. (1981). Teacher interviews. In J. Millman (Ed.) *Handbook of Teacher Evaluation*, (pp. 41-57). Beverly-Hills: Sage Publication.

Hoffman, J.R. (1980). The use and abuse of part-time instructors. *The Community Services Catalyst, 10*(1), 12-18.

Leatherman, C. (2000, January 19). Colleges continue to hire more part-time faculty members, government study finds. *Chronicle of Higher Education*. Available E-mail: http://chronicle.com/daily/2000/01/2000011902n.htm, pp 1-2.

Lyons, R. (1999). Adjunct instructions a priceless resource. *Community College Week*, pp. 4, 16.

McGuire, J. (1993). Part-time faculty: Partners in excellence. *Leadership Abstracts, 6*(6), 1-2.

Miller, R.I. (1987). *Evaluating faculty for promotion and tenure*. San Francisco: Jossey-Bass.

Moore, D. (1998). *A comparative evaluation of financial and activity-based cost accounting systems in a private university*. Unpublished dissertation, Texas Tech University, Lubbock, TX.

Murray, J.P. (1998). Hiring the faculty for the next millennium. *The Journal of Staff, Program, & Organizational Development, 16*(1), 5-14.

Murray, J.P. (1999a). Interviewing to hire competent community college faculty. *Community College Review, 27*(1), 41-56.

Murray, J.P. (1999b). Improving the hiring interview. *Academic Leadership: Journal for Community and Technical College Leaders, 6*(2), 13-19.

Nichols, J.O. (1995). *The department guide and record book for student outcomes assessment and institutional effectiveness*. New York: Agathon Press.

Osborn, R. (1990). Part-time faculty development: What do we know and what can we use? *Catalyst, 20*(2), 17-21.

Preskill, H., & Torres, R.T. (in press). Evaluative inquiry for organization learning. In M. E. Smith, L. Araujo, & J. Burgoyne (Eds.), *Learning around organizations: Developments in theory and practice.* London: Sage.

Roueche, J.E., Roueche, S.D., & Milliron, M.D. (1995). *Strangers in their own land: Part-time faculty in American community colleges.* Washington, DC: AACC Community College Press.

Roueche, J.E., Roueche, S.D., & Milliron, M.D. (1996). Identifying the strangers: Exploring part-time faculty integration in American community colleges. *Community College Review, 23*(4), 33-48.

Roueche, S.D. (1999). Making friends of strangers. *Community College Week,* pp. 4-5.

Seymour, D.T. (1993). *On Q: Causing quality in higher education.* New York: American Council on Education/Macmillan.

Tuckman, H.P., & Pickerill, K.L. (1988). Part-time faculty and part-time academic careers. In D.W. Breneman, & T.I.K Youn (Eds.) *Academic Labor Markets and Careers.* Philadelphia, PA: Falmer Press.

Wergin, J.F., & Swinger, J.N. (1999, November). *Evaluation of academic departments: A national survey of best practices.* Paper presented at the Annual Meeting of the Association for the Study of Higher Education, San Antonio, TX.

Dr. Albert B. Smith is Professor and Coordinator of the Higher Education Program at Texas Tech University. Dr. Bonita Butner and Dr. Brent Cejda are Assistant Professors of the Higher Education Program at Texas Tech University. Dr. John Murray is an Associate Professor of the Higher Education Program at Texas Tech University.

Index